The Avatar Faculty

ETHNOGRAPHIC STUDIES IN SUBJECTIVITY

Tanya Luhrmann, Editor

The Avatar Faculty

ECSTATIC TRANSFORMATIONS IN
RELIGION AND VIDEO GAMES

Jeffrey G. Snodgrass

UNIVERSITY OF CALIFORNIA PRESS

University of California Press
Oakland, California

Library of Congress Cataloging-in-Publication Data

Names: Snodgrass, Jeffrey G., author.
Title: The avatar faculty: ecstatic transformations in religion and video
    games / Jeffrey G. Snodgrass.
Other titles: Ethnographic studies in subjectivity; 16.
Description: Oakland, California : University of California Press, [2023] |
    Series: Ethnographic studies in subjectivity; 16 | Includes bibliographical
    references and index.
Identifiers: LCCN 2022015210 (print) | LCCN 2022015211 (ebook) | ISBN
    9780520384354 (cloth) | ISBN 9780520384361 (paperback) | ISBN
    9780520384378 (ebook)
Subjects: LCSH: Ecstasy—Psychological aspects. | Ecstasy—Religious
    aspects. | Avatars (Virtual reality)—Psychological aspects. | Avatars
    (Religion)—Psychological aspects. | Video games—Psychological aspects.
Classification: LCC BF575.E4 S66 2023 (print) | LCC BF575.E4 (ebook) |
    DDC 154—dc23/eng/20220729
LC record available at https://lccn.loc.gov/2022015210
LC ebook record available at https://lccn.loc.gov/2022015211

32   31   30   29   28   27   26   25   24   23
10   9   8   7   6   5   4   3   2   1

CONTENTS

LIST OF ILLUSTRATIONS

PLATES

FIGURES

TABLES

KEY TERMS AND ABBREVIATIONS

See the Glossary for more terms.

AVATAR (HINDI): an agent who is understood to be the vehicle or embodiment of another's consciousness; in the original Sanskrit, *avatar* literally means "descent"—joining *ava* (down or below) with the verb root *tr* (float or pass over something, such as a river)—and refers to the way that Hindu deities incarnate in earthly vehicles in order to combat evil and restore balance in the universe; contemporaneously, a digital self-object in a computer-generated environment

BHAV A GAYA (HINDI): lit., "feelings have come," conventionally used by Rajasthanis to describe a state of spiritual possession

BHUT (HINDI): ghost

CS-GO: *Counterstrike—Global Offensive*

CULTURAL CONSONANCE: defined by William Dressler as "the degree to which individuals approximate widely shared cultural models in their own beliefs and behaviors"

CULTURAL DISSONANCE: an extension of cultural consonance, refers to the stresses, strains, and psychological processes associated with embodying and negotiating potentially competing or conflictual cultural norms or models

DEVI (HINDI): goddess

DISSOCIATION: experiences and behaviors that seem to exist apart from the mainstream flow of one's conscious awareness and identity; likewise, psychological *absorption* refers to a profound narrowing or concentration of attention, and *immersion* to the sense of losing oneself in another reality such as a computer-generated gaming world

DUNGEONS AND RAIDS: special events in games like *World of Warcraft*, where groups of players battle powerful monsters (termed *bosses*) to win treasure and items like weapons and armor (called *gear*); these events generate new copies of an area in the game for a particular group (referred to as *instances*)

ECSTASY: experiences that allow one to step outside or transcend a current identity and situation, from the Greek *ekstasis,* which literally means "standing outside a current state"

ERTL: the author's Ethnographic Research and Teaching Laboratory, at Colorado State University

ETHNOGRAPHY: case study accounts of a group's practices and points of view, relying largely on qualitative field-based methods like participant observation

GAMING DISORDER: a mental-health condition recently judged by the American Psychiatric Association (APA) and the World Health Organization (WHO) to warrant formal inclusion in their latest diagnostic manuals; sometimes glossed as *gaming addiction* and *toxic immersion*

GW2: *Guild Wars 2,* a multiplayer online role-playing game produced by the company ArenaNet

GUILD: associations of like-minded players in games like *World of Warcraft;* the Knights of Good is a *progression guild,* in the manner its members aim to systematically progress through the game's new raiding content, but less *hardcore* than more competitive guilds

HEALED HEALER: a term used to describe spiritual specialists such as mediums and shamans, who, in overcoming their own life problems, gain the ability to help others

HEALTH DISPARITIES: differential mortality and morbidity across social groups, related to, e.g., cardiovascular disease, cancer, and metabolic problems such as diabetes, which are understood to be driven importantly by factors such as poverty, educational attainment, and racism

KOG: The Knights of Good

MMORPG: massively multiplayer online role-playing games; examples are *World of Warcraft* and *Guild Wars 2;* also abbreviated MMO

PIR BABA (HINDI): a Muslim saint; Mastanna Baba is an example

PVP: Player-vs-Player, a play mode in games like *World of Warcraft,* where players test their skills against each other

RL: real life, in gamer talk; sometimes also *IRL,* "in real life"

SAKTI (HINDI): in Hinduism, spiritual power or divine energy

SDT: Self-Discrepancy Theory, a framework developed by Edward Higgins, to examine how discrepancies between a person's perception of their actual and ideal selves can predict mental and emotional health

SHAMAN (ORIGINALLY TUNGUS): a spiritual specialist believed to have the ability to project his or her consciousness outside the physical body; from *saman,* lit., "one who shakes," referring to experiences involving trance and physical shaking

SPIRIT MEDIUM: a spiritual specialist believed to have the power to channel into their body outside spirits and deities, becoming the *medium* or *channel* through which spiritual agents communicate with humans; Bedami eventually transitioned into the role of spirit medium; Kani Bai, a tribal woman, is another example of a medium

SPIRIT POSSESSION: an altered state of consciousness associated with the feeling that one has become the vehicle of an intrusive spirit or deity

STATUS SYNDROME: Michael Marmot's idea that the social-health gradient was importantly driven by social-status differences, for example, via stress mechanisms and pathways

TRANCE: a termed used by anthropologists and others to refer to the altered states of consciousness experienced by shamans and spirit mediums

WOW: *World of Warcraft*, a multiplayer online role-playing game produced by the company Blizzard Entertainment

PREFACE

I focus in this book on therapeutic processes involving *avatars*. An avatar is an agent who serves as the vehicle or vessel of another's consciousness and will. In this book, I comparatively examine health processes involving spiritual and digital avatars. In the spiritual case, I focus on folk Hinduism in India, where gods, ghosts, and other spirits are said to project themselves into human-avatar vehicles, or mediums, whom they spiritually possess. In the digital case, video-game players, godlike perhaps, extend themselves into character-avatars, their second selves in games like *World of Warcraft*. In each case, avatars can provide the possessed and gamer alike with perceived superior second identities and social standings, which, even if only temporary, can help reduce experiences of psychosocial stress and thus positively impact health.

Although I focus on the therapeutic potential of avatars, I have written in the past on the psychosocial *risks* associated with avatar identities. In the Indian spiritual case, some people get stricken with so-called ghost illness, giving up their will and identity to "dirty spirits" who use human vehicles for nefarious aims. In the digital case, certain gamers get overly enamored with second-avatar identities, playing compulsively and "addictively" in ways that erode offline commitments and mental well-being. These negative processes also feature in the book. But the primary focus is on the health-promoting, rather than health-eroding, potential of avatars. Further, I show how the problems associated with some avatars typically emerge from attempts at bettering a life situation by imaginatively remaking oneself, which can veer off track. So readers interested in topics like "internet addiction" or "gaming disorder" will find something of interest here. But I hope that this book's analysis will encourage those readers to see such problems in a new, and not entirely negative, light.

In fact, I further show how there is no essential way to distinguish a healthy from an unhealthy avatar experience. This is because the nature of avatar experiences and the value of avatar alternative identities vary according to the social contexts in which those identities play out. In this book's central spiritual-avatar case study, a young Indian woman, Bedami (a pseudonym), experiences possession by a spirit. But it is not clear, at least not at the outset, whether that spirit is a beneficent goddess or a pestering ghost. And in the end, whether her avatar experiences ultimately help or hurt her depends on how she negotiates her new identity in relation to demands from her husband and from others in her caste community. In the digital-avatar cases that feature in this book, what might be perceived as passionate play by one's online gaming guildmates can in certain offline contexts be interpreted as "addictive" and undesirable. Here, the value of avatar second identities, in these digital contexts as well, is also shaped by context and audience. And whether gamers experience their avatar identities as ultimately enhancing or eroding their health, I argue, depends importantly on how they successfully balance and negotiate commitments to their offline and online lives. In both spiritual and digital settings, then, the positive or negative quality of avatar identities, as I interpret them, depends less on essential traits of the person or their avatar per se, and more on how avatar identities are enacted within culturally variable social contexts that can fundamentally change how they are experienced.

This book brings together in one place over twenty years of my thinking on health and well-being processes associated with avatar identities. Bedami's case study featured in my PhD dissertation in anthropology completed in 1997 at the University of California, San Diego, with a focused description and analysis of her possession experiences published in 2002 in *American Ethnologist*. I continued to investigate spirit possession while a postdoctoral research fellow from 1997 to 1999 at the University of Alberta, Edmonton, working with Jean DeBernardi, a specialist of spirit religions, and then as a new assistant professor of anthropology at Colorado State University (CSU) in the early 2000s up until the present. I started my gaming research in 2008, as part of an experimental ethnographic research-methods class at CSU, which I taught *inside* the game *World of Warcraft*. I completed what might be considered this book's first draft back in 2011, in the form of a research article, where I compared digital gaming to "shamanic magical flight," published in the journal *Culture, Medicine & Psychiatry*. Back in 2015, I presented in earnest the idea of this book to a colleague. In 2017, I even wrote a book prospectus for these ideas, which I circulated. But my thinking had not fully crystalized, with my working out further strands of the book's key "cultural-norm incongruity" argument about avatar therapeutics only recently, in December 2021 in the journal *Current Anthropology*.

This book's spiritual-avatar analysis focuses most on Bedami's possession, and thus on folk Hinduism as practiced by a low-status Indian community I knew well. In the digital-avatar analysis, I focus most on *World of Warcraft*, a "massively multiplayer online roleplaying game," and *Counterstrike—Global Offensive*, a "first-person shooter" game. I hope that my descriptions of these case studies will inspire readers to dig deeper into avatar processes enacted in other spiritual and digital contexts, which I reference throughout the book.

In presenting these spiritual- and digital-avatar case studies, I have included insider terminology related to Hinduism, gaming, and social science. Typically, I italicize cultural-insider terms and analytical terminology the first time I use them substantively, and then later typically only for emphasis or if there was a large gap since I had last discussed the term. I have done my best to explain and contextualize that terminology to readers. But explaining each term in fully satisfactory detail would have taken me in many cases too far afield from my primary aims. And simply removing that cultural and analytical detail would have limited my ability to evoke the case studies and social-scientific debates that are the heart of this book. I have thus generally walked a middle path by providing enough explanation for readers on specialist topics so that they get the gist of my meaning without getting bogged down in extraneous details. And again, I hope my admittedly sometimes-passing references to certain cultural processes and social theory, even if appearing opaque at times, will encourage readers to dig deeper into this book's numerously evoked yet not fully pursued threads.

By drawing parallels between the magical flights of spiritual specialists such as shamans and the playing of video games, I put into dialogue scholarship on spiritual and digital avatars, with the aim of stimulating new avenues of thought. While writing, I kept foremost in my mind the interests and concerns of scholars from anthropology, religious studies, and media/game studies. To a certain extent, I also wrote this book for specialists in psychology and psychiatry, or, more specifically, for psychologists and psychiatrists who appreciate sociocultural forces and processes. I hope that my book will encourage scholars to explore lines of thinking developed in disciplines and debates they might not have previously conceived as relevant to their work. Directing my book at specialists means, as alluded to above, that I sometimes assume knowledge of topics that would not be apparent to a generally educated reader. However, though engaging specialist debates, I aimed to do so in a clear and evocative way, and especially in the opening chapter, with my references to popular culture. I did this to appeal to (and ideally inspire) students and the next generation of social-science researchers and practitioners, and to address a generally educated audience as well. Keeping students in mind also led me to include discussions of research methods at various points in the book. I hope that such material helps demystify the research process in ways that make anthropology and other fields more accessible to newcomers. Nevertheless, I did not want to overburden either students or a general readership with *too* detailed of consideration of either specialist debates or of my research methodology. To protect the flow of my narrative, I have thus moved scholarly references into endnotes, and detailed engagement with methodological issues into appendices. With the aim of reaching a broader audience, I have also simplified quantitative analyses in the presented case studies, focusing instead on qualitative ethnography and interviews. Interested readers can visit earlier published work of mine, which I reference throughout the book, for fuller accounts, analyses, and arguments presented here in curtailed form.

Finally, I speak throughout this book of *avatar therapeutics* to refer to the psychosocial and emotional benefits derived from spiritual- and digital-avatar selves. In 2017, King's College (UK) researchers published in *The Lancet* results related to the prospects for what they called "avatar therapy" in the treatment of patients suffering from auditory hallucinations. This study is premised on the idea that those patients can benefit from materializing and subsequently confronting troublesome hallucinatory voices in a computer-mediated interface, where those voices are represented as digital avatars. The voices-cum-digital avatars are therapeutically animated by a supportive clinician, which seems to help patients rob negative, tormenting entities of their hostility and threat. I see promise in the procedures these UK researchers describe, and I invite readers to learn more about this creative clinical strategy. But as an anthropologist familiar with the Hindu history of the term *avatar,* I am somewhat taken aback when I hear Western researchers talking about (as clinicians related to this study do) the recent *invention* of avatar therapy. I would say that these researchers have developed a clinical procedure that is inspired by a contemporary notion of digital avatars, which, as I explain in this book, is a c. 1980s co-optation of a Hindu religious principle. That is, these researchers and clinicians describe one form of avatar therapy, but, as I argue, the principles of avatar therapeutics are both historically much older and contemporaneously much broader. Or, to put it another way, these researchers develop a clinical application based on certain avatar principles. But as analogous principles can be found both in ancient Hinduism and in contemporary ethnomedical practices and leisure activities, it might be of benefit to dig deeper into those other contexts. Doing so could help illuminate the psychosocial dynamics and thus therapeutic potential of connecting to avatars, as that unfolds either in daily life or in still yet unimagined clinical applications. This book, then, compared to the King's College research, explores the potential therapeutic benefits derived from relating to avatars in the wild, so to speak, rather than in the clinic.

CENTRAL CHARACTERS AND SETTINGS

BEDAMI AND RAMU: a married couple in their twenties, who are members of the Bhat caste and live in the Rajasthani city of Udaipur; Bedami was believed to be possessed by her husband Ramu's lineage goddess (referred to as a *kuldevi*)

BHATS: low-status puppeteer performers originally from western Rajasthan (a region referred to as Marwar), but now also living in the city of Udaipur and throughout Rajasthan and India

CHAVANDA MATA: Ramu Bhat's lineage goddess, who was said to possess Bedami

COUNTERSTRIKE—GLOBAL OFFENSIVE: a multiplayer first-person shooter game (FPS) developed by Valve and Hidden Path Entertainment

GAMING ZONES: face-to-face gaming parlors found in Udaipur and throughout India; also referred to as *gaming lounges*

KNIGHTS OF GOOD: a guild in the game *World of Warcraft,* founded in 2008 by Lainey and Vern, who suggested this pseudonym; also refers to a gaming guild in the popular web series, *The Guild*

LAINEY AND VERN, A.K.A. TESSA AND STEELY: a married couple, Lainey in her forties, Vern in his mid-thirties, who first met in the game *World of Warcraft;* founders of the Knights of Good guild; Tessa and Steely (or "Stee") are this couple's gaming characters

UDAIPUR: a city in the Indian state of Rajasthan

WORLD OF WARCRAFT: A multiplayer online role-playing game made by Blizzard Entertainment

Introduction

SACRED AND SECULAR AVATARS: A BRIEF HISTORY
OF A SECRET SYNERGY

In the 1986 novel *Count Zero,*[1] William Gibson describes the proliferation of what appear to be voodoo gods inhabiting a virtual-reality data space referred to as the "matrix." The novel's protagonist, Bobby Newmark, a young computer hacker, meets these entities as he plugs himself into the matrix and transforms into his digital second self, the novel's eponymous Count Zero. It turns out that the seeming gods are the fragmented remains of two Artificial Intelligences (AIs), who are named Neuromancer and Wintermute. The AIs' choice of voodoo-god form is a fitting testament to their technological powers and an effective way to communicate and interact with humans in the matrix.

Reading *Count Zero* in the 1990s as a graduate student of anthropology, I was struck by Gibson's joining of religion and technology. That creative fusion stuck with me for a long time and is on some level the spark for this book written decades later. For me, Gibson evokes what I refer to in this book as *avatars*[2]—material embodiments of consciousness, which, as second selves, allow humans (or other agents such as gods and AIs) to accomplish things in realities alternative to their own.[3] In this case, computer hackers enter cyberspace via their digital avatars (though Gibson did not use the term *avatar* in this novel, which entered popular culture later). And the AIs Neuromancer and Wintermute do the same, each having the ability to enter cyberspace in the form of multiple voodoo gods, the exact character of which depends on the AIs' current needs.

It is interesting—and appropriate—that Gibson chose a religious idiom of voodoo gods to frame a story detailing technological embodiments in digital realities. The spirits of Haitian (and Haitian diasporic) voodoo are referred to as *loa*—also, in French creole, *les mystères* and *les invisibles*. They are understood to be vehicles or intermediary forms via which God, the supreme deity, enters the world to communicate with humans. Le Bon Dieu, the supreme "Good God," takes specific form depending on the task at hand. If battle is necessary, that form could be an aggressive and warlike *Petro loa* such as the red demon spirit, Met Kalfu, the "master of the crossroads," who is associated with the Christian Satan. Met Kalfu has a taste for rum infused with gunpowder and the power to grant (or deny) access to all the other loa. Or le Bon Dieu could take an older, "cooler," and less aggressive water-spirit form such as the white *Rada loa*, Papa Legba, who remains closely connected to ancestral Africa. Papa Legba, also an intermediary spirit, is again closely associated with the crossroads and thus understood to have the ability to grant permission to speak and interact with the other loa. All the loa, then, are vehicles through which le Bon Dieu becomes embodied in earthly reality and thus in this instance able to intervene in human affairs—*avatars* in the language of this book. But Met Kalfu and Papa Legba, as spirits of the crossroads, represent the very principle of crossing over into other realities, given the way they control and manage that process. They are thus simultaneously examples of avatars and a kind of metacommentary on processes that facilitate crossing over into realities alternative to one's own—again, what I refer to as an *avatar principle*. Given the importance voodoo places on crossing boundaries and realities, this sacred tradition becomes an appropriate touchstone for avatar processes in general, whether religious or digital.[4]

Gibson intuited an underlying parallel between what I would call *sacred avatars*, such as voodoo loa, and *secular avatars*, including the second selves many now commonly use to enter online gaming or other internet-based virtual worlds. Indeed, Gibson was not the only North American artist to make this connection. One need only think of James Cameron's hugely popular and profitable 2009 epic science-fiction film *Avatar*,[5] which is perhaps the first thing some readers think of when picking up this book. Cameron's film is set in the twenty-second century on Pandora, a densely forested and habitable moon of a fictional gas-giant planet in the Alpha Centauri star system. The film's drama centers on conflicts between colonizers from Earth extracting the mineral unobtanium, used to make room-temperature superconductors and thus very valuable on an Earth increasingly depleted of natural resources, and the Na'vi, the moon's ten-feet-tall, blue-skinned indigenous humanoid inhabitants, whose ecologies and life-ways are threatened by the extraction.

What is important here is that the Na'vi's religion allows them to journey outside their own bodies and take other forms. For example, the Na'vi are able to access the consciousness of other animals in the forest, including their flying dragon-like predator mounts, thus joining with them in some important way. They can also join their own consciousness with that of the sacred Tree of Souls, via which they can then communicate with their supreme mother goddess, Eywa. Those acts of instantiating their consciousness in alternative bodies and realities, religiously based in these instances, are what I am calling a *sacred avatar process*. But the colonizers also have the ability to transport their consciousness into other vehicles and thus enter alternative realities. Specifically, the earthling colonizers have genetically engineered compatible Na'vi bodies, which, via technology, their brains can operate remotely at a distance, giving these human operators the ability to interact with the indigenous Na'vi in their native environment. Thus, for example, the film's lead human character, Jake Sully, a paraplegic former marine, has his own Na'vi body that gives him the ability to walk again—a technologically facilitated and thus secular avatar process. These Na'vi bodies are explicitly referred to in the film as "avatars," which in turn is the inspiration for the film's title. And the sacred-secular avatar parallels are most pronounced at certain moments, as when the Na'vi try to save a dying Dr. Grace Augustine (played by Sigourney Weaver), the head of the humans' scientific avatar project, by permanently transferring (with the aid of their deities) her consciousness from her dying body into her new Na-vi body. That attempt fails, but with the help of the Tree of Souls Jake does succeed in permanently entering his genetically engineered Na'vi body through a now-seamless fusion of sacred and secular avatar processes.

Even though some artistic renderings fuse sacred and secular avatars, the latter are now most closely associated with the term *avatar*. For example, the onscreen visualization of one's gaming character or online self is commonly referred to as an *avatar*, which now is understood to mean "a self-object in a virtual environment." Nevertheless, the history is in reality reversed, with sacred avatars inspiring the idea of a secular digital avatar. In 1985, working for George Lucas's LucasArts, Randy Farmer and Chip Morningstar created the video game *Habitat*,[6] the first attempt at a large-scale commercial graphical virtual world and what is considered the precursor of today's massively multiplayer online role-playing games (MMORPGs, or simply MMOs for short) such as *World of Warcraft*.[7] In *Habitat,* Farmer and Morningstar improvised the term *avatar* to refer to the digital representation of a character, the first instance of such usage. But the inspiration for this was Hinduism. In the Hindu religion, *avatar*, a Sanskrit term, literally means "descent" or "incarnation." And avatars most typically refer to the material incarnation or embodiment of a deity on earth. The most famous Hindu avatars are the Dashavatars—literally, the "ten avatars," referring to the Hindu god Vishnu's ten forms, which this deity took at various times to restore earthly and cosmic order (see plates 1–10). These included the animal-based Vishnu avatars Matsya (fish), Kurma (tortoise), Varaha (boar), and Narasimha (lion), as well as other powerful deities such as Rama, Krishna, and Buddha (though scholars often do not count the Buddha a god).[8] Hinduism, like Eastern spirituality more generally, had been popular in California since the 1960s, closely connected to hippie counterculture, rock 'n' roll, and spiritual experimentation. The Beatles, for example, met the Maharishi Mahesh Yogi in 1967, from whom they learned transcendental meditation, propelling transcendental meditation and Hinduism to popularity in the West. Farmer and Morningstar, working in California and inspired by the idea of spiritual "alters," deemed *avatars* the in-game character vehicles through which players entered their *Habitat* game-world. In their reasoning, just as heavenly Hindu gods incarnate into human avatars to battle demons, so might video-game players, godlike in their powers in scaled down video-game worlds, become embodied in technological second-self avatars to defeat virtual monsters.[9]

Count Zero is the second novel in Gibson's *Sprawl* trilogy, which is credited with solidifying and popularizing the cyberpunk subgenre of science fiction—stories set in typically dystopian near-futures, with emphases on street-smart characters, technology, and evil corporations often fomenting social disorder, or, as Bruce Sterling frames it, a combination of low life and high tech.[10] Just a few years after *Count Zero,* in 1992, Neal Stephenson published the popular cyberpunk novel *Snow Crash,*[11] another book I enjoyed in graduate school. The story features Hiro Protagonist, a hacker and pizza deliveryman, whose "avatar" in the computer-generated "metaverse"—unlike Gibson, Stephenson explicitly used the term *avatar*—is a sword-wielding, black-garbed samurai. In terms of historical sequence, it is of interest that Cameron's eighty-page treatment for the film *Avatar* was written in 1994, just a few years following the publication of *Snow Crash.* These were followed by an eventual avalanche of fictional works featuring avatars, even if all of

The first Indian AVATAR, denominated that of MATSE, representing the incarnation of VEESHNU in the form of A FISH: in the opinion of S.r William Jones, pointedly allusive to the GENERAL DELUGE.

PLATE 1. Vishnu's fish avatar, Matsya. This is Vishnu's first of ten primary avatars, or Dashavatara—literally, "ten avatars or incarnations." From Maurice Thomas's "Indian Antiquities; or, Dissertations Relative to the Ancient Geographical Divisions." London, England, 1806. British Library.

PLATE 2. Vishnu's second avatar, as a tortoise, Kurma. From "The Churning of the Ocean of Milk." Punjab Hill, Mandi, India, c. 1780–90. The Metropolitan Museum of Art. Gift of Mr. and Mrs. Alvin N. Haas, 1977.

PLATE 3. To restore cosmic order, Vishnu descends to earth as Varaha, the Boar, his third avatar. From "Vishun as Varaha, the Boar Avatar, Slays Banasur, A Demon General: Page from an Unknown Manuscript." Punjab Hills, Guler, c. 1800. The Metropolitan Museum of Art. Gift of Jeffrey Paley, 1974.

PLATE 4. Vishnu's fourth avatar, Narasimha, the man-lion, disembowels a demon king. From "Narasimha." Pune, Maharashtra, India, 1886. The Metropolitan Museum of Art. Purchase, Peter Louis and Chandru Ramchandani Gift, 2018.

PLATE 5. Vishnu's fifth avatar, Vamana, the dwarf. From "Vamana (incarnatie van Vishnu also dwerg)." Anonymous, Jaipur, Rajasthan, India, 1825–1875. Rijksmuseum. Gift of P. Formijne, Amsterdam, 1993.

PLATE 6. Vishnu's sixth avatar form, Parashurama, lit., "Rama with an axe." From "Parasurama (incarnatie van Vishnu als Rama-met-een-bijl)." Anonymous, Jaipur, Rajasthan, India, 1825–1875. Rijksmuseum. Gift of P. Formijne, Amsterdam, 1993.

PLATE 7. From the concluding scene of the Ramayana epic, Vishnu as Rama, his seventh form, restores order and benign governance to the world, accompanied by his family, priest, and a kneeling Hanuman, his monkey-general. From "Uttara Rama Charitra, The Assembly of Rama." India, undated, c. 1910. The Metropolitan Museum of Art. Gift of Mark Baron and Elise Boisanté, 2015.

PLATE 8. Vishnu as Krishna, his eighth form, triumphs over a river snake-king (nagaraja) who has been poisoning the waters of the Yamuna River where the cowherd maidens (gopis) bathe, while the snake-king's wives (nagini) plead with Krishna to spare their husband's life. From "Krishna subduing Kaliya." Calcutta, West Bengal, India, 1885–95. The Metropolitan Museum of Art. Purchase, Barbara and David Kipper Gift, 2021.

PLATE 9. Vishnu's ninth avatar, as the Buddha. From "Boeddha als een incarnatie (avatara) van Vishnu." Anonymous, Jaipur, 1825–1875. Rijksmuseum. Gift of P. Formijne, Amsterdam, 1993.

PLATE 10. Vishnu's final form and tenth incarnation, Kalki, who, typically portrayed as a white horse or a warrior on a white horse, will end the age of evil (Kali Yuga) and usher in a new age of truth and righteousness (Satya Yuga). From "Future Incarnation of Vishnu." Basohli, Jammu, India, c. 1700–1710. The Metropolitan Museum of Art. Gift of Cynthia Hazen Polsky, 1991.

them did not explicitly refer to computer-generated second selves as *avatars*. Among the most notable and influential is the 1999 film *The Matrix*[12], which I viewed the year it was released, two years after completing my PhD.

One notable feature of many technologically facilitated avatar stories is their explicit merging of sacred and secular processes. I point to this earlier in the discussion of *Count Zero* and the film *Avatar*. But in *Snow Crash,* we also find religious themes alongside the technological ones. In its fictional universe, the Semitic goddess Asherah takes form in a computer virus; the Sumerian god Enki creates another computer virus that causes all humanity to speak different languages, as protection against Asherah's attacks and influence; and a religious organization, the Reverend Wayne's Pearly Gates, distributes Asherah's virus in the form of an addictive drug and via infected blood to establish control over the consciousness of the drug's users. Reader's might also recall that *The Matrix*'s Neo is described as "The One"—an explicit messiah reference or God's avatar in Hindu terminology. This equation makes sense when one thinks of the godlike powers Neo exerts in the matrix's digital reality.

This is to say that we now think of avatars as second selves found primarily in video-game worlds, given the way that the term *avatar* is now commonly used in those and other internet and virtual-world contexts. But as the examples here drawn from fiction show, a sacred history and concept of avatars animates the now-common secular usages. One of the main tasks of this book is to draw out and explore more explicitly these sacred/secular avatar parallels, in order to clarify foundational processes underlying human psychosocial functioning and well-being. I have used these examples from popular culture in part to better draw readers into my thinking on avatars. But the fictional examples are also relevant in this context in their own right, in the way that imagined realities such as these allow us to transport ourselves into alternative spaces and bodies. Fiction itself, then, is also informed by avatar principles, an idea that readers might keep in mind over the course of this book.

AVATARS AS VEHICLES OF SELF-TRANSFORMATION IN SPIRIT RELIGIONS AND VIDEO GAMES

I use the parallel between sacred and secular avatars to explore the role that symbolic second selves—*avatars*—can play in regulating human well-being. I am an anthropologist who studies both religion and new technology. In the first case, I have written, for example, on spirit possession in India, and am

FIGURE 1. A tribal spirit medium in India channels the goddess, or *devi*, becoming her divine avatar. Photo by author.

currently interested in the cultural therapeutics of Hindu rituals. In the second case, I study games such as *World of Warcraft* (WoW) and *Guild Wars 2* (GW2),[13] with an interest in how those games might enhance or compromise players' mental health. In one of my first gaming papers, published in 2011, I describe playing WoW as akin to a shamanic "magical flight."[14] That is, gamers' journeys to magical worlds to battle monsters, I argue there, resemble spiritual healers' travels to other realms, where they fight forces that torment them and their kin. And importantly, I identify in that earlier work similar psychological forces at play, in that both activities could help individuals (gamers, shamans) manage stress. In this book, I push the argument further, arguing that each of these processes is animated by what I am calling an *avatar principle*, or *the ability to project consciousness into second selves and alternative realities*. As I see it now, this principle is a universal human faculty, which is tightly linked to the regulation of psychosocial well-being. (Figures 1 through 3 show spiritual and digital avatars.)

Beyond William Gibson, Neal Stephenson, and others, another important inspiration for this book is something I learned through my cross-cultural study of health and healing: most of the world's local medical traditions (some-

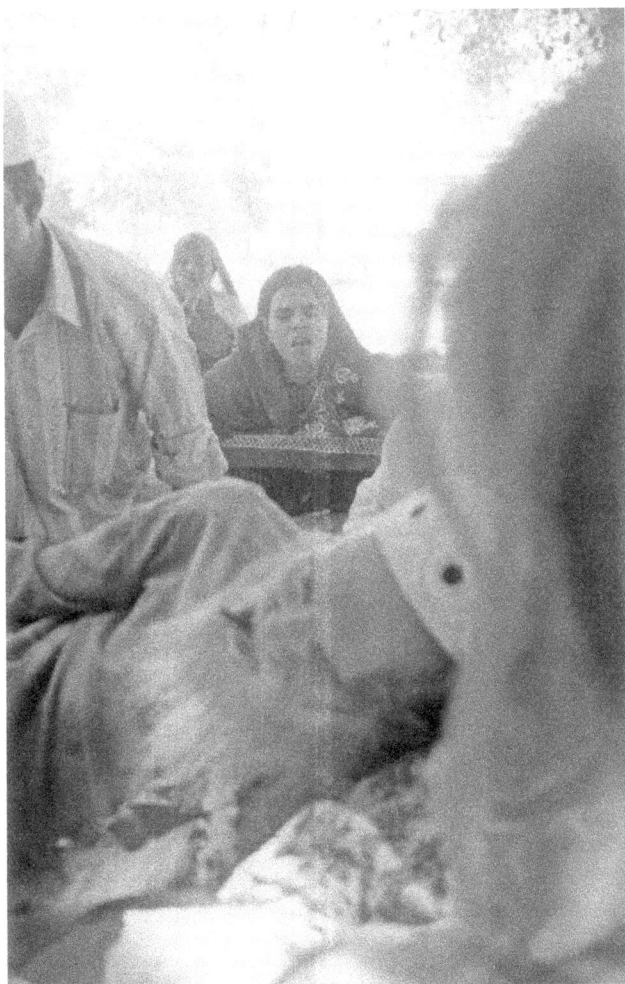

FIGURE 2. An Udaipuri woman possessed by a ghost begs forgiveness from a local saint. Photo by author.

times referred to as "ethnomedicine") have important spiritual dimensions. Specifically, the world's healing traditions often center on individuals believed to possess abilities to channel spirits and supernatural forces in ways that help themselves and members of the community, abilities which include using those spirits and forces to heal. In the Indian state of Rajasthan where I have conducted long-term research, these individuals are typically referred to as *bhopas* or *ojhas*—which we might translate as "spirit mediums" but also "healers." That is, they are the very *medium* or *channel* through which God communicates

FIGURE 3. Video-game players act via in-game avatars—digital self-objects in computer-generated environments. Image by Annette Pendlebury (pendleburyannette) from Pixabay.

with humans. Locally understood, healers such as these are said to be "horses" or "vehicles" that are "ridden" by gods and spirits. In being "ridden" in this manner, spirit mediums are said to become "possessed" with divine power. Or, as locals say it, mediums have powerful "feelings that have come to them"—*bhav a gaya,* in Hindi—with those feelings signaling in ritual contexts the presence of divinity. In those special states of consciousness, Rajasthani bhopas have the power to heal others. In the terms of this book, then, the avatar principle I describe—here, God projecting him/herself into the vehicle of a spirit medium—is tightly intertwined with human health and healing.

My experience with Rajasthani and other ethnomedical traditions around the world leads me to argue that avatar processes are psychosocially important to us and have therapeutic potential. This might seem surprising to some readers, given the way so-called internet addiction, another research interest of mine, seems tightly connected to digital avatars and internet-based second selves. From certain popular-cultural points of view at least, avatars are more commonly thought of as vehicles of harm rather than health. Nonetheless, I show that avatars provide us with the means to escape ordinary reality and to accomplish things not possible according to the rules of everyday existence. In the Rajasthani healing traditions that I know, the avatar principle—in this context, channeling god—provides spirit mediums with powerful second selves. Of interest, most mediums I knew in India were once themselves afflicted individuals, suffering from physical or mental-health problems, which were typically experienced and framed locally in spiritual terms as "ghost attacks." But they overcame their problems, mastering the spirits that once tormented them and turning those spiritual forces to their own aims. In doing so, they gained the ability to heal not only themselves but also others. This is why anthropologists often describe spirit mediums such as these as "healed healers"—in overcoming their own life problems, they gain the ability to help others, a common cross-cultural pattern.[15] We might say that spirit mediums such as these identify themselves with certain powerful divinities, which, as ego ideals of a kind, provide them with the mental fortitude to master their life problems—defeat their demons, so to speak. In local terms, these mediums are the very embodiment of divinity on earth, with superhuman powers—truly, a powerful second self!

Key to the therapeutic processes I describe in this book is what anthropologists call *ecstasy*. This might seem like an odd word choice, given the term's modern English-language connotation of deep pleasure. Although *ecstatic* experiences can also feel very good, etymologically, the English term *ecstasy* goes back to the original Greek *ekstasis*, which means "standing outside oneself" or "self-transcendence"—i.e., getting "out" (ek) of one's current "place" or "state" (stasis). And being chosen as god's vehicle or avatar provides powerful means through which individuals can achieve "ecstatic" states, thus escaping current (potentially unhealthy) situations.[16] Rajasthani spirit mediums, for example, channel god and in the process temporarily "dissociate"— that is, separate—from their current situations (often stressful), patterns of behaviors, and definitions of self. In doing so, religious practitioners and, as I also argue, online video-game players become closer to their idealized versions of self, in many cases carrying such changes back to their everyday lives. I thus suggest that the "ecstasy" characteristic of spiritual traditions with ancient roots is now also promoted by modern technologies such as online video games, with the latter providing new therapeutic escapes from the self that nevertheless retain core features of the archaic traditions. Archaic ecstasy,[17] then, is now also found in online virtual worlds, so to speak, where that faculty is activated and thus "comes online."

Intuitively, I think most readers would accept that games such as WoW and other virtual game-worlds such as *Second Life*[18] are "ecstatic" in this sense of the term: in entering magical play spaces, virtual-world inhabitants escape current everyday realities. In fact, the "magic circle"[19]–type escape they provide has been identified as what centrally makes a game a game. But for many readers, these escapes precisely capture the psychosocial risks, rather than the benefits, that games present to us. They are escapist and thus dangerous. And vulnerable individuals particularly risk overplaying them, overidentifying with second-self avatars and thereby removing themselves from daily life. But avoiding life problems does not make them magically disappear. Instead, they tend to accumulate, seeming bigger than ever, when exiting one's game of choice and having to confront them.

Nonetheless, I sketch in this book a now-robust body of research that demonstrates how games and virtual worlds can provide us with secondary imagined selves or identities—*avatars*—that are experienced as superior in certain ways to our "first" lives. Online gamers, for example, report that their play gives them the feeling of belonging to something bigger than themselves, with a "gamer" identity often perceived as central to players' self-conceptions and sense of purpose in life.[20] In some cases, gaming worlds allow players to pursue alternative racial, gendered, and sexual identities, as well as appearance- and age-based identities, that are somewhat (though not entirely) separated from so-called real life—*RL,* in gamer terminology—providing players with cathartic breaks from the stresses and strains of offline existence.[21] Such modes of identity, purpose, and stress relief typically unfold in the context of gaming-specific social relationships, which give players a sense of connection that can relieve loneliness.[22] As such, some researchers have proposed that online games can play the same role as taverns or coffeehouses that came before them, by serving as congregational "third places" between the "first space" of home and the "second" of work.[23] Summing up video-game research, one group puts it recently: "We propose that video games, by their very nature, have design elements aligned with attributes of well-being, and that playing video games can provide opportunities for flourishing mental health."[24] In this book, I suggest that many games' virtual worlds are specifically designed to facilitate avatar experiences, providing users with alternative ego ideals of a kind, which open up paths for positive growth and well-being. In the right doses and properly managed, temporary escape, or ekstasis, can be a healthy thing, whether experienced in spirit religions or in online virtual worlds.

Some readers may already be attuned to one potential complication in what I say. In relation to sacred experiences, some healers *channel* god. In those instances, divinities are believed to project their consciousness into an earthly body, the spirit medium, who becomes god's avatar vehicle (in this book's language). Other healers are not god's channel or vehicle. Rather, they *project* their own consciousness into other vehicles (again, in the analytical language employed in this book), as when a shaman magically merges with an animal familiar such as an eagle or a fish to travel to the moon or to the bottom of the ocean, as Inuit (Eskimo) shamans are said to do.[25] In the anthropological literature, these processes have been described as *mediumship* in the first instance (the healer is god's vehicle) and *shamanism* in the second (the healer's magical flight to alternative realities). Video-game avatars are typically described in ways that resemble more the latter, shamanic case—i.e., a video-game player, shamanic or even godlike perhaps, projects his or her consciousness into a digital avatar, which becomes a "self-object" (more on this later). Nevertheless, popular culture and scholarship alike describe some video-game players who seem to be taken over—possessed?—by their favorite game, which resembles more a mediumship experience (if demonic rather than divine).

Despite their differences, I treat each of these as avatar processes. In each case, some *agent* (in the sense of a willful actor) takes form in an alternative second-self vehicle—the avatar—though the nature of the agent can vary: god, ghost, or human. In terms of avatar processes being potentially therapeutic for human persons, it is important for the person, either as the agent herself or as the vehicle of other agents, to experience exchanges with an alternative self, no matter what the direction of movement between consciousnesses. In the case of shamanic flight, shamans might project their spirits into animal-familiar forms to journey to other worlds. Such journeys are therapeutic when the shaman retains experiences and treasures even after returning to everyday reality—e.g., the shaman and his patients experience actual-world relief after a battle with monsters and demons, having retrieved, say, amulets that they perceive as protective in the actual-world. In the spirit mediumship case, god takes human form, infusing a chosen vehicle with divinity—a clear benefit to the medium's primary self, both in the moment of actual possession and afterward in terms of the status accrued. These same therapeutic principles remain in place in the case of contemporary digital avatars. For example, by playing with actual-world friends, who can help one recall and relive video-game experiences long after a game has ended, a video-game player can transfer positive "magical flight" experiences back to the actual world, rendering play potentially psychosocially beneficial, as I argue elsewhere.[26] The important point here is that there are multiple avatar processes, with human persons alternatively serving as agents themselves or the vehicles of other agents. But whatever the process, the therapeutics depend on exchanges between first and second selves, which result in the transfer of magical avatar experiences back to a primary self—whether a shamanic healer or a video-game player.

Further, these avatar processes and therapeutics, as I show, are shaped by social forces. In hierarchical India, for example, individuals may be more likely to experience being overpowered by external forces greater than themselves, whereas in places such as the US, where individuality reigns, persons may have more a sense of being an active agent who directs the avatar processes. And as a result, cultural systems that emphasize the power of external forces impinging on the individual may be more effective in an Indian context, whereas those that stress individual agency and control over the therapeutic processes and interventions might work better in the US.

The French anthropologist Claude Lévi-Strauss writes of magical healing as also being dependent on shamans cultivating relationships with helper spirits. In the case of the Cuna Indians of Panama, for example, subordinate spirits helped a shaman during a difficult childbirth, as Lévi-Strauss shows, by journeying into the womb of the afflicted woman and retrieving the baby.[27] Lévi-Strauss argues that this symbolic process comforted the mother and helped her relax—she felt she was protected and in good hands—which in turn facilitated the birth of her child. For Lévi-Strauss, the shaman acted much like a psychoanalyst, in the sense that he was a master of manipulating symbols in ways that connected to and effected change in the actual world. Returning to *Count Zero* and the other works of fiction considered earlier, I would note that Bobby Newmark, like *Avatar's* Jake Sully and *The Matrix's* Neo, has spiritual allies helping them advance their agendas and achieve remarkable feats when in avatar form—the loa for Bobby, the Na'vi for Jake, and Morpheus and the crew of the Nebuchadnezzar for Neo. This is important for the argument of this book, in the sense that avatar therapeutics, as I interpret them, also depend importantly on social processes that involve learning to develop new positive relationships with other persons or agents.

Despite the many benefits to the avatar processes that I describe, research by me and others has revealed risks associated with ecstatic states. In the spiritual "ghost illness" case, some individuals encounter—and embody—disruptive forces such as ghosts, demons, and angry ancestors who erode rather than enhance one's state of being. In the video-game case, some players become so enamored of their new second selves that they do not want to leave their virtual lives, playing in disordered and addictive manners, patterns of behavior that can compromise offline well-being. This book also explores such negative avatar processes. But I generally emphasize how negative experiences such as these can result from positive intention and striving. That is, some spiritual healers and gamers alike assume alternative avatar selves to escape difficult and painful situations, though their success varies. They struggle to overcome, manage, and even turn to positive ends bothersome entities, experiences, and conflicts; yet they sometimes fail. And the presumed medicine (the avatar escape) can instead magnify rather than eliminate the illness (the pestering spirit, the life problem). In also paying some attention to these negative processes, I aim to provide a balanced assessment of the therapeutic potential of ecstatic—self-escapist—processes, as well as of the limits of such therapeutics. The book thus also examines what has been called "ghost illness" and "gaming addiction," though from an alternative anthropological perspective, which considers how avatar dynamics contribute to health and illness processes alike.

TOWARD AN INTEGRATIVE PSYCHOLOGICAL ANTHROPOLOGY OF AVATAR THERAPEUTICS

I aim in this book to lay out what we can know about the therapeutic potential of avatars. To do so, as readers have seen, I draw heavily from studies of spirit religions and from research on video games. Beyond my own work, the studies of religion I cite are primarily from anthropology, the research on gaming from health psychology, communication, and interdisciplinary games studies. But I also engage research from other fields such as psychiatry, sociology, and epidemiology.[28]

Although interdisciplinary, the book's concerns are centrally located in anthropology, and specifically the subdiscipline of psychological anthropology, which represents my own background and training. Psychological anthropologists focus on the relationship between culture and mind. They argue that the social milieu powerfully shapes individual psychology—

including processes related to cognition, emotion, motivation, and selfhood. In the avatar case, societies such as India posit that individuals are "permeable" in the sense of being open to intrusion from external agents such as spirits, with these frameworks of meaning in turn shaping the nature of avatar experiences there. Of course, similar beliefs exist in places such as the US: one need only think of Pentecostal Christian notions of "speaking in tongues" and being filled with the spirit of the Holy Ghost, still common in places such as Appalachia. Nevertheless, more mainstream US cultural beliefs center on the almost limitless potential of human ingenuity and technology, which in turn shapes US avatar experiences centered more commonly on human agents actively embodying themselves in digital, rather than spiritual, avatar vehicles. Yet, once again, such secular thinking is now global, finding its way to places such as India as well. My young-adult gamer respondents in India also referred to gaming and internet self-objects as "avatars." Although the book's argument focuses on avatar therapeutics, a secondary aim of this project is to help readers better appreciate the tight interrelationship between culture and the human psyche. On some level, I think of this book as a primer in psychological-anthropological ways of seeing the world, which also provides a roadmap for this field's important questions, both narrowly in relation to avatar studies and more generally.

In chapter 1, "Sacred and Secular Settings," I provide readers with background that will help them better appreciate the book's case studies and arguments. I begin with a fuller description of the Hindu origins of the avatar concept, tracing its resonance in folk Hindu traditions of spirit possession in the Indian state of Rajasthan, where I have conducted anthropological fieldwork since the 1990s. Then, I sketch the tight interconnection between sacred avatar identities and mental health in Rajasthan. Subsequently, I introduce a single instance of Rajasthani spirit possession, which serves as a frame story and introduction to analysis presented in chapters 2, 3, and 4. The case concerns a young woman in her early twenties at the time (the 1990s)—Bedami Bhat[29]—who was said to be tormented and possessed by an unknown spirit, which was subsequently identified as the Hindu Mother Goddess, or *devi*. In learning to better control her possession states—where Bedami was understood to be an avatar of the devi—Bedami transitioned into the role of spirit medium. And what was once framed locally as illness was later construed as therapeutic to Bedami and to others in her community. Bedami belongs to a caste known as Bhats, low-status performers with whom I conducted three years of ethnographic research in the Rajasthani cities of

Udaipur and Jaipur between 1991 and 1998, as part of my PhD dissertation and just beyond, and then again in the early to mid-2000s.

Next, I turn to secular avatars in typically computer-generated environments, beginning by describing the first references to digital avatars in 1980s computer games such as Farmer and Morningstar's *Habitat*. In this section, I touch on the historical relationship—however tenuous—between sacred Hindu and secular digital avatars. Subsequently, I summarize a now-robust literature on relationships between digital-avatar identities and mental health, focusing particularly on the psychological-anthropological dissociation literature and the immersive gaming literature in health psychology and interdisciplinary games studies. I point to both the positive therapeutic potential of digital avatars and the health risks associated with "toxic immersion"[30] or overidentification with digital avatars in computer-generated virtual worlds. From there, I describe the setting of my own studies of digital avatars, focused largely on two online games, WoW and GW2, both termed MMOs. I also delve more deeply into my study of associations of like-minded players—termed *guilds*—found within games such as these. This includes a US guild, the Knights of Good, whose leader was one of my students at the time of my early (c. 2008) games research.[31] My research on that US guild features in chapters 2 and 3. I also describe my 2016–17 research on gaming in Udaipur, India, which focused on the first-person shooter game *Counterstrike—Global Offensive* (CS-GO).[32] My India CS-GO research is the focus of chapter 4.

In chapter 2, "The Psychology of Avatar Therapeutics: Absorptive Experiences and Stress Relief," I describe what has been called *absorption,* or "the profound narrowing or concentration of attention and focused deployment of cognitive resources; [whereby] the absorbed individual becomes unaware of the external environment, self-awareness and critical thought are suspended and time perception may become distorted."[33] Working together, psychological anthropologist Rebecca Seligman and cultural psychiatrist Laurence Kirmayer suggest that absorption exists on a continuum with more "intense and prolonged" forms of experience, associated with functional alterations of memory, perception, and identity, which they dub *dissociative,* a term I mention earlier.[34] The central quality of such experiences is that they get disconnected—*dissociated*—from more familiar, everyday life. As the American psychologist Stanley Krippner puts it:

> "Dissociative" is an English-language adjective that attempts to describe reported experiences and observed behaviors that seem to exist apart from, or

appear to have been disconnected from, the mainstream, or flow of one's conscious awareness, behavioral repertoire, and/or self-identity. "Dissociation" is a noun used to describe a person's involvement in these reported dissociative experiences or observed dissociative behaviors.[35]

Building on theorists such as Krippner, the anthropologist Chris Lynn prefers to speak of dissociative experiences as *partitioned* as opposed to fully disconnected from consciousness and awareness, which even more closely approximates my own usage in this book.[36]

As I treat them in chapter 2, avatar identities are *dissociative* in the sense that they are somewhat separated from one's primary experience of self. Importantly here, escaping into an alternative dissociative identity has been linked to improvements in health. Specifically, individuals can dissociate or separate from stressful or even traumatic situations in ways that protect them from the harmful effects of such stress and trauma, as a robust literature in psychology and psychiatry has shown.[37] Indeed, anthropologists have long argued that distressed individuals use dissociative states such as trance, often framed in local traditions as spiritual possessions or shamanic magical flights to distant mythic lands, as a way to combat the stresses of human existence.[38] This claim makes sense of the observation that spirit possession and similar forms of dissociation are more typically found among poor, marginalized, and otherwise socially stressed and distressed persons, who, in dissociating "into" spiritual levels of reality, escape their humble surroundings to assume identities of gods, ancestors, and other more idealized forms of being.[39]

In similar terms, in chapter 2, I connect anthropological approaches to spiritual forms of absorption and dissociation to what games studies and communications scholars have called *immersion*—the sense of losing oneself in a computer-generated fantasy landscape and attributing dimensions of self and experience to in-game characters.[40] Here, I conceptualize immersive gaming experiences, facilitated by digital avatars, as technologically enhanced forms of dissociation in which dimensions of self and experience become separated or partitioned from primary consciousness and awareness. That is, in theorizing gamers' experiences of immersion through the anthropological-dissociation literature, I argue that some gamers concentrate so fully on the reality of their play world's fantasy landscapes as to divert attention from their ordinary offline lives. These players can be said to "dissociate" into both their characters and the spaces surrounding those characters, thus coming to importantly identify with virtual second-self avatars who inhabit lands that can come to feel as real as offline places. In some cases, players grow to feel at certain moments as if they actually *are* their characters and really *in* the game, with such fantastic characters and places potentially only loosely connected to offline selves and realities. Given the documented positive character of some forms of immersion,[41] I argue that such a partitioning of self and consciousness might be firmly tied to the therapeutics of games such as WoW, with the potential to enhance offline selves and experiences. As in the spiritual cases described above, it would also make sense that socially marginalized or otherwise distressed individuals might seek fuller relief in online play, which helps explain known connections between social distress such as loneliness and intensive internet gaming.[42] Once again, it is socially distressed persons who would be most eager and likely to want to escape into alternative and potentially superior virtual realities, with the stress relief and health benefits magnified there for such individuals.

Of note, spiritual and secular forms of dissociation such as those described in chapter 2 work most therapeutically if they are valued by members of a given society. For example, research suggests that many everyday absorptive activities—losing oneself in a good book or film, communing with nature, daydreaming and reverie, fantasy play, running and also team sports, driving, and yoga and meditation—can lead to positively altered, dissociative experiences in which the dominant stream of one's consciousness feels distorted and fragmented.[43] These activities contribute to the textures and pleasures of daily life in Western and non-Western contexts alike, in some cases tied to deeply pleasurable "flow" states of consciousness, described by the psychologist Mihaly Csikszentmihalyi, as where individuals feel naturally and pleasurably engrossed in an activity.[44] And the dissociative experiences associated with such activities are typically judged normal and healthy by cultural insiders and scholars alike, which allows individuals to experience them without feeling that they are doing anything wrong or weird.[45] Indeed, the anthropologist Christopher Lynn even argues that such states of consciousness are so important that we should also theorize pathological *under*-dissociation, as when one does not dissociate enough and thus misses out on the positive and even therapeutic experiences associated with such states.[46]

Yet the pathological character of some forms of dissociation is well recognized by clinicians and scholars. For example, Dissociative Identity Disorder (DID), or so-called Multiple Personality Disorder, is associated with extreme and dysfunctional discontinuities of experience.[47] Such seeming overdetachment from the real world, alongside distressful accompanying symptoms such as amnesia, depersonalization, derealization, and disruptions to interpersonal relations, has led clinicians and researchers to frame this condition as a mental disorder. In this book, I show that dissociative experiences linked to avatar identities—feeling like one is spiritually possessed, identifying almost fully with a digital character—possess therapeutic potential. As I have discussed, religious trances and other spiritual states of consciousness are often closely tied to healing rituals. Similarly, in losing themselves in the absorptive tasks and adventures provided by online games, some players find stress relief by temporarily escaping into virtual "sandboxes" and "tree houses."[48] However, these activities' therapeutic potential is unlocked most fully if and when the members of a given society consider normal and even desirable the experiences and behaviors associated with special avatar states of consciousness. And when those avatar states are not socially valued, those very same experiences (spirit possession, immersive gaming) can instead produce distress and even be considered illnesses (ghost illness, gaming addiction), both of which, in clinical terms, might in some circumstances be deemed identity disorders.

That stress processes—not just negative *distress* but also positive arousal or what Hans Selye refers to as *eustress*[49]—are closely linked to the therapeutic dynamics of dissociation in various cultural contexts has led scholars to seek underlying, potentially universal mechanisms. One approach for understanding such mechanisms involves considering neurobiology. For example, neuroscientists examine dissociation as a product of the brain's attention (or inattention) to the environment, homing in on the manner in which the regulation of attention to environmental stressors activates or deactivates the autonomic nervous system with ensuing health consequences.[50] Similarly, physicians have studied how trance-like states (e.g., meditation), can elicit the body's natural relaxation response, potentially limiting the negative health impacts of both acute and chronic stress.[51] Others note that dissociative states associated with meditation and trance might be accompanied by the release of feel-good opioids produced by the body itself and referred to as endorphins. Such naturally produced chemicals lead to even deeper states of pleasant relaxation with subsequently lowered stress responses and thus improved health.[52]

Anthropologists, too, have linked dissociative states to underlying physiological mechanisms and pathways with potentially important health consequences. For example, they have argued that the dissociative states of shamans, spirit mediums, and others might stimulate actual physiological changes in the body similar to the effects of placebos.[53] Others have argued that altered dissociative states of consciousness might cause healing through processes akin to hypnosis and suggestibility,[54] biofeedback,[55] and the cultivation of therapeutic mental images now sometimes employed in modern medicine.[56] Nevertheless, anthropologists are typically careful to identify how culture, in the sense of socially transmitted and distributed information and practice, enhances psychological and even neurobiological faculties related to dissociation, stress, and health. For example, pointing to the interaction and indeed tension between sociocultural contexts and underlying mechanisms, Seligman and Kirmayer argue: "Dissociative experiences may be *highly* socially scripted, yet have a neurobiological substrate that is not 'merely' socially scripted, and can occur in forms that are independent of, contradict, or subvert social scripts."[57]

Guided by such perspectives, I argue in chapter 2 that spiritual- and digital-avatar experiences are dissociative. Combining universalizing and context-dependent perspectives, I specifically show how spiritual and digital avatars provide culturally enhanced forms of absorption, with religious practitioners and gamers alike attributing dimensions of self and experience to secondary avatar identities. I further show, following literature highlighted in this chapter summary, how such avatar experiences are associated with health improvements when secondary avatar identities help individuals regulate psychosocial stress in their lives. Here, avatars are the material identity vehicles that activate deeper, even evolved, systems of relief from stress and trauma involving attention-regulation mechanisms.[58]

In chapter 3, "The Psychosocial Dynamics of Avatar Therapeutics: Enhanced Self-Image and Elevated Social Standing," I turn my attention to how dissociative avatar processes are shaped by identity issues and social contexts. To formulate these ideas, I draw, first, on Edward Higgins's self-discrepancy theory (SDT), in order to clarify why individuals might be driven to dissociate into avatar second selves.[59] First formulating his ideas in the late 1980s, Higgins, a health psychologist, identified three separate aspects of the self: what he called the *actual self* (the traits one actually possesses), the *ideal self* (the traits one would ideally like to possess), and the *ought self* (the traits others believe one should or ought to possess). Research in the SDT tradition shows that discrepancies between an individual's perception of their actual and ideal selves are associated with dejection, sadness, disappointment, and depression, whereas discrepancies between perceived actual and ought selves are linked to agitation-related states such as anxiety, nervousness, and guilt.

For the spiritual avatar cases of chapter 3, I link the SDT framework to anthropological accounts of spirit possession, and especially those involving women's experiences. As I show, in becoming a Hindu goddess's avatar, Bedami Bhat, the focus of this book's central spiritual case study, challenges everyday Rajasthani gender norms related to how women should speak and act. In fact, cross-culturally, women, while spiritually possessed, frequently lodge complaints that cannot otherwise be voiced in the open. In his seminal study, I. M. Lewis, for example, argues that in gender-stratified societies women's spiritual possessions are a "thinly disguised protest against the dominant sex."[60] In another classic account, Gananath Obeyesekere investigates how female ascetics in Sri Lanka redefine themselves through their spiritual practices and possession experiences.[61] This includes one case where fifty-two--year-old Karunavati Maniyo refuses to have sexual relations with her real-life husband, who is abusive, and instead marries the god Kataragama. In Southeast Asia, Aihwa Ong, in a similar vein, documents the spiritual attacks of young women working in Malaysia's free-trade zones during the 1970s.[62] Ong interprets these fits in part as gendered critiques against harsh factory work, which include long hours, unsafe and unsanitary labor conditions, and sexual harassment and disrespect by male supervisors. Janice Boddy's study of *zar* cults in northern Arabic-speaking Sudan makes a similar kind of interpretation, noting that women are more likely to find a voice through spirit cults, which are marginal to mainstream, male-dominated Islam.[63] More contemporaneously, Rebecca Seligman investigates the experiences of spirit mediums of the African-derived Candomblé religion in northeastern Brazil.[64] Many of Seligman's study participants are poor black and brown women who lead difficult lives. One of these women, Lucia, after becoming a spirit medium—in this book's terminology, a divine avatar—transforms from an agitated, high-strung, and emotionally volatile person to, in her own words, the calm and tranquil person she had become at the time Seligman knew her. As Seligman interprets this situation, Lucia finds ways to rewrite her life story and remake herself in ways that fosters greater emotional stability.

In Higgins's SDT terms, women like Bedami find in spiritual avatar identities such as the Hindu goddess a more *ideal self.* Dissociating into ideal avatar selves allows possessed persons such as Bedami to redefine themselves in more satisfying ways, which can be particularly important for women in the context of patriarchy. Further, building on chapter 2, inhabiting those new identities provides women (and others) needed breaks from everyday reality. Those breaks divert attention from life problems, which can help reduce stress and improve mental well-being. But importantly, these processes depend on cultural ideas about the perceived value of the avatar vehicle as alternatively desirable or undesirable. If the new avatar identity is not perceived socially as a positively evaluated *ought self*, in SDT terms, then those new avatar identities will not help alleviate stress and distress, a cultural-norm argument I further develop in chapter 4.

For gaming, I focus in chapter 3 on the manner that WoW guilds, in-game associations of like-minded players, promote different levels of gaming achievement, which, together with players' own motivations, determine whether online avatar identities enhance or detract from players' health and well-being.[65] I show how online gaming guilds establish normative cultures that differentially help players regulate stress emerging from challenging online activities such as *raids,* in which groups of ten or twenty-five players battle some of the game's fiercest enemies (termed *bosses*). To explore these issues, I examine most closely the WoW guild I knew best, the previously mentioned Knights of Good (KOG), a US gaming group I describe in some detail in chapter 1. For greater perspective, I also present survey results examining the way different guilds' normative cultures condition how members experience the relationship between stressful play such as raiding, on the one hand, and gaming experiences, on the other. Some guilds help members frame arousing and even stressful play—what one raider described as that "jittery" feeling—in ways that enhance the positive potential of stress—Selye's eustress—and even transform it into exhilaration, while minimizing negative feelings of being out of control, overwhelmed, defeated, and *distressed*. So-called *friends-and-family* and *casual-raiding* guilds are examples of this. By contrast, other guilds, such as those devoted to *hardcore raiding* can push their members to more extreme forms of online engagement, demanding total commitment and long hours of online activity. In doing so, those latter guilds potentially exacerbate the stressful arousal emerging from raiding or other challenging WoW activities, transforming potentially pleasurable eustress into distress.

I use Higgins's SDT thinking to again help me make sense of the avatar identity processes that feature in the gaming examples in chapter 3. In fact, researchers investigating avatar processes in video games and other digital environments specifically use Higgins's SDT framework to help explain well-being in these contexts.[66] Adapted for such research, the relevant self-dimensions are the actual self (defined in this context as the characteristics of the offline user), the ideal self (again, the traits one would optimally possess), and, interestingly, the *avatar self* (characteristics of the user's online personas). A recent review of the literature suggests that the avatar self is typically created as "better than the user, resembling the ideal self more closely than the actual self."[67] This trend was found for both physical and psychological features of video-game players' various selves. Even more relevant for this chapter's arguments, a now-substantial body of research suggests that gamers suffering from low self-esteem—predicted by SDT as resulting from felt tensions emerging from the perceived disjunction between the actual and ideal self[68]—tend to create avatars even more closely resembling their ideal selves, possibly in order to compensate for perceived shortcomings and thereby bolster psychosocial well-being.[69] SDT, then, helps to further clarify avatar-therapeutic mechanisms: as approximations of individuals' ideal selves, avatars provide opportunities for the enactment of one's best self. That those second avatar selves are often idealized and thus superior in some sense—one's avatar is often better, stronger, smarter, and of higher status than the primary self—keeps one's attention on the second self and its accompanying virtual reality, rendering fuller the dissociative escape from life's vicissitudes described in chapter 2. But again, here and in greater depth in chapter 4, I also draw attention to the manner that offline and online *cultural norms* related to how one *should* be from the point of view of social others—as an *ought self*—also shape these digital-avatar therapeutic processes.

In chapter 3, I also turn, second, to what has been called "health disparities" research to further advance these arguments about avatars as alternative ideal self-objects. In the celebrated Whitehall study of British civil servants, Michael Marmot, a professor of epidemiology and public health at University College London, explained that the social health gradient—the fact that we find health differences across social groups—reflected in part what he called a "status syndrome." In his work, Marmot pointed to a substantial literature showing how social factors such as poverty, educational attainment, race, and ethnicity drive health disparities within and between countries, including differential mortality and morbidity rates related to cardiovascular diseases, cancers, and metabolic problems such as diabetes. That is, Marmot showed how material deprivation related to low income, lack of access to clean water, poor sanitation and shelter, inadequate nutrition, and poor medical care can explain many of the health inequalities between social classes. But importantly for Marmot's (and for chapter 3's) arguments, he also demonstrated that health disparities remained *even after controlling for all the relevant material factors*. This led Marmot to his famous *status-syndrome* formulation, where he posited that the symbolic status or prestige dimensions of social subordination also contributed to poorer health outcomes. Specifically, he postulated that occupying low-status positions reflected (among other things) lack of control over one's life. That lack of control produced the psychosocial experience of stress, a known contributor to a variety of health problems including cardiovascular disease, diabetes, immune disorders, and depression. Overall, Marmot effectively argued that a stress-driven status syndrome could account for the symbolic portion of health disparities—i.e., those disparities remaining even after controlling for material factors such as income, nutrition, and access to health care.[70]

Dissociating into an avatar second self, then, plausibly lessens one's perception of life problems, which relieves stress and improves health, as I show in chapter 2. SDT research in turn helps clarify why some individuals would be compelled to dissociate into those alternative selves in the first place: those selves are perceived as superior or *ideal* in some way, and thus compelling, an argument I broach in chapter 3. But health disparities research such as Marmot's, a further focus of chapter 3, helps me refine understandings of these stress-relief mechanisms and health processes, by better specifying the exact nature of self-improvement experienced in avatar form. Specifically, when in alternative avatar form, individuals can temporarily improve their *social position* and thus *status*. For example, a spirit medium in India or elsewhere might originate from a low social caste or class; however, when channeling god, they experience dramatic (if temporary) improvements in social standing and status. Moreover, a video-game player might be a self-professed loser in the actual world but a wizard of immense power in a virtual setting. Improved social standing, then, might help explain more precisely what makes an avatar feel like a superior or even *ideal* self, which clarifies SDT health processes. Feeling more socially appreciated while in avatar form, the spiritually possessed and gamers alike dissociate more fully into those alternative identities. That more complete form of dissociation in turn can magnify stress relief, which, as work by Marmot and many others now convincingly shows, could also mean lower rates of cardiovascular disease, diabetes, mental disorders, and the like. Something akin to Marmot's status syndrome, then, can explain certain avatar-therapeutic processes described in this book, helping to propel forward dissociation and self-discrepancy theories of health in these contexts, as I argue in chapter 3.

In chapter 4, "Distinguishing Therapeutic from Toxic Avatar Experiences: Norm Conflicts and Felt Dissonance," I argue that health disparities research does not go far enough in explaining the *sociocultural* dimensions of avatar therapeutics. Specifically, health-disparities researchers do not typically aim to explain how the status syndrome Marmot identified might unfold differently according to the cultural setting, despite that anthropologists have demonstrated how social status can vary dramatically in kind and consequence from place to place. Even in the twenty-first century, Indian society is still largely structured around caste principles, where one's status is determined by the community in which one is born. By contrast, in the US, individuals derive most of their status from wealth, education, and their (seemingly) more flexible socioeconomic class. Also, both India and the US differ in the value they place on religion and secular leisure activity, which means that being a spirit medium or by contrast an aspiring pro video-game player is associated with different degrees of social prestige in each context. The latter point means that simply living out the best version of oneself—as defined from one's *personal* point of view—cannot completely account for the health impacts of that process. It is also important to understand how the alternative avatar self-cum-ego ideal—the spirit medium's or the pro gamer's—is *socially* valued. That social value ultimately determines the prestige assigned to alternative avatar identities, which, as Marmot and others have shown, shapes health.

To better understand the sociocultural shaping of avatar therapeutics, I draw on psychological anthropologist William Dressler's theory of cultural consonance, which provides key analytical language for chapter 4. Based on research now spanning almost three decades, Dressler more recently defines cultural consonance as, "the degree to which individuals, in their own beliefs and behaviors, approximate the prototypes for belief and behavior encoded in cultural models,"[71] with *cultural models* understood to be "mental representations shared by members of a culture."[72] With the idea of cultural consonance, William Dressler develops a framework to assess how individuals' greater consonance—or congruity with—any locally meaningful and culturally defined social hierarchy of value is associated with improved health. Dressler and his associates have repeatedly shown that Brazilians and others who fail to embody societal models of success and the good life have more compromised health—for example, higher rates of depression and elevated blood pressure—which can be partially explained by the social sanctions experienced by less culturally consonant individuals, findings replicated in numerous cultural contexts.[73] Dressler's approach thus allows researchers to understand not only how a Western civil-service hierarchy like Whitehall (the focus of Marmot's research) might affect that system's administrators' health; it also helps researchers understand how any culturally defined system of social value influences health anywhere in the world that system is found.

In chapter 4, I focus on how *conflicts* between *competing* mainstream and subcultural values effectively explain the way secondary avatar identities influence mental well-being. In developing this argument, I combine William Dressler's concept of cultural consonance (an individual's consistency with his or her culture) with Leon Festinger's concept of cognitive dissonance (psychic tension associated with conflicting beliefs and attitudes).[74] I refer to the resulting stresses, strains, and psychological processes associated with embodying and negotiating potentially competing or conflicting social norms as *cultural dissonance.*[75]

In the Rajasthani spirit-possession case, for example, Bedami Bhat dramatically elevates her status and mental health when serving as the avatar vehicle of the Hindu mother goddess. But Bedami's new avatar identity also places her in conflict with her husband, as I show in chapter 4, which puts stress on her marriage and psyche. Her avatar identity's elevation in status is thus not simple and straightforward, given how a divine Bedami is pulled in different directions and valued differently by members of the community. Thus, whether Bedami's new avatar identity helps her to improve her life or further erodes her well-being depends importantly on how she manages to navigate and successfully resolve these tensions, processes I refer to as *cultural dissonance* ones. As I further show in chapter 4, similar norm-conflict ideas can be applied to help explain the avatar-therapeutic processes associated with other spirit possession cases around the world. And in this chapter, I examine the work of Lewis, Obeyesekere, Ong, Boddy, Seligman, and others through a cultural consonance/dissonance framework.

In relation to chapter 4's gaming discussion, now-classic studies of virtual worlds—e.g., Tom Boellstorff's (2008) study of *Second Life* and Edward Castronova's (2008) and T. L. Taylor's (2009) writings on the pre-WoW MMO *Everquest*—suggest that online virtual worlds form communities and cultures.[76] As such, local group standards, or what social scientists call *norms,* shape gamer understandings and behaviors in those worlds in ways that can also filter into players' offline lives. Gamer culture, for example, channels play in certain ways, directing players to pursue specific goals and social relationships and to recognize good and successful play when they see it. And gamers' relative achievement of normative notions of in-game success shape whether gamers experience their play as wondrous adventure and good fun or as an important source of life satisfaction and self-esteem. In the specific ethnographic focus of chapter 4, Udaipur's emerging adults who play CS-GO in face-to-face gaming zones can find in their play the success and recognition that eludes them in their offline lives, with their secondary avatar identities contributing positively to these individuals' life satisfaction and mental well-being. But these individuals also experience themselves pulled between competing offline and online worlds, in this case related to these young Indians' impending marriages and careers, on the one hand, and their gaming community's time demands, on the other. Some gamers in this Indian context thus come to feel like they inhabit two lives simultaneously, an infeasible and thus distressing situation, which can erode their mental and physical health.[77] As I show in chapter 4, the social-norm theories of cultural consonance and dissonance provide a flexible approach for explaining interrelationships between social status and avatar therapeutics in these Udaipuri gaming-zone contexts as well.

In the book's conclusion I emphasize the importance of positive ego ideals—avatars being one instance of those—for maintaining mental balance. I stress how spiritually based ethnomedical traditions and everyday leisure activities such as gaming can activate such ego ideals in ways that render them more compelling, motivating, and thus therapeutically effective. I conclude with big-picture ideas on the future of research on avatar therapeutics, giving readers a glimpse of how I see this field progressing in the coming years.

Overall, in exploring processes related to avatar therapeutics, I aim in this book to establish via an evocative case-study approach—Rajasthani spirit religions, online video games—the value of psychological-anthropological perspectives on religion, media, and health. I also hope to influence readers' perception of psychiatry—dominated for decades now by a focus on biology and pharmaceuticals[78]—in ways that better recognize the importance of folk psychiatric practices found in spiritual traditions and video games for regulating linked mental and physical well-being.

As I claim earlier, *avatar,* the book's central term and concept, derives from Hinduism, a religion originating in the Indian subcontinent. However, throughout the book, I also use avatar as an analytical category to describe the process by which an agent embodies her consciousness in an alternative vehicle also termed an *avatar.* My analytical use of this term deviates somewhat from that of my anthropological respondents. In India, for example, the term *avatar* is typically reserved to refer to occasions where God—with a capital *G*, e.g., Vishnu, one of Hinduism's three most important deities—takes earthly (sometimes human) form to battle evil and restore cosmic balance. Now, some Rajasthani spirit mediums I have known were said to be precisely this—incarnations and thus "avatars" of Vishnu—but those individuals were rare and not typical. By contrast, video-game players commonly refer to their digital avatars in ways consistent with my use of the term. But they would not typically think of their avatars as related to the sacred Hindu processes I describe, though they might agree to the logic of agents projecting their consciousness into other agents, say, after hearing my arguments. This is to say that I do aim to do justice to my many respondents' words and worldviews, which includes trying to accurately represent their own points of view on avatar experiences. Yet I pursue the additional goal of developing the idea of avatar as an analytical category—and an underlying human faculty—that in some sense transcends any single cultural setting. I am like Farmer and Morningstar in this sense, extending a Hindu religious concept beyond its original meanings. Although in my case, I remain particularly careful to acknowledge my intellectual debts to Hinduism, as demonstrated by my focus on Bedami's case, and I aim to advance the field of psychological anthropology rather than build a better virtual world.

A UNIVERSAL (BUT NOT UNIFORM) HUMAN AVATAR FACULTY

Avatars are vehicles of consciousness that agents—whether gods or humans—use to experience and accomplish things in alternative realities. In this book, I conceptualize avatars as *self-objects*—alternative representations of the self that serve as vehicles for new identities—found in both spiritual and digital settings. The spiritually possessed and video-game players alike inhabit these alternative identities, which, though in some sense only imagined, can feel deeply meaningful and real. When alternative avatar identities are valued and realized in these manners, individuals can psychologically absorb into them—or *dissociate*—in ways that disconnect them from everyday life. In many cases, those disconnections provide therapeutic relief from felt stress of various kinds. This is especially the case for suffering or marginalized individuals who can benefit more from temporary respites from life's vicissitudes. But that relief comes most readily if the alternative identities are socially valued rather than despised. Culture thus plays an important role in shaping avatar-therapeutic processes, especially local cultural norms through which individuals frame or model dissociative avatar experiences in particular ways, say, as godly rather than demonic or as skill and commitment rather than technological addiction.

On some level, this book represents a direct application of anthropological accounts of spirit possession to the analysis of new technological avatar experiences. As details presented earlier show, anthropological accounts focus on how the spiritually possessed use religious experiences to voice concerns and to redefine themselves in relation to others, key themes in my analysis of digital avatars. Spiritual experiences of these kinds also can alleviate or further magnify felt psychosocial stress, as the possessed renegotiate their relationship to their communities and to dominant cultural norms (such as those related to gender), which are again important themes in my analysis of video-game avatars. More generally, anthropological studies such as these draw attention to the importance of sociocultural context in shaping personal experience, which can help scholars in other fields such as communication, psychology, and epidemiology provide fuller accounts of avatar identity and health processes. Communication scholars, for one, might then understand why avatar identification processes often play out differently around the world. Driving those differences, in part, are the cultural values attached to physical beauty, material wealth, personal achievement, lived experience, autonomy and control, a concern for factual reality, intimacy, and sympathy/empathy, as well as the bodily and experiential distinctions between men and women. All these factors and variables, obviously, demand more consideration.[79] As discussed earlier, psychologists and psychiatrists might better see how local cultural norms can shape the productive or pathological tenor of dissociative experiences related to spiritual states of consciousness, video-game play, and other domains of human experience.[80] And epidemiologists could test if the structure of a social-status system, such as a more class- or caste-bound one, might influence relationships between subcultural identities—religious and gaming ones being two possibilities—and human well-being, by using, for example, Dressler's cultural consonance framework, as I do in this book.[81]

Likewise, anthropology can profit from disciplines such as communication, psychology, and epidemiology, and the scholarly benefits flow in the opposite direction, too. Researchers in communication, for example, illuminate with admirable clarity how avatars function as personal identity vehicles in computer-generated environments.[82] They pinpoint the features and dimensions of digital avatars, such as the degree to which gamers feel embodied, emotionally attached, and attentionally absorbed in relation to their technologically enhanced avatar bodies.[83] And the degree of avatar involvement can in turn influence gamers' felt presence and embodiment in larger virtual worlds—what has been called digital *immersion*—a concept treated earlier.[84] Of note, anthropologists of spirit possession working outside India do not refer to religious-identity vehicles—such as Bedami's alter ego, a Hindu devi or goddess—as *avatars*. In part, this practice reflects that anthropologists typically treat the word *avatar* as a cultural "insider" term that would only be appropriate in certain (but not all) Hindu or Indian contexts. This is fine as far as it goes, and in fact it is a perspective in which I was trained and sometimes still pursue. But in the process, anthropologists (and others) miss a chance to develop the term *avatar* as a more general analytical construct, here, following in part communication scholars, referring to *avatars* as *personal identity vehicles that can serve as idealized self-objects*. In my experience, anthropologists of spirit possession (including me at times) are generally reluctant to think at this higher level of abstraction, or at least to write at that level in their typically highly locally grounded religious case studies. My intention, then, is to run the gauntlet of that abstraction in this book. Doing that promises to highlight the potential of universal identity and health processes related to avatars in religious practices and the digital world—and perhaps in other applications yet to be determined.

Similarly, researchers in psychology and related fields examine how digital-gaming avatars allow players to enact in virtual game-worlds their best and most ideal selves—their *ideal elf* (in the sense of a digital-gaming pixie or elf), in one well-known early formulation by Katherine Bessière and colleagues.[85] Here, avatars, as idealized second selves, have the potential to help players compensate for their perceived life failings, thereby bolstering their psychosocial well-being, as previously discussed.[86] Likewise, and also as discussed earlier, games-studies scholars have focused extensively on the psychological experience of *immersion,* sometimes framed as an underlying mental *motivation,* where players lose themselves in computer-generated fantasy landscapes and attribute dimensions of self and experience to in-game characters.[87] This focus on the individual self and inner experience, typically the purview of psychology, is notable in this context given anthropologist Clifford Geertz's (1973) influential critique of Ward Goodenough's cognitive and psychological definition of culture. Goodenough's definition of culture, which is a cornerstone of modern cognitive anthropology theory and method, is defined as "whatever one has to know or believe in order to operate in a manner acceptable to its members."[88] According to Geertz, Goodenough was wrongheaded and anthropologists should focus on public symbols rather than private meanings; this is because, according to Geertz, "Thinking consists not of 'happenings in the head' ... but of a traffic in significant symbols."[89] Although Geertz acknowledged that sensory data are also processed in "a secret grotto in the head,"[90] he upbraided cognitive anthropologists who "psychologized" and thus trivialized the anthropological trade, instead encouraging them to focus on the material vehicles of thought—public symbols—that are open to inspection and study. By contrast, I will show in this book how a careful analysis of inner mental experience—assessed via, say, a gaming *absorption-immersion* self-report scale measure—can help researchers identify with greater precision relationships between avatar identities and well-being. However, I first adapt the scale measures—themselves originally developed by psychologists[91]—so that they are more sensitive to local cultural processes.[92] I hope readers will appreciate how employing *cultural-psychological* measures and approaches such as these can help researchers better illuminate the tight interconnection between social processes and mental experiences, and more generally the way that culture and the mind mutually constitute each other.[93]

Finally, epidemiologists such as Marmot who study health disparities have identified a general *status syndrome* that appears around the world.[94] In this book, I do aim to show how sociocultural factors—for instance, the psychosocial compensations provided by secondary avatar identities—can help to minimize social inequality's corrosion of mental and physical health. But this should not divert analytical focus from the general health processes Marmot and others identify. Of course, Dressler's consonance framework can help ensure that researchers assess in culturally meaningful ways relationships between social status and health as they move beyond Western settings such as Whitehall. But we should remain open to the possibility that sociocultural factors modulate rather than determine these health processes.

In all these senses, this book is less an *application* of perspectives developed in cultural studies of spirit possession to new digital-avatar settings and more an attempt to identify the *interplay* of local cultural and more universal psychosocial factors shaping both religious and digital-avatar identity and well-being processes. Anthropological studies of spirit possession centrally inform the book, keeping it focused on the importance of local cultural factors, such as how socially learned norms shape whether secondary avatar identities are experienced positively or negatively. But drawing from other fields, I also attend to factors that characterize both religious and digital avatars, aiming to identify a more general avatar faculty in the sense of an abstract human potentiality or capacity.[95] Here, I specifically refer to the human capacity to personally identify with external and often idealized self-objects—avatars—in ways that can improve (or compromise) well-being. In a memorable phrasing, the cultural psychologist Richard Shweder referred to similar projects as aiming to capture "universalism without the uniformity."[96] By this, he meant that researchers could examine how general human capacities emerge in unique ways in specific cultural settings. Shweder often spoke of this idea in relation to moral reasoning and development, in the US compared with India, for example.[97] Here, I use this idea to argue that the avatar processes I describe are at once universal and importantly shaped by local cultural contexts. As I. M. Lewis, Mircea Eliade, Erika Bourguignon, and others have shown in classic works, spiritual trances are human universals found in religious systems around the world.[98] But those same scholars show how local socially learned *theories* of trance—spirit possession, madness—shape how those experiences play out. Depending on the cultural frame, trance states might be experienced as socially productive rather than debilitating, as also argued in the more contemporary spirit-possession case studies of Obeyesekere, Ong, Boddy, and Seligman. In this book, I push this argument further to suggest that Eliade's "archaic techniques of ecstasy"[99]—attention-diversion techniques that facilitate escapes from normal realities and everyday selves—are now also found in online virtual worlds. An archaic-human avatar faculty can thus be said to be activated by modern technologies found on the internet. But to say this does not imply that ecstatic experiences facilitated by new internet technologies do not emerge in unique ways. All-night religious seances characterized by drumming, chanting, and music can focus attention in ways that facilitate trance-like and stress-relieving dissociation into alternative identities and realities, as can beautifully rendered digital-gaming worlds that often include all-night rituals of their own. But the two avatar experiences look (and feel) quite different, illustrating how a universal avatar faculty need not unfold in a uniform manner, to borrow Shweder's idea.

Methodologically, ethnographic fieldwork, the method used for example in the spirit possession cases I cite, has centrally informed my understandings of how spiritual- and digital-avatar identities affect human health and well-being. *Ethnography* refers to case-study accounts of a group's practices and points of view, relying largely (at least in contemporary versions) on qualitative field-based methods like participant observation. In my experience, there is no better method to illuminate local cultural processes. Although typically centered on qualitative methods, ethnographic projects can be enhanced by incorporating more structured data-collection methods and systematic analytical strategies, including field questionnaires, analyzed quantitatively, which have been important to my US and India gaming research that features in this book. Questionnaires feature prominently in the communication, psychology, and epidemiology literature I have cited, which has also influenced my own "mixed methods" qualitative-quantitative approach to digital avatars in particular. For example, field questionnaires have allowed me to confirm with quantitative-analysis insights into gaming processes that I first identified ethnographically through my fieldwork, illuminating relationships between avatar identities and health processes that are more difficult to see with qualitative analysis alone. In relation to these methodological issues, I thus again integrate anthropological approaches with those from other fields, rather than simply extend insights garnered from anthropological approaches to religious avatars to their modern digital analogues.[100]

These theoretical and methodological commitments lead me to a particular approach to social and cultural processes that draws from anthropology, linguistics, psychology, and the cognitive sciences. Loosely, I ascribe to cognitive-anthropological definitions of culture as socially transmitted and thus learned knowledge and practices—*social conventions,* so to speak—which differently shape and influence the personal lives of individuals within a group.[101] In this book, I focus importantly on the *knowledge* and thus cognitive or symbolic dimensions of culture, though, as readers will see, that knowledge is importantly expressed in behavior as well. In an early influential version of this approach to culture that I reference earlier in this chapter, Ward Goodenough described culture as that which one must know to function adequately in a given social system.[102] This approach to culture has been developed extensively within contemporary psychological anthropology and cultural psychology, and it also has links in linguistics and the broader field of cognitive science.[103] For example, psychologists, linguists, and philosophers have devoted considerable attention to the study of *schemas* (or *schemata)*—simple cognitive elements or prototypes which help individuals organize and process information in relationship to their social and natural environments, as well as to *models* or *frames,* understood to be more complex concatenations of schemas, which help individuals understand the world around them and attribute meaning and significance to events and experiences.[104] Rather than ambitiously trying to grasp the totality of culture, psychological anthropologists typically try to understand how *socially learned* and thus *cultural* schemas, models, and frames (the terms often used interchangeably) structure individuals' reasoning and practice.[105] *Cultural* models or frames, as opposed to idiosyncratic or *personal* models, are understood in this context to be mental representations of the world that are socially transmitted and variably shared within a group.[106] In this book, I examine the way culturally learned models or frames (about success and the good life, and also about spirit possession and gaming themselves) shape whether avatar identities are experienced as positive and productive or alternatively undesirable and distressful. As I view them, certain learned models can become more widely shared and even dominant within a particular social setting—becoming what are called social or cultural *norms*—with individuals within a group feeling pressure to conform to those normative understandings and values. These ideas are most critical to my cultural-consonance and dissonance arguments about avatar-therapeutic processes, which I develop in chapter 4.

Although I focus in my analysis on culturally learned mental representations and thus the *symbolic inheritance* dimensions of culture, I also consider culturally informed *practices,* as I have said earlier. The cultural-consonance framework, for example, leads researchers to assess the manner and extent that individuals embody culture in their thinking and (importantly) *their behavior.* And the way that individuals more or less closely embody social norms in their own personal thinking and behavior—are *consonant* with them, in Dressler's terminology—shapes the avatar-therapeutic processes that feature in this book. Here, I would draw attention to the fact that even Goodenough's early "cognitive" or knowledge approach to culture also featured how persons *function* and thus behave in cultural settings. In fact, in an influential later cognitive-anthropological formulation of culture, Naomi Quinn and Claudia Strauss drew explicit parallels with Pierre Bourdieu's *practice theory,*[107] in the manner that thinking was literally *embodied* in human bodies, mind-brains, and behaviors.[108] Similar concepts have also been developed elsewhere, such as Roy D'Andrade's concerning culture as located both inside and outside individual minds, Ed Hutchin's on *distributed cognition,* Andy Clark and David Chalmer's formulation of *extended cognition,* broadly developed perspectives on *4E* or *embodied, embedded, enacted, and extended cognition,* and Bruno Latour's *actor-network theory.*[109] All these have shaped my own approach to culture and are highly compatible with the arguments I develop in this book, in the way they emphasize how individual thinking and behavior is in constant exchange with local environments and networks of persons, objects, and meanings in those environments.

As socially learned, cultural thought and practice can in many instances become broadly shared among members of a group and thus normative. However, I would clarify that my formulation of culture in no way implies that all members of a group think or behave in uniform or consistent manners. Part of the confusion arises from the fact that one influential psychological-anthropological method for assessing cultural knowledge, which also features in my own analysis of avatar therapeutics,[110] is referred to as *cultural-consensus analysis,* thus seeming to imply cultural uniformity.[111] However, I would point out that psychological anthropologists have typically been interested in both cultural consensus and (importantly) *dissensus.* Even in the original cultural-consensus article, where commonly shared group meanings can be identified (in what is called the cultural *answer key*), there still is attention to how individual members variably instantiate that culture (each member's cultural-knowledge *competence scores*). In effect, this means that some degree of shared thought and practice is expected within a group, which is encoded in social norms, though with much variability or what I have called in other writing "dissensus within consensus."[112] The focus on individual variation from cultural ideals or norms, and the way such deviations can influence behavior and well-being, is even more centrally highlighted in my cultural-consonance and dissonance modeling of avatar therapeutics, as readers will see in chapter 4. After all, it is the manner that individuals approximate group norms in their own thought and behavior, albeit with great individual variation, that shapes the well-being processes that are the focus of my analysis of avatar and health processes.

Further, I would emphasize my overall pragmatic approach to cultural theory and method. Cultural-consensus and consonance techniques provide me with useful ways to identify quantifiable proxies for more complex cultural processes, which complement the book's qualitative analyses and deepen my understanding of avatar therapeutics. In fact, these structured approaches to cultural analysis have spread in part because of the way they allow researchers to identify and even quantify associations between cultural knowledge and practice and other processes of interest, including motivational, experiential, and well-being processes such as those featuring in this book but also others related to human biology and the environment. Due in part to these pragmatic considerations, cognitive and psychological approaches to culture have become widespread and even dominant in certain areas of psychological, medical, and environmental anthropology.[113] However, researchers should not confuse the thing itself—here, culturally informed understandings and behaviors—with the various analytical strategies used to identify and evaluate those understandings. To do so would be to commit a fallacy associated with "operationalism," where a concept is equated with its measurement, a methods argument I develop elsewhere.[114] Readers should therefore keep in mind that the cultural processes I describe in this book—and sometimes quantify—are assuredly more complex in reality.

All in all, compared with research in anthropology, communication, and other fields, I examine avatar health processes at a higher level of abstraction, in ways that treat avatars as a general human faculty that takes specific form in spiritual or digital contexts. As I construe them, avatars are personal-identity vehicles that can serve as idealized self-objects and thus promote health and well-being. In comparing spiritual- and digital-avatar processes in this way, I do not mean to equate unequivocally the two. For example, in cultural-insider terms, and as referenced earlier, spiritual possessions are typically felt to be *seizures* of a kind, in the sense that human vehicles are *seized* by gods, ghosts, and other supernatural entities. Human beings are the avatars of higher-order supernatural entities, and those experiencing these events will often say the experiences feel beyond their personal control. By contrast, gamers choose games that appeal to their individual sensibilities, and they project their consciousness into digital pixies during play. Gamers thus seem to be active agents who manipulate digital characters as secondary identity vehicles or avatars.

Yet I also show in this book how drawing sharp contrasts like this between spiritual and digital avatars can be deceiving. In the spiritual cases, possessed individuals do in fact make many conscious choices on their path to becoming a spirit medium. To begin, there are decisions about the nature of the invading presence: Is it a ghost? A disgruntled ancestor? A god? As readers will see, the afflicted, along with priests and members of the community and possessed person's family, at some point decide how to frame the spiritual presence's identity and name it. That frame and name then set in motion processes whereby the possessed start to identify more strongly with the named entity, which shapes the avatar experiences. This includes deciding when, where, and whether to call back the entity, say, in a spiritual séance, and how to cultivate the experiences through drumming, music, chants, fasting and the like. Further, on some important level, the possessed can be thought to project themselves and their psyche into a spiritual system of representations—say, in acts of meditating on an image on a Hindu altar, as I often witnessed, which further shapes their avatar identity and experiences. Divinity, as represented in specific religious traditions, is thus also in some sense the avatar of human consciousness. And multiple conscious decisions and processes such as these determine whether spiritual experiences of these kinds are felt to be therapeutic or mere madness. In the gaming cases, as also suggested earlier, what starts as a conscious choice can take on characteristics of compulsion. This is the case not only with "internet addiction" or "gaming disorder" but also the general felt "pull" of video games, which most players acknowledge can be a powerful urge. So, yes, video-game players project their psyches into gaming avatars and characters. But in some important sense, the game also takes control of the player, occupying waking consciousness and even, as members of my research team experienced, nightly dreams. So video-game players also seem to be in some sense the avatars of their digital characters. Similarly, some gamers initiate play for certain reasons—say, to have fun—but find themselves drifting into other pleasures and processes—as when video-game characters increasingly become self-objects and identity vehicles, which does not clearly emerge from conscious choices and intentions. These points further clarify why I said earlier that less important than the directionality of agent-avatar projections in spiritual and digital contexts—which are ambiguous—is the fact that bi-directional relationships of exchange open up between conscious agents and their avatar vehicles.

Despite identifying parallels like these between spiritual and digital avatars, my point, again, is not to equate unequivocally the two sets of experiences. Rather, I hope to show readers that there is enough overlap between the two to warrant comparison in ways that might expand our understanding of each and more generally of avatar health processes considered at this higher level of abstraction. Such an effort, I believe, can help advance ideas in anthropology, communication, psychology, epidemiology, and other fields. But in doing so, I do not want to lose that important tension between universal and culture-specific processes. The book's central aim, then, is to unlock avatar-therapeutic processes in ways that point to human universals without implying cultural uniformity, to reference again Shweder's compelling idea.

ONE

Sacred and Secular Settings

SACRED AVATARS IN HINDU RELIGION

Hindu Avatars and Rajasthani Spirit Possession

As explained in the introductory chapter, the term *avatar* literally means "descent"—joining the Sanskrit *ava* (down or below) with the verb root *tr* (to float or pass over something, such as a river)—and refers to the way that Hindu deities incarnate in earthly vehicles to combat evil and restore balance in the universe.[1] In Hinduism, any deity can manifest in alternative avatar form, but the term is most closely associated with Vishnu the "preserver's" ten primary forms or *dashavatara* (*das* literally means "ten") (see plates 1–10). According to Hindu scripture, Vishnu—considered one of Hinduism's three principal deities, along with Brahma the "creator" and Shiva the "destroyer"— descended into diverse forms, including a fish (Matsya, Vishnu's first avatar), a tortoise (Kurma, his second form), a boar (Varaha, Vishnu's third avatar), a lion man (Narasimha, his fourth form), a dwarf (Vamana, the fifth form), a warrior-sage (Parashurama, his sixth form), other deities such as Rama and Krishna (Vishnu's seventh and eighth forms respectively, according to some traditions), the Buddha (his ninth form), and Kalki (considered Vishnu's tenth and culminating final form, appearing at the end of each age, when evil prevails). In those alternative avatar forms, Vishnu battled to save humanity from floods, demons, and general collapse and calamity, restoring truth and morality (or *dharma*) in the process. Of interest, each of Vishnu's embodiments could theoretically also take alternative avatar form, as in when Krishna, a god of deep compassion, tenderness, and love, is said to have incarnated as Baba Ramdev, a fourteenth-century ruler of the Rajasthani region of Marwar and who is considered a folk deity. Further, in Rajasthani folklore,

Baba Ramdev himself is said to have materialized in other forms over the centuries, typically whenever some contemporary individual demonstrated great wisdom, compassion, and sacrifice, as I learned during my own field-work in Rajasthan, with several current Bhat *gurus* (or teachers) said to be incarnations of that fourteenth-century Marwari folk deity. Likewise, well-known forms of the Hindu feminine divine, or *devi*, include Lakshmi, the goddess of prosperity and Vishnu's wife, who herself is said to have incarnated as Sita and Radha, respectively, Rama and Krishna's wives and companions. In fact, Lakshmi is said to have eight primary avatars, or Ashta Lakshmi (literally, "eight Lakshmis"), with each of those embodiments capable of taking their own alternative forms, according to humanity's needs at a given moment in time.

The Hindu avatar concept finds reference in ancient scriptures such as the epic Mahabharata and Ramayana, which were first composed around the eighth or ninth and seventh centuries BCE, respectively. For example, in the Bhagavad Gita, or "Song of God," considered a part of the Mahabharata, Vishnu incarnates as the god Krishna, who, as Prince Arjuna's guide and charioteer, helps that hero fulfill his destiny by pursuing his rightful warrior duty and obligations (dharma). Similarly, the Ramayana, or "Coming of Rama," tells how that divinity, again conceived as an embodiment of Vishnu, defeats evil in the form of the demon Ravana to restore righteousness and harmony on earth. Likewise, most of the primary (c. sixth-century BCE) Indian Puranas—or "Ancient Tales"—center on the lives of divine "avatars," explicitly using that phrasing, with the majority of those deities once again said to be embodiments of the Hindu god Vishnu.

Referenced in ancient Hindu scriptural texts, the avatar concept is often connected to what is called Sanatana Dharma, or Hinduism's "Eternal Duty and Morality." Writing in the middle part of the twentieth century, anthropologist McKim Marriott referred to such ancient texts as belonging to Hinduism's "great" or "classical" traditions, connected as they are to urban centers of learning, established priesthoods, philosophical sophistication, monumental temples, and oftentimes dominant social classes.[2] Indeed, members of certain elite social classes, especially Brahmins, use their knowledge of Sanskrit and ancient Hindu scripture, maintained by certain families, to extend their wealth and social standing, for example, by serving as priests in prosperous temples. Nevertheless, the avatar stories memorialized in ancient Hindu texts are not monopolized by elites. Rather, divine avatars, such as the previously referenced Baba Ramdev—conceived of as an embodiment of

Krishna, who himself embodies Vishnu—are also the devotional focus of members of lower-status and often economically disadvantaged communities, including those of the formerly untouchable Bhats, who feature in this book. That is, avatars, as more immediate and accessible expressions of divinity, are also tied to what has been called Hinduism's vibrant "folk" or "popular" (or in Hindi *lok*) traditions. Local incarnations of typically pan-Hindu deities are worshipped through practices that can vary dramatically from region to region. Likewise, images of such avatars are oftentimes found in inconspicuous urban shrines and dispersed throughout village India and the rural countryside. And knowledge about them is typically transmitted orally, rather than meticulously maintained by literate Brahmin priests connected to prestigious temples.[3]

In fact, the avatar concept's emphasis on embodied or revealed divinity, and thus on the immediacy of godhood, intersects with many common Hindu beliefs and practices found in classical and folk traditions alike. These include the Hindu belief in the possibility and importance of *darsan,* or "divine viewing," where catching glimpses of living gods materialized in stone statues or altar paintings is conceived of as an important act of worship, as expressed both in ancient Sanskrit texts and myriad daily practices. Likewise, informed by classical and folk traditions alike, Hindus strive to access *sakti,* or creative divine energies—understood to be especially redolent in goddesses or devis—in ways that directly improve devotees' material lives. Devis are typically considered active and often empathetic helper divinities who bring health, wealth, and general good fortune, thus contrasting with distant supreme gods such as Brahma, the creator, who is less engaged with the everyday management of human affairs. Sakti beliefs connect with the Hindu notion of *puja,* or "sacred offering," where exchanges with materialized gods are meant to bring divine blessings of health, wealth, and fortune. Likewise, the Hindu belief in *karma,* or the force generated by actions that shape one's future lives, emphasizes the movement of spiritual agents—souls—from body to body. Of course, beliefs and practices related to puja and karma, again widespread in both classical and folk Hinduism, are unique in certain respects. But insistently, like the avatar principle itself, each stresses the ways that spiritual agents and forces can take alternative material forms, which can directly affect human existence.

In the Indian state of Rajasthan where I worked, one of the most direct reflections of the sacred avatar principle, and an important focus of this book, is spirit possession: the movement of a spiritual agent such as a god, demon, or ghost into the body of a human vehicle or mount, which is said to be grabbed, controlled, ridden like a horse, and thus "possessed" by the spiritual agent.[4] Spirit possession is referenced in Hinduism's classical traditions. The Mahabharata, the Puranas, and the *Atharva-Veda* (the last of the four Vedas, the oldest Hindu scriptures) all describe spirit possession, ghost illness, and the Brahmin's power of exorcism. (Figure 2 shows a Rajasthani instance of ghost illness.) As I said earlier, in living folk Hindu traditions, contemporary Rajasthanis most commonly speak of spiritual possessions as *bhav a gaya,* literally meaning "a feeling has come." This phrase suggests that one experiences an extraordinary emotion, but more specifically it can imply, depending on the case and context, as I learned, that one is simply overcome with emotion; that one is so overwhelmed by emotions as to seem crazy; that a person is pretending to be a particular spirit or god; that one evokes in an audience a supernatural being's feeling (bhav) or flavor (rasa), much as would a temple painting or a sacred song; that an individual emotionally identifies with a particular spiritual being and indeed thinks she is that being even though she is not; or, finally, that a person's demeanor and emotional state are so reminiscent of a particular spirit or divinity that she is probably being controlled by that entity. (The latter is sometimes referred to by locals as "true" or *asli* possession.)

During my fieldwork, Rajasthanis did occasionally refer to the spiritually possessed as divine avatars. But that terminology was more typically reserved for spirit medium healers perceived to embody and channel divine power in particularly potent manners. In Rajasthan, mediums who learn to control the spirits that originally controlled them—using spiritual energies to heal, locate jobs, fix marriages, predict the future (as oracles), find lost items, chastise the sinful, and reward the deserving—are called *bhopas, ojhas,* and *bhagats.* Controlling spirits and being able to summon them at will— on auspicious days and at regular intervals—entails knowing the songs, drumbeats, chants, smells, or images that please each spiritual agent. Rajasthani folklorist Komal Kothari describes such powerful persons, avatars of a kind, as "human, or living shrines."[5] A spirit medium, when linked to a particular temple through the observance of that shrine deity's *niyam* (regimen), could also be referred to as a *cauki,* literally a "square stool"—in the sense of a judicial seat where legal court hearings (peshi) are held and justice is dispensed by divine powers.[6] (Figures 4 and 5 feature Rajasthani spirit mediums. Figure 1 shows a spirit medium I knew in the Indian state of Madhya Pradesh.)

FIGURE 4. Possessed by Bhairuji, this god's avatar and medium clutches a healing peacock-feather whisk and trembles with power. Photo by author.

Nevertheless, most spiritual possessions, even those experienced by mediums, were said to be less potent than full-blown divine incarnations, with true avatars believed to have been more common before the current decadent Kali Age.[7] However, Rajasthanis did also speak of revered persons such as their gurus (teachers) as being divine avatars in a metaphorical rather than literal sense, in the way devout individuals embodied divine qualities, say, Baba Ramdev's compassion, without actually channeling that deity. This

FIGURE 5. Possessed by a *pir baba*, Kani Bai becomes that saint's avatar. Photo by author.

latter usage corresponds to an alternative meaning of avatar, first appearing in the English language in the eighteenth century, referring to any figure that gives a face to an abstract principle.[8] Of note, this use of avatar is redolent of certain interpretations of the Rajasthani phrase, bhav a gaya—i.e., a certain divinity's "feeling" has "come" to someone, overtaking or "possessing" them in a symbolic rather than literal sense.

In "true" spiritual possessions, where a god or spirit is perceived to have literally entered a human body, the entities can be good and beneficial, as is usually the case with Hindu gods (devis and *devatas*), not all of which alight (utarna) on human mounts (*ghoralas*, related to the Hindi word for horse, *ghora*). Bhairuji, a lusty bachelor god of the underworld, is said to grab human beings more than any other Rajasthani divinity.[9] Hanuman the monkey god, a popular Hindu deity referred to as Balaji in Rajasthan, is also said to take over human bodies, as do various incarnations of the Mother Goddess collectively referred to as Mataji (also as devis), and other divinities such as Gailaji, a local god of madness, Tejaji, a healing deity of snake bites, and Bhakar, a tribal god of the mountain. Sagasji Baojis, the deceased spirits of murdered kings, also seize human beings, as do Muslim saints referred to as *pir babas*. *Kuldevis* (lineage goddesses), however, were typically said not to possess humans, instead communicating through visions and dreams. *Satis,* or women memorialized for immolating themselves on their husbands' funeral pyres, also were said to possess the living only on rare occasions. And I was told that various "big" Sanskritic gods, such as Brahma, the creator of the universe, avoided entering living human bodies, as those gods possessed such immense power (sakti) as to risk exploding earthly vehicles.

Despite Rajasthan's many benevolent spiritual beings, possessing entities can also be evil and malevolent. These include capricious ghosts trapped between the human world (manushya-loka) and the world of the ancestors (pitri-loka), spiritual agents who are referred to by Hindus as *bhut-prets* or *malris* and by Muslims as *jinds* (from the Arabic *djinn;* Muslims speak of possessing entities as *hajris,* "presences"). Some spirits are said to linger as ghosts because of their immoral defiance of custom, which keeps them bound to their earthly existences and enmeshed in the lives of their friends and family. Others are believed to have passed away before the time allotted to them by Yama, the Hindu god of death, and are referred to as *akal mots* (untimely deaths) reluctant to leave this world. The latter include murder victims, suicides (for example, young women who throw themselves in wells because of premarital pregnancies), accident victims (such as, the author was informed, a foreign tourist who drowned in one of Rajasthan's palace hotels), unmarried male children (who have no descendants to remember them), and stillborn babies (whose mounts are said to open and close their mouths in a sucking motion like a breast-feeding child). Other malicious spirits said to seize humans are dissatisfied ancestors (purvajs, pitr-pitranis), demons (raksas), witches (referred to as *dakan* if they are still living, *meli* if they are dead), deceased widows (considered sexually voracious or "hungry" entities, who lust after the bodies of newlyweds), and still living men, who send their own souls to torment and kill their enemies. However, I would note that distinctions between benevolent and malevolent spirits are not always clear, as even mischievous spirits can be used for good, as when spirit mediums turn them to their healing or other positive ends.

In Rajasthan, spiritual beings, good and bad, are said to possess humans for a variety of reasons. Hindu gods, it is said, want fame and feel that appearances in the world—the performance of miracles and communication of important messages—might boost their popularity ratings. Ghosts, too, are said to want things. They hunger and feel that they can satisfy their desires—to play (khelna), eat sweet and sour things, devour meat and alcohol, smoke pipes, or engage in sexual activities—in human form. Because of their unclean desires, ghosts are drawn to dirty places such as toilets, cremation grounds, and burial sites, and toward beautiful things such as perfumes and brightly colored clothing. This taste for dirt and beauty also is said to draw spirits near women, as females are perceived to be ritually unclean (ashudh) on certain occasions—e.g., during menses for three or four days and after birth for twelve days—yet be nonetheless alluring. In Rajasthan where I worked, women are similarly perceived to have stronger fleshly appetites than men (for rich foods, money, and sex), and to be more vulnerable and fearful than men, thus further increasing their likelihood to suffer spiritual attack.

Gods, ghosts, and ancestral spirits are also easily offended—from ritual neglect or simple human carelessness—which can draw them into the world to express their dissatisfaction and to gain redress. The recently deceased, for example, sometimes feel that their families have not given the priests enough gifts, thus jeopardizing these spirits' safe passage to the realm of Yama. In other cases, sorcerers or conjurers, referred to as *jadugars* or *tantriks,* are contracted to place "dirty" (gandi) spirits in the bodies of their patrons' enemies. It is hoped that these summoned spirits, some who come voluntarily and others who are little more than slaves, will seize and consume their victims' souls. Spiritual hit men accomplish ghostly transfers in numerous ways, for example, by giving victims ensorcelled food disguised as a sacred offering termed *prasad,* which renders their marks more susceptible to supernatural attack. In addition to sorcery (jadu-tona) and poisoned gifts of food, witchcraft can also weaken a person enough to precipitate a spiritual attack. Shamans may even cause the possession of their former patients, if, say, they become angered because their patients turn to other healers. Finally, ghosts are closely associated with liminal places (crossroads, burial grounds) and times (dusk and dawn, noon and midnight). In traveling over these places or at these times, one may inadvertently bring pestering ghosts into one's body, though a host of auspiciousness (*shubh* and *ashubh*) beliefs concerning, for example, when to leave one's house and when not to, are said to minimize such dangers.[10]

Spirit Possession and Mental Health

In Rajasthan, possessions by divinities, even angry ones, are locally interpreted as boons, though the benefits of such experiences may not be clear at the outset. Possession by a lesser spirit such as a wandering ghost (bhut-pret), however, is typically construed, at least initially, as an undesirable illness of a kind. Relinquishing control of one's senses to an external spiritual agent is terrifying, especially until that spirit's wants are made known, so that they can be satisfied by the afflicted and their families. Until that time, possessing spirits can disrupt life—fouling up weddings, business ventures, and love lives, and generating a multitude of debilitating mental and physical illness symptoms.

In Rajasthan, such symptoms cluster together to form what is locally referred to as "ghost illness" (bhut-pret ki bimari). Such illnesses typically begin with the afflicted swaying rhythmically under the spirit's influence, referred to as *jhumna,* literally, "to move as if one were intoxicated, as a drunkard."[11] Some possessions never progress further than this, with the possessed demonstrating a generally calm demeanor and no visible trance. In other cases, however, gentle swaying quickly turns violent, with victims entering clearly altered states of consciousness. Such altered spiritual states can involve voices other than the victims' own speaking through them; trembling and convulsions; moaning (spirits are said to howl in pain from the punishment, *dand,* they receive from exorcising spirit mediums or justice bringing gods); fevers; tearing at one's hair and body, interpreted as ghosts trying to kill their human hosts; rapid breathing; wailing for mercy, since when brought to hallowed ground spirits are forced to appear and account for their sins, which can bring cries for leniency; cursing, threats, uncontrolled shouting, and other expressions of anger (gussa) directed at divine images (murtis), as spirits become enraged when forced to appear before divine judges. These states may also include gurgling, choking, and difficulty in breathing, which are "interpreted as a death rattle because a ghost is trying to take the victim's soul through its throat and mouth"[12]; rolling on the ground in the muck (signifying degradation); complaints of numbness and coldness, followed by uncontrolled shivering (perhaps showing mounts' nearness to death); feelings of being bound up (*bandha,* signaling the imprisonment of human souls by destructive spirits); and moans and movements reminiscent of sexual orgasm, in possessions by Bhairuji, for example, which are interpreted as sexual penetration, and thus especially undignified for men and high-caste women.[13] And any of these symptoms are followed in most cases by weakness, lethargy, and amnesia, with the possessed often claiming to remember nothing about their experiences.

Rajasthanis, spiritually tactical and medically polymorphous, practice a variety of measures to rid themselves of pestering spirits. Some turn to local systems of healing such as Ayurveda (a Hindu healing tradition described in ancient Sanskrit scriptures) or Unani prophetic medicine brought to India by Muslims, with the latter having been described as a "combination of Greek humoral theory (four humors—blood, black bile, yellow bile, and phlegm) and animistic beliefs introduced by the Prophet Muhammad."[14] Nevertheless, at some point in the process, most Rajasthanis also turn to spirit mediums to solve such problems.

As noted, spirit mediums provide a range of services for their clients, from predicting the future, to petitioning for spiritual aid in matters of love and money, to healing. In all these contexts, mediums serve as intermediaries between humankind and supernatural entities and energies, communicating with and often channeling gods and spirits both malign and benevolent for the benefit of humanity. In healing contexts involving possessing spirits, mediums first engage pestering ghosts in conversation, hoping to find out who the spirit is and what it wants. Having pinpointed ghostly identities and desires (though this is difficult, as ghosts are notorious liars and tricksters), mediums proffer deals to the spirits, offering gifts of sweets, coconuts, tamarind fruit, cloth, or money, thus hoping to entice or exorcise (bhut-pret utarna) spirits from the bodies of their hosts. These deals involve considerable pleading, cajoling, and complaining on the part of both healers and ghosts. Spirits are sometimes transferred to another person or thing—even, temporarily or permanently, into the medium's own body. Alternatively, spirit mediums make offerings to sources of divine power, hoping that such powers will chase the spirit from their victims. Such fonts of spiritual vitality—whether gods, saints (in the Muslim tradition termed *pir babas*), or the medium's own spiritual servants—are found near impromptu shrines erected in or near sacred spots (termed *sthans*), temples (mandirs), mosques (masjids), or saints' tombs (pirs).

If these steps do not work, spiritual specialists make ghosts as uncomfortable as possible, hoping to convince them to leave human hosts. Techniques include abusing and insulting ghosts, smoking spirits out with unpleasant fumes such as burning cow dung, beating or electrically shocking the bodies of the possessed (some locals say only villagers and saints, but not mediums, employ electrical shocks), transferring mounts and thus also their accompanying ghostly parasites to holy ground, reciting sacred verses termed *mantras* that summon superior supernatural forces in order to discipline recalcitrant spirits (the term *mantra* is a condensation of *mananat trananat* meaning "thoughts that protect"[15]), providing the possessed with consecrated amulets that offer protection from ghosts, and using bundles of peacock feathers (as seen in figure 4) or branches from the *neem* tree to "sweep" (jhara, jharphuk) disease-causing spirits out of the body.

Although considered undesirable, Rajasthani ghost-illness experiences do provide support for I. M. Lewis's famous "deprivation hypothesis"—i.e., the idea that possession allows women and other dominated classes to express dissatisfactions, thus providing not only emotional catharsis and social support but also covert channels of protest that these persons would not otherwise have.[16] This echoes a broad range of research by anthropologists, psychologists, and others, who frequently point to positive dimensions of such dissociative partitioning of self and experience. Anthropologists particularly show how dissociative trance in religious contexts, framed locally in diverse ways, e.g., as spiritual possessions, shamanic soul journeying, and even prayer, can provide for satisfying and deeply felt experiences. In fact, as noted, religious trances and other spiritual states of consciousness are typically tied to healing rituals, pointing to their connection to positive health.[17]

The anthropologist Graham Dwyer, following Lévi-Strauss, whose work was discussed in the book's opening chapter, saw Rajasthani possession and exorcism as therapy akin to psychoanalysis in the West. For Dwyer, possession and its treatment allow ailing persons to deidentify with pathological states and negative emotions, thus reconstructing themselves in more positive ways and rediscovering what it means to give and receive emotional love and support.[18] Dwyer, however, was less willing to enter into an explicit Western psychological language, or even to speculate on the internal psychic states of the possessed, focusing instead, in an approach he termed *phenomenological,* on local conceptions of self and emotion that grounded spiritual experiences.[19] His work thus contrasts with other theories, where possession is conceptualized as, alternatively, hysteria traceable to sexual disturbances and conflicts within the family,[20] dissociative and somatoform conversion disorders (the latter term used if biological factors are involved) linked to the inability to transition to adulthood,[21] or as a form of dissociation termed "dissociative identity disorder" and "multiple personality disorder" brought about by early childhood abuse[22] or by unresolved Oedipal conflicts.[23]

In this book, following Dwyer and others, I focus on cultural frames of meaning, such as spiritual possession, as locals employ them to make sense of experiences as described above. I do also draw on theories of dissociation to help explain possession experiences and their health consequences. But as readers have already seen, influenced as I am by anthropologists such as Chris Lynn, I. M. Lewis, and others, I highlight the dual positive and negative dimensions of dissociation, with particular emphasis on the therapeutic benefits of dissociating from everyday reality into second avatar selves. In the end, my approach is more social-scientific than clinical-diagnostic. For me, the most important point is that even the undesirable states of spiritual possession—the psychological expressions that seem reminiscent of dissociative identity or multiple personality disorders—can positively influence mental health. In fact, Rajasthani spirit mediums are most typically individuals who have been healed from ghost illness. Now controlling the pestering spirit that once afflicted them or the divinity that formerly overwhelmed their human capabilities, spirit mediums find themselves able to heal others. Spiritual possession, then, begins as an affliction but can be transformed into a gift that plays an important role in a medium's healing repertoire. This is why spirit mediums are often referred to as *healed healers*—or persons, who, once assailed by spirits, now control them in ways that help them cure others.

More generally, spirit mediums, though once considered ill, are typically seen as strong-willed and healthy. And working as a healer can signal gratitude to the spirit or deity that allowed one to survive a difficult affliction. Working as a spirit medium can also bring honor and new income opportunities, though most mediums retain their former employment. In fact, I witnessed this cycle in this book's central spirit-possession frame story—the possession of a young Bhat woman, Bedami, by her husband's clan deity. At first considered an illness, Bedami, eventually learned to (more or less) master her spiritual affliction and came to occupy the role of spirit medium. Her illness, then, once it was overcome, served as an important source of psychosocial well-being for her, as I show. As stated, this event structures opening analyses in the next three chapters. As such, it will be helpful to have more details on the contexts of Bedami's experiences, as preliminary background information to the upcoming analyses.

The Spiritual Possession of Bedami Bhat

Toward the end of my PhD dissertation research in the 1990s, a young Bhat woman, whom I refer to pseudonymously as Bedami, was possessed by what was eventually identified as her husband Ramu's clan devi, Chavanda Mata, with Bedami eventually taking on a spirit-medium role.[24] Insistently, the devi, having taken control of Bedami, ranted at Ramu for his stinginess and antisocial nature. Readers may recall that I said clan deities are not generally supposed to possess human mounts. Such details will become important in my analysis, pointing to, among other things, the contested nature of this spiritual event within the Bhat community, which was alternately judged as real (asli) or fake (nakli). That is, Bhats asked, was this *really* the devi, with Bedami transformed into something akin to a divine avatar? Or, by contrast, was Bedami, consciously or unconsciously, feigning possession, attempting to manipulate her husband Ramu and others in the community?

Bedami is a member of a low-status community of performers known as Bhats, with whom I conducted three years of ethnographic research in Udaipur and Jaipur between 1991 and 1998.[25] Bhats (literally, "Bards") are entertainers from the western desert region of Rajasthan, which is referred to as Marwar. Historically, Bhats were, and currently still are, employed as village genealogists, historians, buffoons, and praise-singers for a Dalit, or formerly untouchable caste, referred to as Bhambis.[26] High-status bards to Rajasthan's former feudal lords (the Rajputs), such as the Charan-Bhats, who famously narrated Rajasthani history to Colonel Tod,[27] are seen as cultural authority figures. My informants, however, are considered by many to be low-status interlopers—the bards of untouchables and thus not true bards like the praise-singers of the noble Rajputs. My Bhat informants are also seminomadic, taking local myths and legends on the road—performing them, for example, before wealthy merchants and military officers who had migrated from Rajasthan to Delhi, Calcutta, and Bombay. (See figures 6 and 7.)

Since Indian Independence in 1947, Bhats have also taken to performing puppet dramas for local and foreign tourists as well as for government officials in five-star hotels and folklore festivals. Bhats have now settled semipermanently in urban areas throughout India, where they are supported by their new skills—thus escaping, at least in part, a degrading traditional status. In the

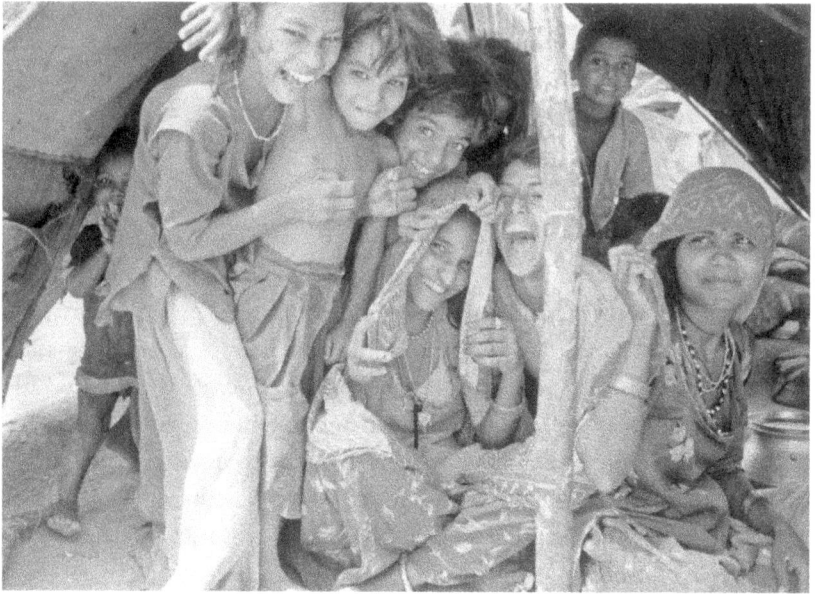

FIGURE 6. Bedami Bhat sits far right. Photo by author.

FIGURE 7. The Udaipur Bhats. Photo by author.

Rajasthani city of Udaipur, where some of the events described in this book unfold, Bhats are more typically referred to as *kathputli-walas* or "puppeteers"—literally, "those of the wooden figures."[28] In post-Independence India, ancient residences—warrior-nobles' mansions referred to as *havelis,* as well as full-fledged kingly palaces called *mahals*—have been converted into guest houses and restaurants. In these palace settings, Bhats put on short five-to fifteen-minute puppet dramas in hotel lobbies next to gift shops or in hotel restaurants as dinner entertainment. These performances are family affairs: Bhat fathers, hidden behind a curtained stage, dance the string puppets and whistle through a reed to create the puppets' voice; mothers sing, play a small double-headed drum referred to as a *dholak,* and narrate; and children help out where needed. Bhats typically celebrate the exploits of knights from Rajasthan's medieval period. For example, the Bhats' signature character is Amar Singh Rathor—a minor seventeenth-century noble from their home district of Nagaur in western Rajasthan, who is said to have served under the Mughal emperor Shah Jahan. Bhats also narrate ballads and epics of *dacoits* or marauders, who once plagued the Rajasthani countryside but, at least in Bhat tellings, renounce their evil ways to fight for good. Dacoit, or *daku* in Hindi, puppets carry torches that are actually lit—a trick that certainly catches tourists' attention but one that I have seen go awry. Bhat puppet shows also feature communities who, while still present in parts of Rajasthan and in fact often inhabit the same slums as my informants, signify a disappearing rural way of life: snake-charmers and black-garbed dancers (like Gulabi Bai, a famous performer from the Saphera caste), performing *hijra* eunuchs, as well as professional mimics known as bahurupiyas who, in puppet form at least, unexpectedly flip upside-down thus switching between male and female identities. Each Bhat nuclear family is linked to one or more hotels, which they guard almost as jealously as they do their village patrons. (See figure 8.)

For financial and emotional reasons, however, Bhats return periodically to their natal villages, especially to perform genealogies and poems of praise on the occasions of their Bhambi patrons' weddings. Bhats, with their history of performing and praise-singing, have also been engaged by the Indian state, as well as by nongovernmental organizations, to propagandize modernization projects. Bhat puppet dramas typically concern ancient kings and battles. My informants, however, now promote a modern vision of the future by dramatizing, in both rural and urban areas, family planning (think of the future, not your own desires), bank-savings programs (a *paise* saved . . .), health care (disease prevention through vaccination and better sanitation,

FIGURE 8. A Bhat silhouetted in the background dances a puppet—
his avatar?—in the foreground. Photo by author.

anti-AIDS propaganda), alcohol abuse (invest in your family, not the bottle),
and life insurance (what will your family do when you are gone?).

Udaipur, founded in 1567 by Maharana Udai Singh, is a relatively small city
by Indian standards, with a population of slightly more than three hundred
thousand in the 1990s.[29] As the administrative headquarters of Udaipur district, this city is situated in southern Rajasthan in a valley in the Aravalli
mountains and is famed for its man-made lakes, palaces, and beautiful scenery.

FIGURE 9. Bedami and her children in their Udaipur tent home. Photo by author.

Its royal family, the Mewars, to which Udai Singh belonged, is also known for holding out stubbornly against Muslim invaders. Folk wisdom has it, though official histories tell us differently, that the Mewars never surrendered to the Mughals, who ruled north India from the sixteenth to the mid-eighteenth century.

The first Bhats settled in Udaipur forty or so years ago in the 1960s. At the time of my PhD dissertation research, about fifteen Bhat nuclear families were settled in Udaipur, having pitched their tents on the outskirts of the city (see figure 9). The Udaipuri Bhats, with a few exceptions, were close kin. Five sisters and a brother, all in their early to mid-fifties, and one of them Bedami's mother, constituted the core of the Bhat community when I knew them. A sixth sister lived elsewhere; a second brother had died before my research, though his three sons also inhabited Udaipur. My key informants came from this older generation of Bhats, as I was especially interested in the Bhat knowledge of the past. Around this sibling core were a mishmash of children, grandchildren, spouses, cousins, friends, and hangers-on, all of whom shaped my experience of the Udaipur Bhat community.

During my time in Udaipur, Bhats inhabited three locales. The first group included Bedami's parents and sisters, my adopted Bhat family, who lived in a two-room house in a *kacci basti,* or unfinished squatter settlement, near Lake Fateh Sagar. Their house was built with profits from a trip to America and was a focal point of much Bhat activity. Near my adopted family's house, in the jungle (from the Hindi, *jangal* or "wild place"), a second group of Bhats had pitched their tents. Finally, five or so Bhat families were situated next to the road leading to Udaipur's Mohan Lal Sukhadia University. These Bhats inhabited tents but were forced to leave this spot whenever dignitaries visited the area, such as during university commencement ceremonies. In fact, most Bhats of Udaipur are squatters, as they typically do not own the property on which they live. After first asking permission—from a local strongman or politician, and perhaps offering money, service, or votes in return—Bhats would pitch their tents. Some Bhats would buy a title to their property, but these purchases were circumspect and Bhats did not put much faith in them. Nevertheless, Bhats, practically speaking, had to maintain good relations with these informal landlords, who did exercise a degree of power and could evict Bhats with hired goons.

As I show, one of the striking characteristics of Bedami Bhat's possession was how the visitation was overtly linked to money and finances, and more particularly to Bedami's husband Ramu's attitude toward financial matters. My Bhat informants typically told me the goddess incarnated because Ramu refused to spend on others—that is, Ramu was stingy (*kanjus*). The goddess was thus said to have overtaken Bedami in order to convince Ramu to spend more on the community, thus "fixing his mind" and "teaching him how to behave." My informants, moreover, explicitly linked Ramu's stinginess to the fact that he had entered the new market economy in a manner unlike other Bhats—as a paid employee at a local folklore institute, a job that regulated his life and values in ways that other new Bhat pursuits did not. Ramu's pursuit of a regular wage, personal savings, and even life insurance, according to many Bhats, instilled in him a destructive stinginess and forgetfulness toward his community, which was said to be the trigger for his wife's possession. Many Bhats claimed that Ramu no longer "believed" in people but only in money. My informants also accused him of "forgetting" his community, stingily refusing to loan other Bhats even five-rupee notes. Ramu was even said to have sold out his own community in his blind pursuit of wealth, for example, by providing his folklore-institute employer with his community's puppetry secrets. Some Bhats suggested to me that money was Ramu's only god (in Hindi, *devata*). Ramu, as he pursued his salaried employment at a local folklore institute, was branded the new economy's greedy, even wicked (setan), agent. Bhats, in fact, referred to Ramu as a ghost (bhut) and demon (raksas)—terms that, in Bhat parlance, referred to evil entities wandering on the fringes of society and not respecting human values.

I have presented details related to the Bhat community and to Bedami's possession because, as I have said, I use this event as a frame story in chapters 2, 3, and 4, as an introduction to each chapter's analysis of psycho-socio-cultural dynamics associated with what I am calling avatar therapeutics. I hope these details help readers appreciate how this possession event was intricately related to Bedami's personal experiences as a member of a poor and socially marginalized community with little control over many dimensions of her life. It was those circumstances that made the devi's visitation so important to Bedami, and to other members of the Bhat community. Here, I follow the anthropological principle of interpreting human experience in relation to social and cultural circumstances. Ultimately, I will argue that the therapeutic potential of symbolic second selves—avatars—resides precisely in how those secondary selves allow individuals to more effectively enact beliefs and behaviors that are socially valued. Or, when the second selves are associated with illness, whether ghost illness or gaming addiction, that distress can be explained in part due to the way the second selves come into conflict with the commitments of socially valued others.

GAMING AVATARS IN ONLINE VIRTUAL WORLDS

Avatars as Self-Objects in Digital Environments

The earliest use of the term *avatar* in reference to computer-generated digital environments was in the 1979 computer role-playing game *Avatar,*[30] run on the University of Illinois's PLATO computer instruction system. Likewise, the Hindu term appears in Richard Garriott's 1985 *Ultima IV: Quest of the Avatar,*[31] where the player's earthly self is conceptualized as manifesting as an "avatar" in a digital-virtual world. In that game, the player-avatar is a virtuous chosen one who has the potential to usher in a new age of enlightenment. Despite the influence of the *Ultima* series of games, it was Farmer and Morningstar's *Habitat* that is largely credited with the most explicit early use of the term *avatar* to refer to a digital self-object in a computer-generated environment, which is how the term is now used in reference to digital settings. That is, in *Ultima IV: Quest of the Avatar,* players strive to become something akin to a divinity, though actuated in a virtual-gaming environment.

FIGURE 10. Via avatars, a video-game player can become a sorcerer or a soldier. Illustration by Kurt Komoda (https://agonyagogo.com/).

By contrast, the game *Habitat* simply used the term *avatar* to refer to self-objects that allowed players to perform tasks in a computer world, a usage closer to contemporary understandings, with such character visualizations in no way seen as embodying high-minded beings striving to improve the world in ways akin to sacred Hindu avatars.[32] (See figure 10.)

I have already noted the parallels between sacred and secular avatars: reminiscent of the way that a divine consciousness incarnates in a human-avatar vehicle on earth, a human agent takes form in a digital avatar in a computer-generated virtual world. Despite the logical parallel, it is nevertheless still curious why these early game designers chose a Hindu religious term such as *avatar* to describe play experiences and activities unfolding on a computer screen that could have been framed in other terms—digital *messiahs* perhaps, rather than *avatars*. I had earlier mentioned the influence of Hinduism on hippie counterculture, which started in the 1960s and unfolded in particularly potent ways in California, where many early game designers lived and were raised. It has been suggested that many early tech designers, whether in California or elsewhere, perceived utopian possibilities in their games and other products. Computers, they thought, might usher in a new era of liberation and prosperity, allowing for new forms of self-expression and social connection that would unleash almost unimaginable human potentials. That sounds a lot like how Hindu avatars are similarly believed to usher in new eras of human prosperity and moral excellence, vanquishing demons and other evils in the process, themes explicitly replicated, for example, in Garriott's 1985 *Ultima IV: Quest of the Avatar*. And such techno-optimism helps explain the transplantation—some would say co-optation, as I do in the preface—of a Hindu sacred language into secular gaming contexts, which evoked an exotic and even magical Eastern feel to boot.[33]

In any case, this avatar language caught on quickly in US popular culture, as noted in the opening chapter. Neal Stephenson used it in his 1992 novel *Snow Crash,* with his references to a "multiverse" said to have influenced Linden Labs' lead developer, Philip Rosedale, who led the design of *Second Life*, first released in 2003.[34] The film industry followed, with movies such as *The Matrix* and *Avatar* further popularizing, even normalizing, the use of the term *avatar* to describe technological second selves. Indeed, the new secular use of avatar has become so widespread that today even my young-adult Indian gamer respondents, many of them Hindu, commonly reference secular digital-gaming avatars while rarely speaking of Vishnu's ten sacred incarnations.

Early computer games such as *Habitat* were the direct precursors of a new generation of online games referred to as MMORPGs, which, as stated earlier, is an acronym for "massively multiplayer online role-playing games" (MMOs for short). As I have said, my own research on digital avatars has unfolded primarily in two MMOs: *World of Warcraft* (WoW), first created in 2004 by Blizzard Entertainment, and *Guild Wars 2* (GW2), designed in 2012 by ArenaNet. WoW has remained the industry leader in MMOs even to this day. In 2008, when my research on digital avatars first started, WoW reached 10 million monthly subscribers, making it the largest subscription-based MMO and virtual community in the West at that time, about 62 percent of the then-MMO population, with significant player populations in East Asia as well.[35] And WoW remains popular, with its 2021 player count still in the millions, despite the ever-increasing proliferation of new MMO and other online-gaming opportunities. GW2, directed toward a more casual player group, had in 2013 about half a million players, with that count ebbing and flowing in recent years.

Two other important influences on the MMO genre of online games, and particularly on the ones I study, are J. R. R. Tolkien's high-fantasy books *The Hobbit* and *The Lord of the Rings* trilogy,[36] and the tabletop role-playing game, *Dungeons and Dragons* (D&D).[37] Written in stages between 1937 and 1949, Tolkien's books had a profound impact on Gary Gygax and Dave Arneson's D&D, first published in 1974. Both in turn deeply influenced early computer games such as *Habitat,* which in turn morphed into later games such as WoW and GW2. For example, WoW has been described as being dominated by a "Tolkienesque high fantasy motif," referring to the fact that its settings, plotlines, and characters owe much to the fantasy writings of J. R. R. Tolkien.[38] Still, there are hundreds of MMOs, many preceding and others existing alongside WoW. In some of these, players take on the roles of space adventurers; in others, pirates and barbarians—forms of play that do not even begin to exhaust the possibilities of these game-worlds.

Nevertheless, what all MMOs have in common is an emphasis on the development of one's gaming *character,* which, in computer environments, is visually represented by a gaming avatar—now the commonly accepted term for such digital self-objects. Central to character experience in these games is that player characters, and thus their related avatar self-objects, inhabit computer-generated virtual environments that are *persistent:* these worlds provide virtual places where thousands of users, represented via avatars, interact in ways that persist independently of any single player's actions. Typically, they persist for twenty-four hours a day, with only brief interruptions for maintenance. In earlier video games, play typically started and ended with any single player initiating or terminating a gaming session. But in these game environments, any individual player may have logged off his or her computer, with that character's avatar thus having disappeared from the game-world. Nevertheless, events continue to happen in the online world, and players also continue to compete and interact in ways that advance and change the contours of the game-space. This helps create the experience of characters—and avatars—feeling more real in some sense, and thus more fully a true second self of a kind.[39]

MMO play spaces are also highly *immersive,* a concept, as mentioned in this book's introduction, that is central to games studies research and to my own concerns. Sophisticated software and computers with powerful 3D graphical processing create spaces that can feel virtually real. For example, WoW forms a fantastical virtual world that stretches over numerous continents and planets. And this game's designers have taken care to render beautiful this virtual reality's landscapes—its craggy mountains and grassy plains, lakes and oceans, and wastelands. Equal attention has been given to WoW's built environments and social settings, for example, its castles, fortresses, dungeons, battlegrounds, villages, and cities. In both natural and social landscapes, players encounter a range of denizens, such as other player-avatars animated by real-life persons, as well as myriad computer-programmed entities, including menacing ones such as monsters and demons (referred to as "mobs" for "mobiles") and friendly and helpful ones such as innkeepers, auctioneers, and quest-givers. Encounters with these animate agents magnify players' experiences of the reality of the WoW game-world, and of their second-self avatar identities, pushing some to feel as if they actually inhabit another space and an alternative identity, no longer aware of the so-called real world that surrounds their physical body and computer play station. In this book, as noted earlier, I refer to this psychological process as *dissociation,* a key concern in these pages, in the way dissociative experiences can provide opportunities for mental relaxation and stress relief.

Perhaps the most important and engaging aspects of WoW relate to character creation and advancement. Each player creates characters who themselves are represented as avatars, their visual bodies in the game-world. Avatars are manipulated through keyboard and mouse commands, and they can communicate through gestures (such as dancing, waving, pointing, jumping, and flirting) that complement chatting through in-game text channels or headsets and voice programs (either built into the game or through third-party modifications such as Ventrilo or Discord, pieces of communications software commonly used by gamers). The way an avatar, or visual representation of one's character-self, responds to commands can add to the sensation of actually *being* one's character.

Character creation, advancement, and manipulation unfold in ways that lead players to feel closely identified with in-game second avatar selves, pushing them to even deeper states of WoW immersion. To begin, one typically does not know the name of the actual-world person controlling someone else's character unless that other player volunteers that information. Even then, players will often continue to refer to themselves and one another in the game, and sometimes even if they were to meet in the real world, by their character names—showing the extent to which many players feel connected to their in-game embodiments. Also, in the case of WoW, characters possess, according to player choices, a variety of attributes—membership in one of two warring factions (the Alliance or the Horde), a *race* (like elf or orc), and a *class* (warrior, mage, priest, et al., loosely an in-game profession and set of roles)—which lend them greater depth. Further, quest completion and level advancement, mentally and emotionally absorbing dimensions of WoW, provide each character-self with an individual life trajectory—whether a player's main character, into which they pour most of their energy and affection, or an alternative character, which allows players to experiment with other roles.

Here, I would note that there is no single way to play WoW, nor any single goal, which is also what makes games such as this seem so compelling and real. This game's persistent and immersive virtual spaces offer players a range of tasks, which they complete via avatars (again, visual representations of the character-self) that respond to player commands. Some tasks are referred to as *quests* with goals given by computer-controlled non-player characters. In completing these goals, players advance in *levels*. Each level acquired, like won *gear* in the form of swords, armor, and jewelry, bestows additional power and ability on a character, allowing a player to complete more difficult game challenges, which in turn allows them to advance even further. After completing the game's highest character level, players compete in challenging in-game content such as multiplayer "instances" such as *dungeons* or *raids*. (*Instances* are special in-game areas that generate new copies of an area in the game for a particular group, as when a multiplayer raiding party descends into a virtual dungeon to fight a particularly powerful monster and its minions.) WoW raiding parties or *raids,* for example, require cooperation between five and as many as forty players, with groups balanced between different character classes. Typically, the most fearsome monsters are faced, and most valuable treasures are won, in these contexts, though comparable challenges can be found in *Player-vs-Player arena* and *battleground* competitions, where players in groups of various sizes are pitted against one another in tests of martial prowess and group organization.

Important to MMO game play and social dynamics are in-game associations of like-minded players called *guilds*. Ranging in size from a small group of players in the tens or twenties to massive numbers even in the thousands, MMO guilds typically represent a group of gamers who, sharing common interests and goals, join together to pursue them. Some of the player associations I knew best were self-proclaimed raiding *progression* guilds (the raid-party groups "progress" through the game instance's increasingly more challenging situations), whose members worked systematically through multiplayer collaborative game content. Other guild groupings declared themselves *casual* and *social,* as opposed to more *serious* and *hardcore.* These more typically represented a coming together of friends and family, whose primary aim was to enjoy their MMO of choice, which included advancing in skill and progressing through game content, but at a more relaxed and less competitive pace.

Overall, games including WoW and GW2 share features with social network programs such as Facebook, in the manner they bring people together in a shared virtual space to chat, share ideas and information, and socialize. Still, distinct from social networking sites, massively multiplayer game-worlds such as WoW set the stage for collaborative and simultaneously shared play interactions that seem as real as they are fun, unfolding as they do in the meticulously rendered world of Azeroth[40] and via avatar-characters who, in many instances, come to feel like actual second selves.

Online Gaming and Mental Health

Games are fun, and they are played for enjoyment and to feel good.[41] Sometimes games seem even better than reality—not only more fun, but *fairer,* with success and advancement driven largely by one's skill, smarts, determination, and hard work, rather than advantages based on one's gender, race or ethnicity, age, wealth, or country of origin. As Jane McGonigal puts it provocatively, games can help us fix a seemingly "broken" reality, helping us to improve ourselves, and making the world a better place in the process.[42] It almost seems obvious that games and play could also help fix our minds, and thus be mentally therapeutic in some important sense.

A now extensive body of psychosocial research suggests that games' impact on mental health importantly depends on why and how one plays. For example, overcoming challenges creates important *achievement* experiences, which are integral to why many online and other games are experienced as fun and rewarding. Similarly, games-studies researchers propose that online spaces, as mentioned earlier, are akin to the pubs or coffeehouses that came before them, and thus serve as important new "third places" between the first space of home and the second of work, with games thus providing positive *social* experiences. And *immersion* gamers also report WoW play can relieve the stress in their lives, producing positive play experiences and temporary breaks from the offline world.[43]

Despite the clear positive health and other benefits associated with gaming, research also shows that a small percentage of online gamers can become unduly involved in video games as to play them problematically, in ways that compromise their ability to function in day-to-day life. This is estimated at 5 percent in one global study[44] and between 3–9 percent in others,[45] variability due in part to the range of employed assessment tools. In these cases, play fosters maladaptive forms of learning that result in obsessive, compulsive, and *addictive* behavior potentially organized on the neurobiological level.[46]

Related to these ideas, on June 18, 2018, the World Health Organization (WHO) officially recognized "gaming disorder" as a mental health condition warranting formal inclusion in the latest edition of its diagnostic manual, the International Classification of Diseases, 11th ed. (ICD-11).

> Gaming disorder is characterized by a pattern of persistent or recurrent gaming behaviour ("digital gaming" or "video-gaming"), which may be online (i.e., over the internet) or offline, manifested by: 1) impaired control over gaming (e.g., onset, frequency, intensity, duration, termination, context); 2) increasing priority given to gaming to the extent that gaming takes precedence over other life interests and daily activities; and 3) continuation or escalation of gaming despite the occurrence of negative consequences.[47]

This follows the American Psychiatric Association's (APA's) introduction in 2013 of "Internet Gaming Disorder" in its emerging measures appendix (Section III) of the fifth edition of its *Diagnostic and Statistical Manual of Mental Disorders* (DSM-5), where it still resides as "a condition warranting more clinical research and experience," not yet formally included in the manual's main section.[48] Both the WHO and APA classify gaming disorders with other addictions: for the WHO, gaming disorder is put under "disorders due to addictive behaviors"; for the APA, Internet Gaming Disorder is tentatively classed alongside "substance-related and addictive disorders," akin to gambling, with the latter currently the only formally recognized behavioral addiction in the DSM-5.

Both scholars and clinicians disagree about the utility of treating problematic internet gaming as an addictive disorder resembling substance abuse and problem gambling, as currently described in both the ICD-11 and DSM-5. Some argue that the addiction formulation brings clarity to a contested field of research and clinical practice, with potential therapeutic benefits to individuals suffering from gaming-related distress.[49] But others say that problem gaming is not dominated by addiction symptomology such as cognitive preoccupation, withdrawal, and tolerance.[50] Instead, they show that gaming-related distress can better be assessed by attending to players' diverse life experiences, rather than applying a scientifically imperfect and potentially stigmatizing clinical category such as gaming disorder.[51]

Important for the present discussion, research once again illuminates how gamers' motivations for playing contribute to distinctive forms of video game overinvolvement and distress. *Achievement*-motivated play, such as one sometimes finds in MMOs, is associated with compulsive online activity, as players stay on longer than intended to accomplish their goals.[52] Other studies explicitly treat extensive online *social* gaming as problematic, with gamers seeking online a life they lack offline, binding them to internet communities in potentially unhealthy, even addictive, ways.[53] Finally, even the motivation to escape offline problems and responsibilities through *immersion* in online worlds has been linked to gamers, in their own estimation, becoming overinvolved in online play to the detriment of their offline lives.[54]

In this book, I concentrate on how so-called "immersive" play shapes video game players' mental health. Specifically, as stated earlier, I consider the idea that *immersive* play in games such as *World of Warcraft* and *Guild Wars 2* might usefully be conceptualized as technologically enhanced forms of *dissociation,* in which dimensions of self and experience become separated or partitioned from overall consciousness and awareness. Further, I emphasize how the therapeutic or toxic tenor of video game *immersion* depends importantly on gamers' related strivings to *achieve* and to *socialize.* For example, I show how some US MMO players seek to *achieve* in avatar second selves the success that sometimes eludes them in their offline lives. This changes their experiences of gaming immersion, and the associated stress relief, in comparison with gamers' experiences in places such as India, where "success" and the "good life" are construed differently. Likewise, in the US, online gamers now typically network individually from their homes, but in the Rajasthani town of Udaipur, where I have also worked, gaming takes place primarily in face-to-face internet cafes referred to as "gaming zones." The extent that gamers play with offline friends and family can greatly enrich the *social* quality of their immersive experiences, which means that avatar therapeutics can play out quite differently in the United States compared with India given the different social dynamics involved.

Though focused most on the positive benefits of immersive gaming, I will also show how some players find it hard to resist the temptation to lose themselves fully—dissociate—in MMOs' persistent and immersive environments, which are available almost always on demand. Nevertheless, I generally avoid, as in the spiritual-possession cases, applying clinical categories such as dissociative identity disorder (as described in WHO and APA manuals) to gaming experiences. Those diagnostic labels can obscure the complexity of players' experiences, which typically include a mix of positive benefits and negative risks, with this book focusing mostly on the positive therapeutics of game play.

Overall, as in the spirit-possession cases, I emphasize in the gaming analysis how positive and negative avatar experiences are tightly intertwined. Intensive MMO play, as I show, often represents attempts to improve one's life. For example, many gamers get involved in online worlds to express and seek to resolve dysphoric moods and life distress, and particularly those linked to social isolation and disconnection. And substantial research now shows that distressed individuals can use the internet to effectively psychologically compensate for such perceived deficiencies.[55] Online environments provide settings where lonely persons can build and develop social relationships that "bridge" them to new ties that help them practically in their lives.[56] Other gamers use the internet to more strongly and deeply "bond" to persons offering emotional support and understanding, building more substantial relationships with other gamers who better understand them and their passions.[57] Such relationships allow some gamers to identify and integrate into communities whose social norms relieve the stigma they might experience as persons with socially marginal and oftentimes misunderstood passions for games.[58] Further, these effects can positively spill into offline life, with newly felt social support leading gamers to more confidently interact with others offline, or to simply re-evaluate their offline lives in more positive terms, whether any real changes have occurred there or not.[59] However, in other cases, attempts to better one's life via gaming fall short, providing only temporary relief and insubstantial life improvements. Or intensive gaming leads individuals to forsake real-life roles and obligations, rather than confronting them directly, with adverse health and well-being consequences.[60]

In the spirit-possession cases presented earlier, possessions often begin as illnesses and then, once controlled, bring health and other benefits to the lives of the possessed. By contrast, highly immersive gaming is more typically mostly enjoyable, rewarding, and *healthy*, evidenced, for example, by the low gaming-disorder prevalence statistics mentioned above in recent meta-analyses. Nevertheless, it is now well documented that problem gamers who immerse toxically do in fact tend to struggle with mental-health problems such as depression and anxiety.[61] For that group of gamers, intensive and immersive play, which involves strong identifications with avatar second selves, is often aimed at alleviating life problems and mental distress.[62] In this book, in addition to examining the psychosocial dynamics of the more purely healthy forms of gaming and their associated avatar therapeutics, I also analyze why gaming-related self-medication can be effective in some cases, while prone to failure in others. Or, to push the spiritual analogy further, I also aim to explain why some gamers find in online play the power to escape the ghosts and demons who haunt them, while others do not.

US Gaming Guilds and Indian Gaming Zones

The Knights of Good (KOG), an association of like-minded *World of Warcraft* players termed a *guild,* has played key roles in my research, and features in chapters 2 and 3. One of this guild's leaders, Lainey, was a former student of mine. She participated in my first spring 2008 experimental-methods seminar taught inside the game WoW, which I describe more in the next chapter, and the KOG were the explicit focus of my ethnographic research during 2011–12. Before the foundation of the KOG in 2008, its married founders, Lainey (forty-four years old) and Vern (thirty-five), first met online in a hardcore (or serious-minded) raiding guild in WoW, where they experienced problems (again, MMO *raids* pit players in a raiding party against power monsters termed *bosses*).[63] The guild in which they first met aimed to progress rapidly through raiding content, competing aggressively with other groups on the server. This guild removed Lainey and Vern when they did not show up for a raid, which was interpreted to mean (unjustifiably in their eyes) that they were not committed enough to the guild mission. As explained to us by Lainey, final-exam week had just ended—they were both students at the time—and they were tired and needed a night off from raiding. Lainey says they were removed despite her being recognized as the guild's best healer and having "exemplary attendance, like 99% raid attendance." Still, she says the guild's council of leaders "got all uppity and pissed off and kicked us out, because we missed one raid." Angry, she considered quitting the game for good. Instead, she gathered the necessary signatures (a WoW requirement at that time) and founded the KOG, presenting it to Vern as a Christmas gift on December 24, 2008. With Lainey the self-proclaimed "guild mom" and Vern the raid leader, they started recruiting others to build the kind of guild "they wanted to be in," soon having enough members to field a team that worked successfully and at a decent pace through the then end-game raiding content ("end-game" because this content is seen as one of the culminating challenges in WoW).[64]

Not wishing to inflict on others the pain and injustice they themselves had experienced—they were serious gamers, and being removed abruptly from their former guild felt wrong to them—Lainey and Vern created a guild with a charter of promoting good. It would be a casual rather than a hardcore raiding guild, in the sense that they would aim to raid a few times a week, but they would not require players to show up for these raids, instead respecting members' offline lives. However, out of consideration for others in the guild, and to plan more effectively, players would be asked to sign up for raids that would meet at a certain time and place in the game. Players who showed up more frequently did have a better chance to make it into the guild's *raiding rotation* (the team members participating in a given mission), but there was no severe punishment characteristic of other hardcore raiding guilds.

Although aiming to progress through WoW's raiding content at a relatively steady pace, KOG did not generally strive to be among the first on their server (and certainly not first across all servers) to complete end-game content, as some guilds did, instead taking frequent breaks from raiding to accommodate member schedules. Likewise, light banter accompanied the sometimes necessarily stricter, military-like, and hierarchically orchestrated raid communications, with raid leaders and other members often taking responsibility for one another's foibles and offering constructive and supportive counsel, rather than berating subordinates and pointing fingers. The guild even organized charity events, encouraging members to donate to worthy social causes. Overall, as the name suggests, the guild strived to create good in their members' lives and in the world more generally, which meant respecting the guild's motto that "real life is more important."

At its core, the KOG had fifteen committed raiders, surrounded in turn by another thirty-five to forty individuals, typically friends and family of the raiders, who showed up more occasionally in the guild via both in-game text-based chat channels and the KOG's own private Ventrilo channels. The KOG attracted members who tended to be older than the average WoW gamer—typically in their early to mid-thirties or above. Likewise, with a few exceptions, the members tended to be well-educated, white, and middle-class, with a relatively equal gender balance. They also typically were gainfully employed, with core members working, for example, as a bill collector, military contractor (who had previous service in Iraq), maintenance worker at a hotel (both husband and wife), nursing assistant in a cardiac intensive-care unit, health-insurance salesperson, assistant-manager at Walgreens, and retail worker at a bookstore. One raider was a medical student, and another was in nursing school. Many of the core raiders had children, as did Lainey, one of whom himself, along with his girlfriend, were also KOG members. Most of the KOG's core raiders were "serious" WoW players, possessing multiple max-level characters (level eighty-five at the time of our research during 2011–12). For example, one member informed us he played over eighty hours a week and had ten separate characters in the guild, many of them maximum level. Of note, many of these core members had left hardcore raiding guilds to join KOG, having also had negative experiences like Vern and Lainey's.

The second gaming study featuring prominently in this book—in chapter 4—was carried out in 2016–17 in the Rajasthani city of Udaipur, the site of my earlier PhD research, which by this time had grown to around half a million people (the 2011 census provides a figure of 450,000[65]). This later study focused on Udaipur's young-adult male gamers, most of whom were either university students or in their final year of high school, and typically in their early twenties. At this age, my respondents lived with their families. In Hindu discourse, individuals up to twenty-five years old are student *brahmacharyas,* whose primary life aim normatively entailed learning to master their passions and "animal selves" in preparation for the next householder stage. Most of these Udaipuri young adults would have their marriages arranged by their parents. And demonstrating the ability to earn a living, necessary to land a suitable bride, was partially premised on school performance, a pressure keenly felt. After marriage, young Udaipuri males would typically either continue to live with their parents or, as was increasingly common, start their own separate households. In either case, they would remain close emotionally (and often geographically) to their parents, for whom they were obligated to care.[66]

With widespread broadband technology, mobile phones, and Wi-Fi, Udaipur at this time was well connected to the internet. Among the young adults featuring in this study, social-media use was common, with apps such as Facebook, WhatsApp (with social groups very common), Instagram, and Twitter particularly popular. Many young people also played casual mobile games—games which are played on cellphones and other mobile devices, and generally have a minimalistic interface, simplistic rules, and intuitive gameplay. However, striving to be "true" or "real" gamers, the individuals

FIGURE 11. An Udaipuri gaming *zone* or *lounge*. Photo by author.

featuring in my study also played more "serious" and "hardcore" games (again, their words), such as *Counter Strike—Global Offensive* (CS-GO). CS-GO is a multiplayer "first-person shooter" game—i.e., players can view the game in first-person fashion through the eyes of their character-avatar— where teams of players compete against one another as either terrorists or counter-terrorists. Playing CS-GO at a competitive level required a high level of commitment, requiring players to display not only fast gaming reflexes but also an intimate knowledge of gameplay *maps* (3D landscapes where play unfolded), anticipation of enemy-player movements, and coordination with other squad members. There were only about fifty such committed players of CS-GO in the entire city of Udaipur, most of whom I knew personally.

Playing CS-GO competitively required not only stable broadband but also expensive computer equipment. This meant that my respondents, though typically middle-class and up and often having their own computers, played CS-GO in local gaming zones, where both the computers and the internet service were superior. Gaming zones typically charged between twenty and thirty rupees per hour (less than half a US dollar), with reduced prices offered to regular customers (see figure 11).

The gaming centers were located near high schools and universities, as the bulk of the CS-GO players were students. During the week, gamer customers frequented zones between day classes for two to three hours, or after classes in the late afternoon and early evening, or both. Sundays were a "full rush" day, with some gamers spending much of their time there. Groups of friends generally coordinated with one another their visits to their preferred gaming zones. Computers were typically arranged in rows of five, with rows facing each other. Shops were kept dark to enhance the viewing and game-play experience.

In a typical gameplay session, my respondents would visit the online CS-GO game lobby, where they would chat and invite friends to play with them in their group, some from their same gaming zone, others networked online. Players would communicate with others both via text-based and voice chat. A quick CS-GO match might be over in under thirty minutes, though more engaging matches lasted between forty-five and sixty minutes, with my respondents taking frequent breaks to smoke, sip chai and colas, snack, and simply hang out with friends.

Focused as it was on a different cultural context and genre of online game, this latter India gaming zone study provides me opportunities to extend this book's gaming avatar therapeutic arguments beyond the United States and MMOs. Finally, I would also add that much of my gaming research, in both the United States and India, have focused on experiences related to emerging adulthood, which encompasses a period of development from the late teens through the twenties and even early thirties and beyond, though Lainey and Vern were older.[67] Emerging adults are drawn in a potent manner to online places,[68] which makes sense given how virtual worlds provide fertile ground for role exploration and identity formation, key themes in this stage of development and in the avatar therapeutic processes that feature in this book.[69]

CONCLUSION

As the details of this chapter should make clear, second-self avatar identities need not be positive and therapeutic. That depends on the nature of the transformation: feeling like one is a god is not the same as feeling like a ghost. And the positive or negative nature of the transformation, in turn, depends on how that alternative self is socially judged by meaningful others: heroically saving one's WoW raid team from certain annihilation might produce ecstatic shouts of joy from one's entire gaming guild, all connected via communications software such as Ventrilo, Discord, or TeamSpeak (as I have witnessed); but that same activity might be judged by offline friends and family, watching that play and perhaps feeling ignored, as evidence of a gaming "addiction" (as I have also seen).

These examples illuminate why I take a psychological-anthropological approach to avatar therapeutics in this book. Psychology, or the study of the individual self and mind, is of course important to my inquiry, in the way it delves deeply into human personality, self-concepts, motivation, and mental health. But those psychological processes unfold in specific sociocultural contexts, the domain of anthropology, with group-specific beliefs, values, and behaviors importantly shaping the psychological and therapeutic processes I describe. For me, avatars, as personal identities projected into not only secondary bodies but also alternatively full-blown sociocultural realities, illustrate well these psychological anthropological principles and processes.

In the following chapter, I delve more deeply into the nature of sacred and secular avatar self-transformations and their potential therapeutic quality, examining Bedami's and other Rajasthanis' spiritual possessions as well as avatar transformations associated with online gaming.

TWO

The Psychology of Avatar Therapeutics

ABSORPTIVE EXPERIENCES AND STRESS RELIEF

INTRODUCTION: BEDAMI'S SECOND SPIRITUAL SELF

In late 1994, the terrible "feeling" (bhav) seized Bedami, a young Indian woman, around midnight. She and her husband Ramu were making an offering (puja) to Ramu's lineage goddess (kuldevi). This gift was intended both to ensure the health of their newly born son and to supplement Ramu's salary at a local folklore institute by inviting a return from his clan's patron goddess. Incense and a single candle were lit near the kuldevi's image, before which sat a blindfolded Bedami, forbidden to view the image because she originated from a clan other than her husband's. Clarified butter was poured over coals of burning cow dung, emitting a soft light and sweet smoke, both of which the goddess was said to relish. Pleasing the goddess is central to such offerings, which Bhats spoke of as bribes (rispat) intended to win divine favor.[1]

Bedami and Ramu, along with fifteen or so other Bhat families, most of them close relatives, had settled on the outskirts of the city of Udaipur (Rajasthan), where these events unfolded. Except for their sleeping children, the young couple was alone, the other Bhats dozing peacefully in their own quilted tents and ramshackle homes. All was quiet until Ramu presented rupee coins and notes to the kuldevi, at which time his wife was grabbed by the "feeling" that convulsed her body and sent her tumbling on the floor, beating her head against the walls and tearing out strands of her hair. A gust of wind blew through the house, flinging open the door; Ramu and his bawling children rushed out, closely pursued by a wailing Bedami. At some point, this young woman's blindfold flew off, apparently of its own accord, exposing the puja and revealing—in the words of the couple's now

FIGURE 12. Bedami Bhat appears far right. Photo by author.

very awake neighbors, who tried and failed to restrain their normally staid relative—Bedami's eyes glowing like an automobile's headlights. (See figures 12 and 13.)

Bedami's first rush of emotion lasted a few minutes and departed as abruptly as it arrived. I did not witness this initial fit that occurred late one night, for I lived in Udaipur's Old Town with a Jain family, spending only my days with the Bhats. But I was sharing an early lunch with the Bhats the next day—I supplied the goat meat, the Bhats the rest—when Bedami's feeling returned. My interest piqued, I spent the following days and some nights with Bedami's parents, whose home neighbored their daughter's. During this time, I witnessed a succession of outbursts that filled Bedami's body alternately with mute energy and silent trembling, or raucous anger and incomprehensible shrieking. As the days passed and the attacks showed no sign of abating, the small Bhat community, perched on the edge of town in the jungle, grew fearful. Bedami's own family, afraid to be left alone in the darkness with the "feeling," started to spend evenings in the homes of reluctant Bhat neighbors. Bedami herself also grew afraid of her own increasing loss of control. Although she always sensed the onset of her attacks, she could do nothing to stop them. Instead, she became empty (shunya), only able to watch

FIGURE 13. One site of Bedami's possession. Photo by author.

herself, in her words "like one watches a Hindi film"—somewhat detached and curious, wondering what might happen next.

My Bhat informants were not only frightened but also confused by these events. Bedami was not considered volatile and had no history of mental illness. Her parents also were known to be levelheaded and the stabilizing core of this small Bhat colony. Bedami's father, the first Bhat to settle outside of his natal village, supported himself by entertaining soldiers, pilgrims, and tourists with puppets. He was the leader of the Udaipur Bhats, to the extent that this community of fiercely independent persons can be said to have had a leader. I, too, was caught off guard by the sudden outbursts of emotion from the mild-mannered Bedami, who was my *dharam ki bahen* (adopted sister) and a member of a family I had known for nearly two years.

From her first attack, Bedami had always spoken while transformed, but her laments were typically fragmentary, brief, and ultimately incomprehensible to her scared relatives. Even when they succeeded in making out the literal meaning, the import of her words eluded them. After a week of breakdowns, however, Bedami began to speak more often and more clearly, but my Bhat informants noted that her voice, staccato and breathy, was unfamiliar and even unearthly. It was suspected, and had been from the beginning, that this was no ordinary flood of emotions. In fact, though one literal meaning of *bhav a gaya* is "feelings have come," the phrase, as mentioned earlier, is conventionally used by Rajasthanis to describe a state of spiritual possession.[2] I have relied on the literal meaning of this expression not to mislead my readers but to suggest the Bhats' own inability to make sense of Bedami's outburst—just as likely interpreting the event as an emotional fit, or even insanity, as a spiritual possession. Spiritual explanations, however, gained ascendancy. Indeed, given that gods and spirits in Rajasthan are said to travel with the wind, the gust that had coursed through the house slamming open the door appeared a likely sign of divinity. Bhats soon began to refer to Bedami's condition not only with the common Hindu phrase for spiritual possession, bhav a gaya, but also with the Muslim term for an intrusion of supernatural energy and desire—*hajari* (lit., "presence").

As this interpretation grew in the hearts and minds of the Bhats, Bedami's speech and movements gradually came in line with the stereotypical forms of spirit possession. Before long, Bhats even thought they had identified the spiritual intruder. Bedami, who bucked like an unbroken horse during her attacks, was probably being used by Mataji, or the Mother Goddess, as a mount (*ghorala,* an archaic term originating from *ghora,* the Hindi word for "horse"). I was told by one excited Bhat informant after one of Bedami's seizures, "She had the strength of ten men! She was transformed one hundred percent completely [in English] into Mataji! Just like Kali!"

A few days later, the "presence" herself announced her identity through her mount, clarifying that she was Kali's sister, Chavanda Mata. The Bhat caste (jati) is composed of sixteen intermarrying patrilineal clans (*gotras*), each of which is presided over by a clan goddess (kuldevi). Each Bhat clan goddess is viewed as an incarnation (avatar) of the Mother Goddess believed to have performed a miracle that saved the clan's founder. Chavanda Mata, being the oldest of the Nine Durgas or "Nine Sisters"—who are seen to encompass the forms of the Mother Goddess—had special authority within the Bhat community. Most importantly for the discussion here, Chavanda Mata maintained authority over Ramu himself—for she was Ramu's own lineage goddess.

Bedami's claim was not immediately accepted by the Bhats—and certainly not by Ramu—for possession by a clan deity was unprecedented. Male ghosts (bhut) and female ghosts (churail), dead witches (dakan) and living witches (meli), and demons (raksas), yes. Ancestors (pitra) with a grudge, or merely lonely, are commonplace. Bhairuji, a minor god (*devata*) of the underworld, seen as a fragment or son of Shiva, is not infrequent. Even certain incarnations of the goddess, such as Kali, were known to grab (pakarna) humans, but in Bhat recollection, a clan deity had never done so.[3]

Bhats had other reasons to doubt this was the goddess, for a force for good would surely not allow Bedami to so deteriorate physically. If this were a possession by the goddess, it was also questionable why Bedami should be chosen to receive such a gift. She was not devout, had no special talent (gun) or sixth sense that allowed her to see into the spirit world, and unlike her father, who was said to commonly wrestle demons, she had never even seen a spirit. Some suggested that Bedami was faking. Yet, even this was a less than satisfactory explanation, for the adjective most frequently used to describe this young woman—Bedami was about twenty-three years old at the time, Ramu, twenty-nine—was *bholi,* best translated as "simple," or honest and straightforward with a touch of naivete. Bedami was the opposite of clever (chalak), a phrase typically applied by outsiders and Bhats themselves to members of this community of players. It thus seemed unlikely that she was staging a drama (natak karti) for illicit gains, as her kin were known to do.

An exorcist was called. After being paid handsomely—too handsomely according to my Bhat informants, themselves ritual specialists working for the low-caste Bhambis of western Rajasthan—the spiritual specialist informed the community that this was in fact Ramu's lineage goddess, Chavanda Mata, and she appeared benevolent.[4] With the exorcist's blessing, and after cleansing the devi's vessel according to her regimen (niyam) or command (hukam), Bhat believers and nonbelievers alike actively began to summon Chavanda Mata into Bedami's body. "Come and sit with us, our power, our Mother" (Hamari sakti, Mataji padaaro), Bhats would chant. After ten or fifteen minutes at the most, amidst the relaxing smells, rhythmic drumming, and devotional songs, the devi would alight (utarna) on her medium. Bedami performed a series of miracles during these ritual invocations, such as one remarkable incident in which she was seen to cure a baby who was expected to die within the hour. This event electrified the Bhat community and made them more willing to believe that the goddess was real (sach) and not a lie (jhut), that Bedami was not merely crazy (pagal) or playacting (natak karna).

Despite these wondrous happenings, many Bhats, and even Bhat believers, still advanced natural explanations for Bedami's seemingly supernatural strength. They pointed out that, only weeks before her possession, Bedami had given birth to her fourth child and was therefore in a weakened physical state. Bhats, like many Indians, believed that a mother should eat fatty foods, such as *ghee* (clarified butter), to restore her strength following childbirth, but Bedami did not do so, mainly because her husband refused to buy them. Without the rich foods, Bedami, who was still breastfeeding her new son, complained frequently that her new child, her other children, and even her husband were "eating" her. On numerous occasions (well before her spiritual transformation), because of her weakness, Bedami fainted, becoming unconscious, in some ways resembling her state when possessed by the devi.

More importantly, Bedami, on her husband's insistence, had been sterilized a few days before her first spiritual attack. (Ramu believed that his paltry salary could support no more children.) Moreover, the institution that performed the operation reneged on its promise to pay Bedami for her sterilization through its incentive program. This left Bedami unable to purchase the foods needed to regain her strength, which further contributed to her dizzy spells and fainting. In short, though Bedami appeared a simple person with few conflicting emotions, her integrity, as Bhats themselves pointed out, had been threatened long before the devi's intrusion: she had given birth to a child, and thus quite literally had been separated from a part of herself; the violent intrusion of a medical sterilization had also cut her off from an important part of her body, as well as from her ability to reproduce; and the resulting weakness caused her to dissociate from her conscious self. Aptly summing up the situation, though taking the metaphor of a battery and not of physical dismemberment, my Bhat informants told me Bedami had been losing power and that the devi, real or imagined, recharged her.

. . .

In addition to the language of feelings (bhav) and presences (hajari), many Bhats, themselves performers paid to aesthetically represent and critically comment on everyday reality, referred to possession with the Hindi terms *nakal karna* and *nakal utarna,* which mean "to copy," especially in reference to acts of artistic creation. Bhats even used the English-Hindi phrase *double karna* (taken from a Hindi cinema frequented by lost twins and usurping doppelgangers), which literally translates, "to make a double." In the case of Bedami, some Bhats said that she imitated or copied the devi's ways, assuming them as her own. In doing so, she brought supernatural levels of reality populated by gods, demons, and spirits into her immediate body and experience.

In other writing, I have pointed to the utility of an artistic and performative language for explaining spirit possession's therapeutic effects: by imitating threatening others—suicides, stillborn infants, widows—the possessed gain some modicum of control over perceived threats in ways that help them imagine their way out of unsatisfying identities and promote self-healing.[5] As such, the spiritually possessed wield power similar to that of language, theatre, and art—as well as other communicative and expressive forms—an imaginative power that not only replicates but also reworks dominant mores and ways of being and thus potentially transforms illness to health.

This performative language parallels the more explicitly psychological terminology I employ in this book and especially this chapter: that of *dissociation*. Bedami *dissociates*—or psychologically separates—into a second identity, which, from certain Bhat points of view, resembles in some ways how actors take on dramatic roles.[6] As in many cases of dissociation, Bedami feels not only a partitioning of her experience of self but also other symptoms such as so-called *depersonalization*—the feeling of alienation from her own body—as evidenced in the way she speaks of watching herself as she might a film. Importantly, that dissociative process, though initially experienced by Bedami as disruptive and stressful, seems at this point to also promise relief from her life problems. The disruption is identified as a Hindu goddess trying to communicate with Bedami, Ramu, and others in the Bhat community. That is an auspicious sign, and an indication that the "presence" is there to help—in the Bhats' words, to *recharge* the suffering Bedami with divine power, or *sakti*, much like one would a battery.

Her dissociative experience interpreted in spiritual terms, Bedami also goes from feeling afflicted by an illness to starting on the path to becoming a spirit medium. Bhats in the community begin to make offerings to the young Bedami while she is transformed into what is increasingly interpreted as the devi. On those occasions, Bedami becomes the focus of attention, care, and adoration, which, amidst the relaxing puja offering, again promises to provide her with relief from her suffering. Further, if Bedami were to fully take on the spirit medium role, she would become a powerful individual, who, far from being helpless, would help others recover from their own afflictions. Early indications here are that Bedami will assume this mantle: after all, the transformed Bedami announces herself as Chavanda Mata, and on one occasion Bedami, as the devi, is believed to be responsible for curing a sick infant. In moving into that new sacred status, a process that takes time, Bedami would experience greater and greater control over her dissociative experiences. Already we see some sign of this control, as when Bedami-cum-the devi clearly announces her identity as Chavanda Mata, Kali's sister. Paralleling the health trajectories of spirit mediums around the world, Bedami seems on her way to becoming a healed healer, as she learns to control the powerful feelings that course through her body, to both better her own situation and help others. Again, psychologists refer to experiences such as Bedami's as *dissociative,* a language I employ in this chapter. But as the Bhats point out, these experiences also resemble acts of artistic imitation: Bedami duplicates divine levels of reality, an act that allows her to spiritually reinvent herself as the devi, improving her health in the process.

. . .

As I said earlier, I use Bedami's spiritual experiences as a frame story to introduce and help explicate this chapter's spiritual- and digital-avatar therapeutic themes, as well as those of chapter 3 and 4. I now describe digital-avatar parallels to Bedami's experiences, focusing on dissociative experiences in gaming contexts, and how such experiences can promote stress relief and thus enhance gamers' mental well-being. To better set up that material and analysis, I first present more detail related to the context of that research and to my own personal gaming experiences. This chapter's introduction gives a sense of my relationship to Bedami and the Bhats, and I want readers to understand my gaming research in a similar way. I follow those reflections with ethnographically informed interview and questionnaire results from my US *World of Warcraft* studies. I use those more structured research results to help convince readers of the *dissociative* character of gaming and how dissociative gaming relates to *stress-relief* processes, which might sound implausible to some who more typically think of gaming as harmful and "addictive." This structured analysis of dissociative processes central to gamers' avatar experiences sets up later chapters' findings, which foreground more clearly my ethnography, first in chapter 3 in the United States with a focus on the KOG and then in chapter 4 in Indian gaming zones, though with further support provided in both instances by interview and questionnaire results. Before proceeding to this chapter's culminating discussion of parallels between spiritual- and digital-avatar therapeutic processes in relation to dissociation and stress relief, I also present additional examples of spirit possessions I witnessed in the Indian state of Rajasthan, which help further contextualize dissociative experiences such as Bedami's.

A passion for stories first brought me to India in the 1990s, where I hoped to learn more about Rajasthan's vibrant oral traditions. Having finished my MA thesis (on the Renaissance mathematician and magician John Dee[7]), I took a summer trip to India, where I met the well-known folklorist Komal Kothari, who introduced me to the Bhats.[8] They were Rajasthan's famous puppeteers, but much more than that, given their genealogical, oral-historical, and poetic performances. Working with them, though, meant gaining proficiency in Hindi and local Rajasthani languages. This took me first to UC-Berkeley, to learn Hindi from Usha Jain, and then to the towns of Udaipur and Jaipur in Rajasthan, where I further advanced in local languages with tutors and while living and working with the Bhats over several years.

During my 1990s and early 2000s research with the Bhats, I participated in and documented almost all aspects of Bhat daily life, both sacred and secular. In my Bhat research, I worked as what has been called a *lone ethnographer,* taking it upon myself to document Bhat culture.[9] Simultaneous with fieldwork, I conducted qualitative interviews with Bhats. These were typically informal and conducted with groups of individuals, many over daily lunches of stewed curried goat, others on ritual occasions, for example, during Bedami's spirit medium seances, where I elicited Bhat perceptions of those events. In the Bhat case, I got to know the Udaipuri Bhat community quite well, sharing their lives for almost three years, during which time I spoke to them about their lives, aspirations, and daily practices.

In fall 2007, refreshed and energized after a recent sabbatical and receipt of tenure, I was imagining a research project on gaming. This related to something I had been discussing with Colorado State University (CSU) faculty and students since I was first hired. Though I worked in India, I spoke during my job interview of a project on US LARPing or "live-action-role-playing"—that is, role-playing dramatically acted out in the world rather than confined to a tabletop. Such a project seemed suitable for my own "halfie" gamer identity (half gamer and nerd, half something else).[10] It also felt like a potentially interesting extension of my ongoing study of the social and psychological implications of story and the imagination, as in my work with the performer Bhats of Rajasthan. In games, I saw stories lived and embodied in particularly powerful manners—in LARPing, for example, one actually becomes a character in the stories as opposed to simply reading or viewing such stories.

Compared with my study with the Bhats, I knew that this new project would require learning a different kind of language, gamer-speak perhaps, which I partly knew, along with WoW's intricate rules and informal community norms, which were new to me.[11]

These ideas intersected with my attempts as a still relatively new professor of anthropology aiming to teach students how to do what I did and finding that things that came naturally to me—like ethnography—were not as easy for my students. My goal of demystifying the research process for my students intersected with a growing personal enthusiasm for mixed qualitative and quantitative research methods. A diverse methodological toolkit did more justice to my own background in the sciences and humanities (a BS in molecular biology, but with lots of literature, history, and philosophy on the side), as well as to the complexity of the subjects I studied. Importantly, in mixing multiple methods, I felt both more confident in my own understanding of a research subject and also more able to illuminate for students links between theory, data, and conclusions.[12]

At that time, I met weekly with a group of Fort Collins friends to play tabletop role-playing games. A mix of faculty, grad students, and community members, our favorite game was White Wolf's *Vampire the Masquerade*, though we sometimes also pretended to be werewolves or Tolkienesque "high-fantasy" creatures like elves, dwarves, and hobbits. I had also reconnected with an old friend from high school now living in Los Angeles, Howard, who was deep into the online role-playing game, *World of Warcraft* (WoW). As a gamer and anthropologist, I was intrigued by this game's social dimensions. As a "massively multiplayer online role-playing game"—"MMORPG" or simply "MMO" for short, as referred to in earlier chapters—many thousands of players simultaneously logged into WoW via the internet to connect with one another in shared fantasy realms. With Howard as my guide, I first dipped my toes into this online virtual world in that fall of 2007. It also turned out that many of my local gaming friends themselves played WoW, which further fueled my enthusiasm for the genre. (See figures 14 and 15.)

In a process now partially opaque to me, I thought to myself at some point: Why not teach a research methods class *inside* the game *World of Warcraft*? A virtual fantasy world like WoW, I reasoned, could be thought of as a foreign land with its own customs and culture. And it seemed to be a particularly accessible one to boot: with just a personal computer and a relatively affordable subscription fee (about twelve dollars a month at the time), one could access this land from the convenience of one's own home.

FIGURE 14. Games like *World of Warcraft* unfold in a Tolkienesque "high-fantasy" land-scape. Image by Jim Cooper (jcooper2) from Pixabay.

I imagined forming a research team with my students and venturing together into this internet-based reality. Initial participant-observation would help us understand the concerns and experiences of this world's denizens, which we would document in field notes. This could lead to more focused research questions and hypotheses, which we could further explore and test in semi-structured "key-informant" interviews and online "field" surveys, thus mixing qualitative and quantitative cultural-anthropological methods. Indeed, such questions might reveal contours of a new internet-based era, which was transforming both the way we accessed information and how we interacted

FIGURE 15. In *World of Warcraft*, orcs, who in Tolkien's *Lord of the Rings* trilogy are monsters, are a playable character race. Image by Annette Pendlebury (pendleburyannette) from Pixabay.

with one another. I also had this feeling that as quickly as traditional cultures and communities were disappearing, new internet-based ones were being born, which called out to the anthropologist in me.

I approached some of the graduate students in my local gaming group with the idea of such a methods course. They were enthusiastic. I also approached my then department chair, Kathy Pickering, who was similarly excited by the idea. We decided that I could teach the seminar under the prefix and title of an already existing graduate class, Advanced Ethnographic Research Methods. "Experimental" methods might have been more accurate, but that title was good enough and allowed me to proceed immediately in the following spring of 2008. I did not need to recruit students. They were already there, ready and excited: eleven of them, a talented mix of graduate students from anthropology and sociology, along with a physicist (a spouse of one of the anthropologists), and a few undergraduate students too, largely anthropology majors, who had taken previous courses from me.

Given what I judged to be that original 2008 seminar's success, I aimed to replicate it over the years that followed, running roughly every year or every other year some iteration of that first seminar, with findings from those collaborative research endeavors informing what appears in this book. For example, in fall 2011 and spring 2012, eight CSU students and I, two graduates and six undergraduates, ethnographically documented the Knights of Good's (KOG's) *raiding* activities, which feature in chapter 3. Early on, I also created a dedicated virtual-worlds lab space to better accommodate the research and training, which I dubbed my "Ethnographic Research and Teaching Laboratory" (ERTL).[13]

Unlike my earlier India research with the Bhats, my gaming research was from the outset highly collaborative. The original spring 2008 seminar was more of a fly-by-the-seat-of-your-pants kind of affair, as there was no model we knew of that explained what we as a research team should be doing. As a group, we played *World of Warcraft* extensively, often together, typically at least two to four hours a week. When we played together as a class— sometimes even face to face with our laptops tapping a team member's home's Wi-Fi—such play also became the focus of our scrutiny and reflection. By the end of the semester, many of us had reached the game's maximum level cap (then eighty), of which we were proud, and had engaged in a wide range of WoW activities. Some of these were collaborative and involved groups of five, ten, or more individuals, in which teams pitted skills against the game environment and other players. Most of our experiences and observations occurred within the context of our own in-game guild and playgroups, which were composed of both strangers as well as those known to us "in real life" ("IRL," in our respondents' vernacular). Of note here, we trained ourselves to monitor and document our own levels of WoW focus and absorption, as well as the way such states of concentration and awareness seemed to influence our lives offline, serving as a relaxing retreat in some instances and as a time-consuming source of stress and frustration on other occasions. These activities became the source of self-reflexive discussions among members of the research team. We also disciplined ourselves to stop in-game to conduct brief informal interviews with coplayers on these and other topics, noting responses in field journals and then expanding on these notes after the activities had concluded. The 2008 seminar itself, three hours each week, consisted largely of us sitting around a large conference table discussing our past week's gaming experiences, observations, and informal interviews, sometimes observing live in-game activities as a prompt for our discussions.

In the fall 2011 and spring 2012 research of KOG, which informs this chapter but features most prominently in chapter 3, my student collaborators and I followed relatively closely the earlier 2008 ethnographic research model just described. We also formed our own "friends and family" guild, Virtual Worldz, which survives in spirit to this day in *Guild Wars 2* (Virtual Worldz-t located in GW2's land of Tyria rather than WoW's Azeroth). I spent much of fall 2011 semester training my student collaborators in ethnographic research methods, with us again sometimes even playing WoW together in local cafes via their Wi-Fi, which helped the students less familiar with the game (about half the class). Then, as a class, we spent the remainder of fall 2011 and also the spring 2012 semester in KOG, taking notes, conducting informal interviews with its members, and observing raids via live internet streams on YouTube and other online video services such as Twitch, and generally participating in and observing this guild's online and sometimes offline activities. We documented in fieldnotes the sadness we felt as our small close-knit CSU community of researcher-gamers temporarily dissolved as we left to join the bigger and more intimidating KOG. In the latter case, we even observed raids in the actual home of this guild's founder couple, watching them unfold on their big-screen TV, and conducting informal interviews with them about what was happening. We also gamed with KOG's members and were generally privy to their activities and conversations via multiple sources: for example, not just YouTube broadcasts but also WoW's in-game text-based chat channels and the raiders' Ventrilo conversations. Not wanting to overwhelm them, I typically only sent a few student researchers into any given night's raid and limited our questioning there, refraining from talking at all during critical raid moments. I also assigned individual researchers to "shadow" and thus document the words and activities of a given raider, with more in-depth "debrief" conversations saved for after the raid.

In my gaming projects, ethnographic participant-observation has been invariably accompanied by somewhat more formal key-informant interviewing. Members of my research teams and I generally solicited interviews from persons associated with local gaming communities and centers as well as through our own guilds and play networks, followed by network "snowball" sampling from these initial respondents (i.e., one respondent refers another, with the sample growing like a rolling snowball). Some interviews were conducted face to face, when the gamers were local, though many were conducted over Ventrilo, a voice-over-internet-protocol commonly used by online gamers. I sometimes had students do one of each type, which became a focus of discussion. The gaming interviews, which feature in this chapter, were more typically based on interview protocols—that is, a written-out set of questions—which I developed collaboratively with my students. All interviews were digitally recorded and transcribed.

As MMOs were still relatively new to me during my early phases of gaming research, I personally interviewed many of my students with MMO and other online gaming experience. Then, during fall 2011 and spring 2012, we interviewed members of KOG about their positive and negative play experiences, concentrating especially on their raiding experiences with KOG and other more "hardcore" guilds. The interviews were drawn from a convenience sample from KOG's membership, though we interviewed all the guild's "core" raiders.

Further, these research stints typically culminated with quantifiable surveys, where my teams and I tested key ideas that emerged from our observations and interviews. Of relevance here, surveys allowed us to measure relationships between dissociative experiences and stress processes. And we developed our own WoW-specific scale measure for assessing dissociative gaming experiences and other survey items to assess the extent players believed WoW play either added to their happiness and life satisfaction and decreased stress in their lives or, by contrast, subtracted from their mental well-being and even increased their stress levels. Our samples were obtained by posting links to our survey on WoW blogs and gamer websites and by extending invitations through our own personal play networks, which included KOG.

Turning now to this chapter's substantive gaming findings, my team's qualitative interviews demonstrated how WoW promoted relaxation alternating with mildly stress-inducing states.[14] These two states of experience and consciousness, relaxed in the first instance and slightly aroused in the second, could be best achieved, players reported, if they imaginatively absorbed into this game-world, experiencing Seligman and Kirmayer's narrowing of attention and focus,[15] which I discussed earlier in the introduction.

In the first therapeutically relaxed state, it was only by successfully dissociating *into* the game that players were able to dissociate *away* from real-life stressors. As Richard, nearing forty and working in sales for a technology company, told me of his WoW play:

> Sometimes a beer at night can be a very therapeutic thing. The game can definitely be a very therapeutic thing. Believe it or not, when I'm out there killing *mobs* [mobile monsters] and it's the same stuff over and over and over, my mind will wander. I'm relaxing. The game for some people is a retreat. It's a place where I can run and hide from real life, and I use it to that extent. I can go run and hide from real life.

For Richard, WoW's therapeutic benefits emerged most clearly when performing repetitive tasks in the game. Other players credited WoW's beautiful virtual landscapes as allowing their minds and bodies to relax, temporarily protected from real-world stresses. As Jonathan, a twenty-two-year-old college student, put it:

> Sometimes I just log on late at night and go out by myself and listen to the soothing music in the Barrens [a WoW in-game area] as I run past some gazelle or do a couple of easy quests on my own. It's sort of an African motif, so there's giraffes and zebras. Maybe it's the music or the colors. It's just something about there I like and enjoy.

Playing alone late at night and listening to the rhythmic drum sounds of the virtual world gave this individual a sense of peace and calm. Indeed, such is the feeling of peace and calm created by certain WoW activities that some players compared their gaming experiences as akin to meditation. In the words of another college-age player: "You know, honestly, I like the repetitive activities that don't require a lot of thought but that need to be done. I actually find them to be a calming influence . . . You know, a Zen-like state."

Without the focus and deep immersion provided by this virtual reality, real-world stressors continued to plague players, and these players did not reach their deeply relaxed, even meditative, states of play. Therapeutically, WoW dissociation thus enhanced players' ability to inhabit a fantasy world, where they could temporarily escape real-life troubles, whether with their bosses, bills, or significant others. In a sense, imaginative absorption and dissociation into WoW blunted players' awareness of real-life stressors. Shielded from external real-world stimuli, players' minds thus wandered, and they relaxed. Of importance in these contexts, WoW presented players with a world that was largely regular and predictable. As players pointed out to me and others in interviews,

WoW was characterized by clear rules for how to play and advance in the game, as well as structured tasks that could be completed in a largely timely and predictable manner. It was also characterized by codes of conduct—*honor* even, a common player concern and topic of discourse—that lent the game further regularity. Such structure and predictability, as my research team was reminded repeatedly in observations, interviews, and indeed our own gaming experiences, contributed to a lowering of players' experiences of stress.

As such, the game seemed to function in a manner akin to meditation or other techniques for eliciting the relaxation response and thus lowering the body's levels of stress. As reviewed previously in the introduction, WoW's lightly altered relaxed states of consciousness might be accompanied by, as is argued for shamanism, the release of feel-good endorphins, pushing players into even deeper states of pleasant relaxation, further contributing to the potential therapeutic dimensions of WoW dissociation.[16]

In the second instance of WoW working therapeutically, informants described the game as doing precisely the opposite for them: *creating* rather than *relieving* stress. Sometimes such stress was pleasantly stimulating and thus positive. Consider one individual's description of the excitement he and his other raid members felt completing the Molten Core *instance* (i.e., one "instance" or personal version of this complex dungeon, which only the group's raiders saw), one of WoW's earliest end-game raiding experiences involving forty players and a concerted effort.

> Several guilds ago, before the *Burning Crusade* expansion [WoW has multiple game content additions referred to as "expansions"], the very first forty-man dungeon was called Molten Core. It took us probably six weeks of raiding two to three nights a week to make it all the way through Molten Core. It's very intense, and by the time we finally killed the last boss [a fierce in-game enemy], people were screaming. I mean, *yelling* into their microphones, and you know, "Yah, yah, yah!" *Really* exciting. Everybody was over the top excited about it . . . Just because it had taken so much time . . . But when you invest that much time into something, and to finally succeed . . . It was a real incredible experience. We managed to work together to accomplish this task and then get the rewards for it . . . Everybody felt good. When you succeed at doing something like that, it's definitely a rush. It's a feeling that you and the people you're with have accomplished something that nobody else has done.

Another college-age gamer described the euphoric emotional experiences accompanying his WoW play in the following terms:

WoW is like soda pop. It's bubbly. It's adrenaline, and it's pretty. You can get a wide range of emotions unlike anything . . . *anything*. And the extremes: from rage, to happiness, to jumping out of your chair and going, "Yeaaahhh!" And you don't even realize you're doing it! But yeah, the range of game-world content, from the social, mail, and chatting. You've got the collection of gear and armor, and the intense feeling of success. You have to concentrate to win, you have to be on your guard to avoid dying. It's there, and those emotions will be going for hours. It's the extremes that you get. And I think that's what makes it significant.

Here, too, it was WoW's fantasy-induced stresses—that "you have to concentrate to win, you have to be on your guard to avoid dying"—that ultimately made the feelings of accomplishment satisfying and even euphoric.

In these contexts, dissociative experiences again greatly enhanced the therapeutic process related to positive stress. WoW accomplishments are even more absorptive because they often are felt to be *real* rather than virtual, described by some gamers as just as meaningful as those accompanying real-life successes. If the fantasy monsters and dangers do not at least *seem* real and important, and if one does not feel as if they really *are* their character, the game would be less successful in creating the mild positive stress necessary for the achievement of enjoyable and potentially therapeutic states of consciousness.[17] Thus, somewhat paradoxically, while lowering one's worries and perception of real-world stress, the game also induced fantasy stress. In fact, we might characterize WoW as an endless parade of mildly stress-inducing challenges and puzzles to be completed and solved. Players were confronted by monsters and demons to slay, and by tasks to complete. They experienced competitive challenges from foes, whether members of the rival Horde or Alliance faction (recall that WoW players choose to belong to one of these opposed groups, each allowing for faction-specific races, like Night Elves for the Alliance and Orcs for the Horde) or young duelists eager to make a name for themselves (WoW players can test each other in duels). They were encouraged, often strongly compelled by other players, to collaborate with somewhat unpredictable social others to win the highest rewards in the game. Likewise, treasure was generated largely by chance and only after completing tasks of variable lengths, leading to states of aroused anticipation and delayed gratification, as players speculated on and anticipated their rewards, hoping for the best but fearing ending up empty-handed or getting "ninja-looted" by an unscrupulous play partner (who steals in silent ninja-fashion a reward that rightfully belongs to another player).

Following the Hungarian-American psychologist Mihaly Csikszentmihalyi, such positive stress, I learned, helped players achieve *flow:* the experience of being in the "zone," where players were pushed by the game's tasks and challenges, but nevertheless had a high likelihood of experiencing success.[18] As Csikszentmihalyi argues, the most enjoyable experiences, those that most enhance happiness and satisfaction, are often somewhat stressful. Indeed, the enjoyment stems in part from encountering proper amounts of stress. Without WoW's moderately stressful challenges, players would feel bored, rather than alive, alert, focused, in control. With too much stress, they would become overanxious. As I witnessed, WoW's game mechanics, constantly updated and refined, struck a balance between the two potentially negative states of boredom and anxiety. Pushed to the limits of their skill, many players grew in their mastery of the game rather than quit in frustration and defeat. And as I will show in subsequent chapters, WoW achievement boosted many players' self-esteem, allowing them to rework their less-than-heroic portraits of their actual-world selves. Further, WoW, in its many challenges, presented players with *predictable* forms of stress, very different from the generally vague, unpredictable, chronic, and even undefeatable stresses of the actual world—which certainly added to the experience of WoW fun.

Survey results provided quantitative support for my interpretations of the relationship between dissociative gaming experiences and positive mental well-being. First, I would point out that survey analysis revealed how commonly players reported gaming-related dissociative experiences. For example, 30 percent of the respondents said they became so absorbed in game-play that they always or often became unaware of events happening around them in the actual world. Losing track of the passage of time while playing was also common, occurring at least sometimes to nearly two-thirds of the sample, as was the experience that WoW game events felt *actually* real, as opposed to merely virtually so, though for a smaller percentage of respondents. Some survey respondents also reported experiencing events in WoW as more vivid or memorable than those of their real lives, and a substantial fraction have felt themselves to actually *be* their character. (See table 1 for frequency of respondents' reports of dissociative experiences.[19])

Second, I would highlight how many players felt that WoW contributed positively to their mental well-being. About half of respondents reported that WoW play increased their happiness, and an even larger fraction said that WoW increased their life satisfaction and helped them relax and combat stress. Most respondents denied that WoW play increased stress in their lives, but nearly one-third agreed at some level that it did. (For a summary of these results, see table 2.[20])

TABLE 1 Selected Dissociation-Scale Items, Percent Distribution ($N = 253$)

	Always (5)	Often (4)	Sometimes (3)	Rarely (2)	Never (1)
Lose awareness of real world while playing WoW.	8.3	21.3	36.4	23.7	10.3
Lose track of time passage while playing WoW.	15.0	24.1	25.7	17.8	17.4
Events in WoW feel like they are really happening.	4.0	9.9	8.7	17.1	60.3
Events in WoW more vivid/memorable than real world.	5.6	9.1	11.9	27.4	46.0
Feel like I am my WoW character.	4.8	3.2	13.9	17.1	61.1

NOTE: Originally appeared in Snodgrass et al., 2011, *Culture, Medicine, and Psychiatry* 35 (1): 26–62.

TABLE 2 Self-Reported Subjective Well-Being Outcomes of Playing *World of Warcraft*, Percent Distribution ($N = 253$)

	Strongly Agree (5)	Agree (4)	Neutral (3)	Disagree (2)	Strongly Disagree (1)
WoW increases my happiness.	9.1	35.6	32.8	12.6	9.9
WoW accomplishments and friendships add to my life satisfaction.	14.6	37.2	25.7	14.2	8.3
WoW play helps me relax.	17.8	45.8	22.1	11.9	2.4
WoW play increases my stress.	9.5	19.4	19.4	32.4	19.4

NOTE: Originally appeared in Snodgrass et al., 2011, *Culture, Medicine, and Psychiatry* 35 (1): 26–62.

Most importantly for this chapter's arguments, the survey analysis allowed my team and me to confirm substantive relationships between personal reports of dissociative experiences (as assessed by our WoW-specific scale measure) and *all* this study's positive subjective well-being outcomes, while adjusting for demographic and other "control" variables. That is, such an analysis allowed my team to verify if relationships between dissociative

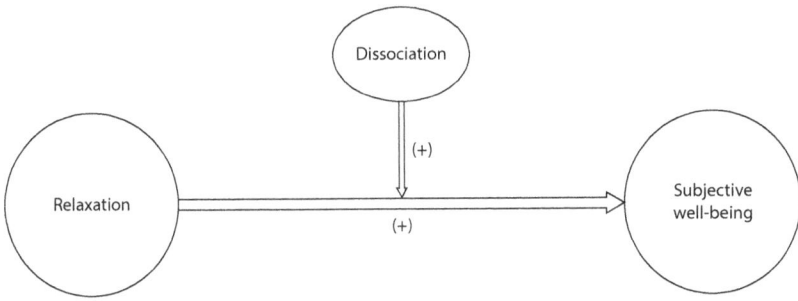

FIGURE 16. Conceptual model of the interactive relationship between Relaxation and Dissociation on gaming-related Subjective Well-Being as the outcome. The more a respondent experiences *World of Warcraft* (WoW) as dissociative, the stronger the positive relationship is between the experience of gaming-related relaxation and reporting WoW as increasing one's happiness and life satisfaction.

experiences and subjective well-being held at each and every value of other variables such as gender, age, and so forth, thus accounting or "controlling" for their impact on the analysis. Specifically, using a technique referred to as *ordinal logistic regression,* we identified substantial positive relationships between self-reports of WoW dissociative experiences (as a sum of an individual's reports of experiencing that scale's items) and the game being perceived, first, to increase one's happiness and life satisfaction (two separate outcomes assessed with different single-question survey items) and, second, to provide for stress relief. Analyzing the survey data in a slightly different way, we also found that players who said WoW helped them relax were more likely to report that the game added to their happiness and life satisfaction. And we also found that players who experienced WoW as increasing their life stress were also more likely to report that WoW increased their happiness.

Finally, results indicated a statistically *interactive* relationship between dissociative gaming experiences and relaxation in relation to the experience that WoW both increased one's life happiness and one's life satisfaction. What this means is that the more a respondent experienced WoW as dissociative, the stronger the positive relationship was between the experience of gaming-related relaxation and reporting WoW as increasing one's happiness and life satisfaction. In both cases, dissociation considerably magnified the positive relationship of the experience of WoW play promoting relaxation to these subjective well-being outcomes. Figure 16 graphically illustrates those patterns. (For a more detailed presentation of this survey analysis, see appendix A.)

As discussed in the book's opening chapters, dissociative avatar experiences such as Bedami's, framed as spiritual possessions, are in fact common occurrence in the Indian state of Rajasthan. For example, at the time of my research with the Udaipur Bhats in the 1990s, I learned that when Bhats experienced financial problems or ill health, they often visited a spirit medium named Kani Bai—or as Bhats referred to her, "the wife of Loharji"—who was a neighbor of my Bhat informants. (Kani Bai appears in figure 5.) Kani Bai, a tribal woman (adivasi), became possessed by the spirit of a deceased Muslim saint called a *pir baba*. Before her transformation into a medium, Kani Bai had been very ill. Her body, in her words, had *sukh gai*—"dried up"—and she was in her telling but "skin and breath." She visited healers, but none of them was able to identify the source of her illness. Finally, she visited the nearby town of Kapasan where a pir baba known to be a powerful healer was buried. On stepping onto the holy ground near the saint's tomb, a ghost "came out" of her and named itself. Speaking through Kani Bai, the ghost declared it was sent to torment her by a magician named Dilip. Dilip, also a tribal, was from Kani Bai's natal village. He had a son whom he had hoped to have married to Kani Bai's niece. Shortly after the engagement, however, Kani Bai had blocked the marriage, declaring that "Dilip's family is not good." Dilip, infuriated, was believed to have then set out to destroy Kani Bai's family with witchcraft. As Kani Bai put it, "This is how adivasis [tribals] fight. Not face to face, but behind the back. Not with fists, but with 'deadly words' [maro boli]." According to Kani Bai, Dilip managed to kill with dark magic both her mother and father, as well as most of her extended family's children. Kani Bai was next, and according to her, this magician would not have rested until her entire lineage was eliminated.[21]

The spirit of the Saint of Kapasan, however, exposed Dilip by forcing the ghost in Dilip's employ to name its master. After he was identified, Dilip was questioned by Kani Bai's remaining male relatives, who were said to have beaten him until he was nearly dead. Then, unsheathing a rusty sword, they threatened to cut off his head unless he would restore Kani Bai to health. Dilip promised to stop his magic. And Kani Bai's health, which had already started improving since her visits to Kapasan, began to improve even more dramatically. At this time, the spirit of the Saint of Kapasan himself started "coming into" Kani Bai's body. The saint began to regularly visit Kani Bai, which pleased her. As she told me, "Now I have the Pir Baba. I am not afraid anymore. He protects me." In time, Kani Bai's fame as a source of spiritual power spread. Her saintly protector was regularly summoned to solve problems both for members of her own community as well as for neighbors like the Bhats. Going into dissociative trance, which I frequently witnessed, Kani Bai would take handfuls of corn, whose kernels were counted, and depending on their odd or even number, gave "yes" or "no" answers to whatever questions were posed. As for Dilip, shortly after having his black dealings exposed, he died. As Kani Bai put it, "A man like that, the Earth won't tolerate him. It swallows him up."

Kani Bai, before becoming a medium, was said to be tormented by a ghost. These beliefs are not unusual. Rajasthani women are frequently said to be tormented by evil spirits. And their spiritual maladies are often preceded by family or caste disputes, such as disagreements over marriage arrangements or a piece of property, which are said to weaken them and open them to supernatural assault. To purge their bodies of pestering spirits, some visit mediums. Others, like Kani Bai herself, frequent the tombs of saints. And still others, I learned, visit living holy men such as the Muslim saint Mastanna Baba, to whom I now turn. (See Mastanna Baba in figure 2.)

Mastanna Baba, which loosely translates, "single world-renouncing man who basks in the divine pleasure of Allah," was an aged Udaipuri saint who lived with his followers and caretakers under an ancient peepal tree in Udaipur's Gulab Bagh park. The park was near my own residence in the old part of town, and I frequently visited it for its lush greenery and zoo. I had many chances to interact with Mastanna Baba over the course of my fieldwork in Udaipur in the 1990s, though he was elderly and ailing at that time and died in the summer of 1998, at which point he was enshrined in a tomb, now a pilgrimage site, outside of Udaipur city proper. Mastanna Baba, while living and dead, was described as a potent demon-slayer, the "Mike Tyson" of Muslim saints, or so locals told me. Mastanna Baba did not get possessed himself. Rather, he was said to have a "direct telephone link" with Allah. And as a conduit of the voice of divinity, Mastanna Baba was said to be a powerful miracle worker.

Surrounded by the peepal tree's twisting maze of hanging roots and branches, Mastanna Baba was fenced in by his mostly female followers, who rubbed his feet, refreshed him with yogurt drinks, draped him with garlands of flowers, and whispered in his ear, all the while hoping their ministrations might result in an illness cured, a job restored, a child granted. The possessed who came before Mastanna Baba to be healed were also almost exclusively women. Sitting at a respectful distance, not wanting their "filthy" spirits to contaminate the saint, they sought to rid themselves of the entities who had invaded their bodies. Their possessions were screams of raw hurt, painful to watch, both for myself as well as for other Rajasthanis. The possessed women panted and ranted; they rolled on the ground, thrusting dirt and filth into their mouths; their tongues lolled; they pulled at their hair and clothing. And in all their actions, they focused on Mastanna Baba, sometimes cursing him and banging their heads against the metal barriers that separated them from him. (Such was the desire to get close to the saint that these barriers were deemed necessary.)

And Mastanna Baba responded. As it was explained to me, he spiritually beat the evil spirits, forcing them to yelp in pain. This thrashing was said to be on another plane, inaudible and invisible, evident only in the mounts' wracked and contorted bodies. The saint also carried on a conversation with the spirits. Without using his actual voice, he asked the spirits what they wanted. The spirits' replies, unlike Mastanna Baba's own voice, were audible. Before they would "release the child" they were possessing, they demanded things. Some spirits craved the sour fruit of the tamarind tree (imli), shouting, "Feed me! I want imli." Other spirits wanted out of the bodies they were occupying, begging, "Release me Baba!", "Please, Allah's Servant, bury me in the ground!", "Get me out of this 'clean' place!" (referring to the holy ground surrounding the saint), "Jinesh put me in this body, I do not want to be here!", "I have brought confusion to this poor thing, now I want to go!", or self-disgustingly, "Kick me, discard me!" Some repented their sins: "I have done so much wrong and evil, please forgive me!", "I am a 'witch' [literally, 'dirty woman' (gandi aurat)]. I have tormented this poor thing. I am such a sinner!" Others would beg for mercy, "Lord, you've really beaten me! Please, Baba, I cannot take your stick!", "Please, Baba, don't burn my eyes, not my eyes!", or "Do not shock me with your electric 'current'!" (Again, in each of these cases, the Baba supposedly magically tortured these spirits.) But not all spirits were so repentant. Some would ask, "What do you care for this woman? Leave me be!" or "You destroy all the magic I do against this innocent, why?!" Some tried to fling dirty substances, such as dog feces or their own urine, on the saint. Others exposed themselves to the saint, flirting bawdily with him.

Some women appearing before this saint were said to be tormented by the spirits of still-living men. These women were believed to have been seized by the spirits of greedy and lustful neighbors or abusive male relatives, who longed for their bodies and property, and who threatened them physically if not given them. Some of these men would brazenly announce themselves before the Baba, "I am Davendra of Rawli village. This one is mine!", or "I live in Hiran Mangri, what about it?" Others, however, were more contrite, sobbing and begging forgiveness for their crimes: "I have had so much greedy magic done against this poor thing. I lust after money! Please, can you ever forgive me?!"

The most interesting example of this kind that I witnessed concerned the repeated possession of a young woman by her uncle (*kaka,* or father's brother), who craved the land and house she had inherited from her father. This man was said to have hired magicians to work black magic on his niece. These magicians, untouchables who inhabited a nearby cremation ground, were said to have directed spirits of the "dirty dead" into this woman's body. But the niece would not die, and so the uncle himself supposedly started to possess her. This young woman regularly visited Mastanna Baba. On each of her visits, at a relatively fixed time, her uncle's spirit would materialize in her body and beg forgiveness. On one occasion, however, the actual uncle had come to the saint to repent his sins, appearing at the exact moment that his spirit was supposedly in his niece's body. It should not have been possible for this man's spirit to simultaneously occupy both his own body and his niece's, which, needless to say, created all manner of conflicting interpretations. Some persons witnessing this event, though not all, thought that the uncle's spirit was inside his niece's body, while the real uncle was either some manner of phantasmic doppelganger or was animated by another ghostly spirit. That is, they doubted not the woman's channeling of her uncle's spirit but the uncle himself, which highlights the abiding power of what I refer to in this book as avatars.

I have also witnessed many spiritual possessions of Rajasthani men. For example, in Udaipur, as mentioned earlier, a class of Hindu spirits who are said to commonly seize humans, and men in particular, are referred to as *sagasji baojis* (roughly translated, "of the same kin" or "ancestor," but also sometimes "brave hero"). These male spirits were once kings, princes, or warriors, and typically of the Rajput caste (jati). They died in the prime of their lives before their "time" (referred to as *akal mot*), and this was usually a violent death by weapons.[22] For example, they might have been cut down on the battlefield defending a territory or murdered by a father or uncle in a palace intrigue. Having passed away in shining health, sagasji baojis are said to possess excess energy (sakti) to burn. They invade the bodies of the living, though usually in an attempt to help in some way, eager to use their power to right wrongs visited on themselves or on their mounts. As Rajputs, sagasji baojis commonly inhabit palaces. These include royal abodes like the City Palace (the residence of Udaipur's *Maharaja,* or "Great King"). It also includes mansions owned by retainers to the king. If properly propitiated, the sagasji baojis haunting these structures can be "installed" as powerful guardians. As an example, many schools in Udaipur's old town—and particularly those which were once aristocratic residences like the Royal Girls High Middle School—have sagasji baojis as protectors.

Many sagasji baojis appear only after their earthly abodes have been sold by their former Rajput owners. For example, I worked with a medium of the Jingar caste of saddle-makers, a man named Om Prakash, who had recently purchased a piece of Rajput property. Jingars, like the Bhats' Bhambi patrons, were once leather-workers (Chamars) and thus formerly referred to as "untouchable." The fortunes of the Udaipur branch of this caste, however, changed dramatically twenty-five years ago when its members took up silver work. Om Prakash, for example, made a great deal of money in his new profession and moved from a tiny hovel on the outskirts of Udaipur city to a former Rajput mansion close to the heart of old town. As Om Prakash explained: "Rajputs don't know how to work. They don't understand labor. After Independence, they drank all their money away and had to sell their land. They got desperate and would sell to anyone, no matter what the community. They got taken, while we got rich." Shortly after the purchase of his new home, however, Om Prakash was visited by a spirit that started "coming to his heart," causing him tension and trouble. He began to experience uncontrollable fits of anger, cracking "one hundred kilogram" [his phrasing] stones on his head, ripping at his clothing, and yelling at anyone within earshot. He also found himself unable to concentrate on his silver work and ultimately lost his appetite and started to physically wither. At night, his spiritual visitor made it impossible for him to sleep, and his health further deteriorated.

Finally, late one evening, Om Prakash gathered his courage and asked the spirit who he was and what he wanted. The spirit, appearing to Om Prakash in a dream and at other times in a dream-like trance, a form of dissociative experience, replied that he was Mann Singh, a young Rajput who had been killed a hundred years ago at the age of sixteen and an ancestor to the previous owners of Om Prakash's home. Mann Singh further claimed that his father was an important retainer to the king of Udaipur, and that he himself was the eldest son of his father's first wife and thus in line to inherit the family name and property. But one of his father's younger wives had him killed so that her own son would inherit the estate. This young wife concocted a story in which Mann Singh was accused of having "dishonored" her—a euphemism here for having tried to rape her. Going before her husband with torn clothes, she convinced him of her tale. Mann Singh's father was so outraged that he ordered his son's beheading. Mann Singh the spirit, desiring the respect he had been denied in life, demanded that Om Prakash construct a household temple in his honor. Mann Singh further insisted that his image be placed on the altar without his head. Only then, his treacherous murder properly recognized, could he finally rest.

Om Prakash, following the wishes of this sagasji baoji, "sat him down in his place," so he wouldn't "restlessly wander." After this, Mann Singh blessed Om Prakash. No longer tormenting this Jingar man's dreams, he even allowed Om Prakash to channel his supernatural energy, which was expressed as dissociative trance that was framed locally as a spiritual possession. Om Prakash became a neighborhood medium (*bhopa* or *ojha*), which further added to his fortune. In fact, the fiscal rewards of being a medium were so great as to draw the unwanted jealousy of Om Prakash's—mainly upper-caste Rajput—neighbors, who supposedly concocted a spell using cow's blood to stop this Rajput spirit from visiting. Following this sorcery, according to Om Prakash, Mann Singh the spirit only visited infrequently.

Bhairuji, a pan-Indian boss of the underworld and lord of ghosts and demons, also possesses Rajasthani spirit mediums, often men, who become that god's vehicle or avatar. Bhats maintain a special relationship to one incarnation of this god referred to as *Malasi Bhairuji.* When a son is born, Bhats perform a ritual sacrifice to this god, who is believed to be responsible for releasing child-spirits into a mother's womb.[23] As the story of this god's link to birth and fertility was told to me, Malasi Bhairuji was a Jat, a member of a Rajasthani agricultural caste. He was visiting his wife's sister in the town of Malasi. He was in a lustful mood, teasing the women of the village, and especially his sister-in-law, with sexual innuendo. He also touched his sister-in-law's body in "dirty" ways, caressing her through her clothing, hoping to entice her into intercourse. In one version of the story, he successfully seduced his sister-in-law, and the two engaged in consensual sex. In another version, he raped her. In either case, the two were caught in the act. And the men of the village of Malasi grabbed the lecherous Jat, hung him upside-down in a well, and slammed him against the well's walls until he was dead. After his death, however, his spirit lingered, haunting the villagers' dreams. Though terrifying, this spirit would inform the women of Malasi when they could expect to become pregnant. A temple was set up next to the well where the Jat man was killed. Now, Malasi Bhairuji is a popular fertility god, and women hoping to be blessed with offspring travel from afar to make offerings to him.

Malasi Bhairuji, as revealed in this story, is reminiscent of a sagasji baoji. His death, an untimely atrocity, not coming when expected, reverses his "natural" life course. He thus clings to life as a disgruntled spirit much like the ghosts of dead Rajputs. Also, he is transformed into a supernatural benefactor, though he protects child spirits and pregnant women rather than homeowners. And, tellingly, Bhats describe him as a watchman (chokidar), as well as a "prizefighter" (using the English), "Durga's bodyguard" (picking up the English "bodyguard" from Hindi films), and a "captain" (again, the English) in the Mother Goddess' Army—epithets equally applied to sagasji baojis.

But in other respects, Malasi Bhairuji is not like a sagasji baoji. To begin, he is a bawdy and subversive god. While sagasji baojis are sometimes referred to as "mischievous" (setan), Malasi Bhairuji's seduction (or rape) of his sister-in-law goes well beyond the playful hijinks of a young Rajput. He totally inverts local morality—or at least Rajput notions of chivalry and honor—actually doing what sagasji baoji was only accused of having done. Bhairuji is also known for his insatiable appetite. He howls, begs, and cries for meat and alcohol (substances especially prized by Rajputs). According to Bhats, this behavior is terrifying—as when he demands food in exchange for sparing a son's life—but also comical in its inappropriate forwardness. In fact, Bhairuji's hunger is so great that he reputedly eats filth on the street, which he shares with his dog mounts. By eating and sleeping with unclean scavengers and maintaining them as sacred mounts, Bhairuji further demonstrates that he is not bound by the same rules as ordinary caste Hindus.

Possessions by these two gods also differ in their related dissociative experiences. When a mount was taken by a sagasji baoji, thus becoming that god's avatar or vehicle, I typically noticed a simple closing of the medium's eyes, a slight sigh, and a minor twitching of the mount's hand or foot. Though the possession and avatar experience might be interrupted by the medium's occasional mad laugh or loud hiccup, for the most part, mediums of sagasji baojis stayed seated before the shrine to the possessing Rajput spirit, all the while calmly answering their congregation's questions. Bhats, like me, could not always tell when a possession by a sagasji baoji had begun and when it had ended—given such divine avatar experiences did not clearly demonstrate altered or trance states of consciousness. In fact, Bhats characterized these seances, using the English-Hindi, as "bore *ho gaya"*—literally, "a bore has happened." Possessions by the god Bhairuji, on the other hand, were inevitably punctuated by the spirit mediums' striking themselves on their backs with iron chains until they drew blood, behavior meant to demonstrate the ferocity of this god as well as the "truth" and "power" of the priests. Mounts of Bhairuji also shouted obscenities, insulting members of the audience, and even lunging menacingly in particular at female onlookers, all of which served to reinforce the reality and power of god's vehicle or avatar.

DISCUSSION: DISSOCIATION, STRESS, AND AVATAR THERAPEUTICS

As revealed in this chapter's opening vignette, Bedami *dissociates*—or psychologically separates[24]—into her second avatar identity, which, in her case, is the devi. Bedami feels her personality become partitioned, or divided, to take the phrasing of anthropologist Chris Lynn.[25] She also manifests classic dissociative symptomology, even as formulated in the DSM-5, such as *depersonalization*,[26] in the way she feels alienated from her own body, watching herself while possessed as she might a film and remembering little of the experience afterward.

Perhaps most importantly for this chapter's (and book's) argument, Bedami's dissociative experiences, though in part stressful, seem to eventually provide her with relief from her life problems as she transitions to becoming the devi's spirit medium. In fact, Bedami's feelings of stress are central to the therapeutics of her avatar experiences. In the following chapter, we see, for example, how Bedami, as the angry devi, confronts her husband and her life problems in particularly direct ways. This is stress-inducing, but it also seems emotionally cathartic, promoting, much like psychotherapy, her mental healing, as other scholars of spirit possession such as Lévi-Strauss, Dwyer, Seligman, and Kirmayer have remarked.[27] Relaxation does not yet seem to play a central role in Bedami's healing, at least not initially, or on the surface of things. In fact, Bedami's possession seems the opposite of relaxing, given the way this young woman, transformed into the devi, screams, pulls at her hair, and rolls about maddingly in the dust. This seems more like a fit of madness, as scholars of ghost illness note.[28] However, I would remind readers that Bedami's experiences might trace the classic healed-healer spirit-medium arc, where what once felt like an illness may eventually become to Bedami a fuller source of power and wellness.[29] Further, as we also see in this chapter, Bedami's possession fits start to settle into a more rhythmic and quiet panting, which, in the context of the burning cow dung, soft light, and communal chanting associated with offerings to her as the devi, were in fact deeply relaxing, both for Bedami and for others in the Bhat community. Further, once she starts to settle into her role as a medium, the avatar embodiment of the goddess on earth, Bedami starts to experience, as I show in subsequent chapters, an overall improvement in her life situation and a reduction in her daily experience of marital tension and psychosocial stress.

Bedami's experiences are echoed in the other Rajasthani case studies. The tribal woman Kani Bai's spiritual experiences, for example, trace a similar healed-healer arc, with Kani Bai going from being afflicted by a ghost to fulfilling spirit medium roles, with similar alleviation of her life stress and distress. Other afflicted women visit the living saint Mastanna Baba to find relief from tormenting ghosts who often repent of their sins, which helped these women recover their spiritual health. Likewise, the Jingar man Om Prakash finds relief from a ghost and bouts of uncontrollable anger, once he installs a sagasji baoji spirit properly in a residential shrine and takes on a spirit medium role, showing how similar dissociation and stress relief processes can work for men as well. Finally, possessions by sagasji baojis and Bhairuji can vary dramatically—from meditative calm in the case of Om Prakash's possession by a sagasji baoji to violent, obscene, and emotionally ecstatic in many Bhairuji possessions I witnessed— illustrating the variety of possible avatar states of consciousness experienced in Rajasthan.[30]

Perhaps surprisingly to some readers, a substantial proportion of videogame players who participated in my research reported their gaming to produce dissociative experiences. These included distortions in perception such as gaming leading players to become unaware of events happening in the world outside the game and to lose track of actual-world time, with 30–40 percent of respondents who completed my survey experiencing these always or often. Smaller numbers of gamers, about 15 percent, felt so *immersed*[31] in games such as *World of Warcraft* as to always or often experience events there as having the same quality as actual-world events, even feeling gaming events to be more vivid and memorable than actual-world ones. About 8 percent of respondents said they always or often felt like they actually *were* their WoW characters, with almost 40 percent reporting at least some experience of this. Overall, experiences such as these led certain WoW players to demonstrate some level of partitioned—dissociated—perception, memory, and identity,[32] which is also characteristic of spiritual experiences such as Bedami's. (See table 1 for more detail on these experiences.)

Likewise, many players in my gaming research felt that WoW was more than just a game, in the way it contributed substantially to their mental wellness. This was vividly highlighted in players describing the feelings of almost meditative peace and calm that came over them while wandering WoW's digitally rendered landscapes, or while performing repetitive WoW tasks such as quests. And the moments of euphoria, like that forty-person raid group's celebration of defeating the final boss in WoW's Molten Core raiding event, signaled this game's ability to foster deep feelings of group solidarity and individual satisfaction. Not surprisingly to me, having played and studied games such as WoW for over a decade now, close to a majority of players said in an early research survey I distributed that gaming contributed positively to their happiness and life satisfaction, with even more respondents remarking on the way WoW play helped them combat stress in their life. (Table 2 gives greater detail on these findings.)

Tanya Luhrmann has argued that many common everyday activities like losing oneself in a good book or film—and I would add to that list *a good video game*—can produce lightly altered dissociative states of consciousness.[33] These temporary breaks from everyday reality can be experienced as deeply relaxing, which, in the case of immersive gaming, can provide for important stress relief.[34] In a different stress process, Jane McGonigal points out that creating some degree of positive challenge and thus eustress—what she calls *fiero*—is integral to why many online and other games are experienced as fun.[35] Rather than being a bad thing, stress *creation*, then, is also important to pleasures associated with games and play. Positive stress helps to unlock, for example, the link between fun and the achievement experiences characteristic of many MMOs.[36] Here, being challenged and thus stressed by a problem or opponent is the first step toward winning and advancing in the game.[37] If the stress is balanced rather than overwhelming—positive *eustress* in Selye's terms—then gamers can experience powerfully satisfying flow experiences, in Csikszentmihalyi's terms.[38]

Stress, then, either its *absence* or at least reduction or its *presence* in the form of positive eustress, is centrally related to gaming rewards and pleasures, including *dissociative* gaming pleasures. In fact, my survey results confirmed important interactive (or synergistic) relationships of dissociation in combination with relaxation on positive mental-health outcomes, such as how players perceived WoW adding to their happiness and satisfaction in life. These results could be interpreted in several ways: one, experiencing WoW as relaxing had a more strongly positive relation to WoW-related happiness and life satisfaction the higher one's dissociation score, as earlier noted; or, two, dissociation was positively related to experiencing WoW as increasing gamers' happiness and life satisfaction, and this tendency increased the more players experienced WoW as a source of relaxation. (See figure 16.) My research did also reveal associations between the way WoW *induced* stress and the way players reported playing this game to enhance their lives. Interviews and survey data alike pointed to how higher levels of WoW stress were connected to the way WoW was seen to add to both players' happiness and life satisfaction. I interpret this to reflect how WoW promotes positive eustress (again, Selye's language, equivalent here to McGonigal's fiero): that players said they often felt stressed while playing WoW pointed in part due to their commitment to the game, that they felt something important was on the line and that meaningful rewards were at stake.

Overall, this chapter's results, spiritual and digital, lead me to affirm the conclusions of scholars who see many forms of dissociation as positive and normal.[39] Spiritual experiences such as Bedami's are for me the prototype for how dissociative avatar experiences can promote well-being through stress-related mechanisms, given my own earlier training in the anthropology of religion. However, I have drawn parallels to similar processes in gaming contexts, theorizing my ideas through games studies writings on *immersion, eustress,* and *flow* experiences, and how those can promote well-being. The altered absorbed states of consciousness that many gamers reach, even the powerful dissociative identification some gamers have with their characters, provide players with relaxation as well as some of the most satisfying, meaningful, and wondrous experiences of their lives.[40] WoW play, then, can lead to states of deep relaxation akin to meditation, which promote positive wellness, much in the way spiritual forms of dissociative allow for separation from stressful situations (such as Bedami encounters). Or, in an alternate positive pathway, WoW play induces mild to moderate stress, leading to deeply gratifying experiences, which, in spiritual contexts, only occur once religious adepts (such as Bedami) gain control of the spirits who torment them. Further, my gaming studies coming later in my career and in the context of my collaborative ERTL, I was able to confirm these play patterns through a wider range of ethnographic methods, including the quantitative analysis of field-questionnaire data, giving me even greater confidence to the findings.

In presenting research both on Indian religious trance experiences and US video-game play, I hope that readers are better positioned to appreciate common health mechanisms associated with absorption and dissociation across different cultural settings. Further, I hope readers also better appreciate the way that dissociative experiences can promote well-being, for example, by helping the possessed and gamers alike better manage life stress. I have focused on how dissociative and absorptive experiences can contribute positively to both stress relief and felt eustress, which I hope has advanced readers' understandings of the therapeutic potential of avatars. But questions remained in my mind, such as, What is it about avatars that promotes dissociation and thus also therapeutic stress management? That is, why are spiritual and digital second selves so alluring, to the extent that they draw the possessed and gamers alike into their alternative realities?

These are complex questions, with possibly multiple answers. In the next chapter's spiritual and digital case-study analyses, I will suggest that avatars can provide individuals with important alternative *social identities*. This leads me to the idea that avatars can provide opportunities for the enactment of superior, even ideal, second selves. Those second selves, more compelling in many respects than primary identities, draw players' attention in powerful ways into alternative spiritual and digital realities, which in turn promote the therapeutic processes I describe in this book. In these terms, Edward Higgins's self-discrepancy theory (SDT), in the way it highlights the role played by ideal self-concepts in emotion regulation, provides an excellent jumping off point for this book's next steps in explaining avatar therapeutics. Further, I will also argue that Higgins's *ideal* and *ought* selves can provide not just alternative therapeutic identities but also enhanced *social standings*. To develop those ideas, I link Higgins's SDT framework to the health disparities research of Michael Marmot and others to more clearly explain avatar therapeutic processes.

THREE

The Psychosocial Dynamics of Avatar Therapeutics

ENHANCED SELF-IMAGE AND ELEVATED SOCIAL STANDING

INTRODUCTION: A STINGY MAN

Throughout Bedami's transformation into Chavanda Mata, her husband Ramu seemed less than pleased to exchange his wife for a goddess. He was frustrated at continually relinquishing his home to the raucous summonsing of the devi. Ramu's attitude gives insight into the primary reason, according to most Bhats, for the possession. My informants said that Bedami's childbirth and sterilization lent this event meaning, or in Hindi, a *matlab*. Nonetheless, most Bhats claimed these contextualities were ancillary. They invariably suggested that the goddess overtook Bedami in order "to fix Ramu's mind," "to make him understand," or "to teach him how to behave." Discussions of Chavanda Mata inevitably became character assassinations of Ramu, fortifying the shared opinion that he was not a good man. According to the Bhat community and, in fact, according to the goddess herself, the root of the problem was therefore not to be found in Bedami's emotional or bodily disintegration—but rather in Ramu.

I was struck by the fact that the Bhat community, like the devi herself, voiced one consistent complaint against Ramu. When asked why the goddess came into the body of Bedami, they said she did so because Ramu refused to spend money on others, just as he refused to spend on his wife after she gave birth. For example, he put off his kuldevi puja to Chavanda Mata because of the expense, though it was supposed to be done immediately after the birth of their child. When he finally did perform the ritual, he did so minimally. No one was invited, and Ramu refused to distribute sweets to the community after the ritual, once again because of the cost. For these reasons, the devi appeared the moment when Ramu was making his meager offering of coins and notes, repeatedly shouting, "Wrong! Wrong! (Galti! Galti!). The devi was dissatisfied with the puja, objecting not only to the filth and disarray in the house (it was soiled with children's urine and feces) but also to the paucity of resources contributed to the worship. Ramu's disrespect led the goddess to ask him, "Why are you mocking me with this pitifully cheap puja?" and to demand that another puja be done festively and from the heart (kushi se), with pomp and show (that bat se)—and most importantly, without regard to expense (karch). One Bhat neighbor woman, gleefully interpreting the deity's request of Ramu, said, "He's going to have to spend a lot of money!"

Ramu, according to many of the Udaipur Bhats, had cut himself off from his community. Long before his wife's possession, he was criticized for not throwing community feasts such as public pujas. Even if he did so, it was said they were poorly done. Bhats claimed it took a herculean effort to get a five-rupee loan from Ramu. If he did lend the money, then he pestered incessantly the recipients until he was repaid. (At the time of my research, one US dollar was equivalent to thirty Indian rupees). Bhats valued those who properly welcomed (swagat dena) and honored (*adab* or *ijjat dena*) guests into their homes with food and drink, or at the least with smokes (Indian *bidis* and foreign-style cigarettes). Ramu, however, rarely visited the homes of the others in this small encampment, much less invited them into his own, as I was told, to avoid the expense of reciprocal entertaining. Not surprisingly, the most common descriptors applied to Ramu were *kanjus* (stingy) and *tere-mere sochte karte hai,* a phrase that has several meanings but here is used to describe a person who clearly distinguishes his property from that of others and thus, literally, "thinks in terms of yours and mine." As one man told me to demonstrate Ramu's lack of understanding of reciprocity (and to say something somewhat indirectly to me), "If we send you a letter in America, then you'll send an answer, right? Ramu doesn't understand this."

As mentioned, it was Ramu's failure to spend properly on his wife after she had given birth that supposedly brought on her weakness (kamjori), thus precipitating her transformation into the goddess. Not only did Ramu refuse to produce the cash for *ghee* (clarified butter), but he supposedly skimped even more than usual on basic expenses. And rather than helping Bedami with her household chores, as a husband in a family without servants often does after his wife has given birth, Ramu refused to take any time off from work, staying at work well into the evenings and even on Sundays. As a result, he was rarely around when Bedami needed him—whether to buy vegetables, carry water from the well, or cook. Moreover, Ramu, unlike the rest of the

Bhats, refused to give money to his children for small candied treats and was thus seen as having a "heart like a stone." Ramu (unlike most Bhat husbands) controlled the family's purse-strings, and so the weakened Bedami could do nothing to stop her children's daily begging.

Most strikingly, shortly after the devi's first appearance, Bhats celebrated Raki, a Hindu holiday in which brothers offer money and small gifts to their sisters in recognition of their mutual affection for each other. Unlike most Bhats, Ramu only gave to one woman, the daughter of his father's brother—in other words, to a woman closely related through patrilineal descent and thus, in the Bhat clan system, more like a true sister. As it was explained to me, he could have, and should have, gifted to many other women within the colony who also were like his sisters—for example, his wife's two younger sisters, his father's sister (who was married), and his many adopted (or *dharam ki*) sisters. Instead, he chose to interpret his fraternal obligations narrowly and thus, according to the community, transformed Raki, a time when one extravagantly expresses love for one's sisters, into a holiday of miserly calculation.

Ramu was also seen to have skimped on his offering to his clan deity, and it was this deficiency in the worship that according to some in the community first caused Chavanda Mata to take control of her mount, Bedami. Accusing Ramu of treating the puja as an obligation to be finished as quickly and painlessly as possible, rather than a gift joyously given, she demanded that he sponsor a second *jagan* (all-night puja) in her honor, sparing no expense and inviting all members of the community. In preparation for this second puja, the devi also demanded that Ramu have a new floor built for his home, as the old one was unfinished and unsightly, and thus an insult to a divine guest. Ramu responded immediately to the request to build a floor, which presented an opportunity to increase the value of his private property. He took out a Rs2,000 advance on his wages from the folklore institute where he worked, which he planned to pay back at the rate of Rs500 per month. He responded less than enthusiastically, however, to the devi's request for the public puja. The devi had to repeat her request, and even then, Ramu remained reluctant. He invited the other Bhats, beginning, "Chavanda Mata has invited you to a puja," and then specifying, "I am not inviting you, and it doesn't matter to me one way or the other whether you come, but Chavanda Mata has invited you." The others, though respecting the wishes of the goddess, were quite understandably offended, asking me rhetorically, "What kind of invitation is that?" and "Who can attend such a puja?" And they did not, in fact, attend. Out of the entire Udaipur Bhat colony, only one old woman, the mother-in-law of Bedami's sister, participated, and she did so because of her failing health and her inability to get money out of her sons for medical treatments, hoping to find relief through the devi.

Not surprisingly, the second jagan, like the first, was a failure, further enraging Chavanda Mata, who now asked not only for a third jagan but also for a goat sacrifice that was to be performed during the Hindu holiday Nav Ratri, the nine days of Durga (an incarnation of the Mother Goddess), a celebration that was quickly approaching. Once again, this was to include the entire community and was to be accompanied by music and festivity. Furthermore, this third jagan would be quite expensive and would require an even larger advance on Ramu's wages, once one calculated not only the price of the goat but also of the spices, rice, and sweets that the goddess demanded. I should add that the devi made her last "request" in the most forceful terms imaginable, informing Ramu, through her vehicle Bedami, "If you do not do as I ask, then I will kill you and your son."

Even after Ramu roughly satisfied his kuldevi's demands, he continued to make mistakes that revealed his selfishness and brought further criticism both from the goddess and from members of the Bhat community. One Sunday night, Ramu returned late from work only to find that the devi had been summoned in his absence, despite his explicit instructions to the contrary and despite the wishes of Bedami who wanted her husband to be a part of the festivities. Ramu was furious, chasing his wife's relatives from his home. Then, later that night, after securing the door to his home, Ramu himself privately summoned the devi. When she arrived, much to Ramu's surprise, she was angry. In a stinging quip, Chavanda Mata zeroed in on Ramu's attempt to hoard her power for himself and asked, "What are you doing? Did you pay for me at the market?" Ramu was speechless, having no answer. Then, the goddess screeched at him, "Open the door! Why do you bother me by closing the door? Why do you stop others from telling me their problems?" With this, the door was said to have flown open without being touched, according to the Bhats, an appropriate symbol for how Ramu's private worship was opened to the community at large. And his wife's relatives, who had been secretly listening outside, poured into Ramu's home and poured out their litany of woes to the devi.

According to my informants, Ramu's selfish attitude demonstrated how little he regarded them. Ramu was often referred to as proud (gamand), thinking himself superior to others in the colony. He refused to feed them or to visit them in their tents. (Ramu had built himself a house.) He even refused to greet elders decked in turbans and *dhotis* (single pieces of white cloth wrapped around the lower body and worn in place of pants)—dress that signaled these persons' village ties and traditional ways, and that Ramu found "backward" (piche). This behavior, my informants said, demonstrated Ramu's lack of *ijjat,* which might be translated as "honor" or "personal restraint." A person of ijjat curtails his own desires, for example, spending on those who share a common history. Ramu, however, preferred to be free like a foreigner—saying what he wanted, when he wanted, to whom he wanted. For Bhats, the manner that Ramu followed his selfish impulses, without regard to the needs of others, implied a lack of social smarts (akal) and decorum (maryad). It demonstrated, as did his refusal to take time off from work, that he had become like an Angrezi (Englishman), whose love of money was stronger than his love of people.

RAMU, THE SALARY MAN

That Ramu was referred to as a foreigner was not coincidental, for he had taken on the values and habits of the bourgeois citizen—beliefs and practices increasingly universal though of European origin. He had been in the Indian army, something unusual for Bhats. Literate, he spent much of his time composing written poems that were commentaries on his inner experience. Also, unlike most Bhats, Ramu had severed all ties with his family's village patrons, remembering none of their genealogies or panegyrical verse. But, most importantly, at least for my arguments here, Ramu was the only Udaipuri Bhat with a regular salaried job (nokri).

Ramu worked at a local folklore institute where he taught indigenous persons (referred to by Rajasthanis as *adivasis,* "tribals" in English, or by these persons' specific tribal affiliations) to make and dance puppets for the tourist industry. This was part of a state-sponsored uplift program for groups that, because of their historically low status and poverty, are classified in the Indian constitution as "backward" or "scheduled" communities (i.e., "scheduled" for participation in Indian-style affirmative-action programs). The folklore institute, a local landmark, was heavily involved in promoting and profiting from the folk arts. It consisted of a museum documenting local folk-art styles, a theater in which local artists performed daily, and workshops where artists crafted their wares. The employees of this institute saw the Bhat community as a valuable resource, given their knowledge of history, story, and puppeteering. Thus, hiring Ramu was a real coup, because most members of the Bhat community assiduously avoided the institute, fearing its staff would steal Bhat caste secrets.

Many Bhats at the time of my field research participated in a patron-client system termed *jajmani*. This moral village-based economy—moral because production, exchange, and consumption were regulated by inherited duties and obligations, often framed in a religious idiom, rather than by mere market mechanisms—was said to revolve around the *grain heap*. Landowning patrons (termed *jajmans,* originating from the Sanskrit term *yajamana* or "patron of the sacrifice") made gifts of grain to clients (termed *yachaks* and *mangats,* both terms literally translating as "beggars" or "suppliants"). Payment levels were primarily fixed by custom and included not only grain but also other gifts in kind such as clothing, sugar, fodder, and ghee. Such a description, as I note in this book's introduction, could be applied to Bhat relations with the formerly untouchable Bhambis. Although also freelancing, Bhats maintained the exclusive right (hak) to work as the entertainers, genealogists, historians, praise-singers, and jesters for this community. They thus referred to themselves as clients (yachaks) of their Bhambi patrons (jajmans).

In the past fifty years or more, however, Bhats had migrated throughout India, so that one now finds members of this community in virtually all of India's major cities and towns—Udaipur, but also Delhi, Mumbai, and Calcutta. In these new urban settings, Bhats had formed economic ties that might be conceived of in terms of money and the market. They marketed traditional (par-amparik) culture to tourists in hotels and folk festivals throughout India and recorded devotional songs for local radio stations. They also performed educational dramas in the name of the Indian state, staging puppet plays concerning AIDS, communal violence (Muslim-Hindu clashes), family planning, hygiene, and the proper use of fertilizer—in short, selling modern values and practices to India's poor. Most Bhats, then, were stuck between an old and a new economy. But, as discussed, Ramu had entered the new economy in a manner unlike any other Bhat: as a paid employee of a local folklore institute. Such an entrance into the modern economy, and the peculiar way it regulated Ramu's life, led to a perceived stinginess of character that was said to have triggered his wife's posses-sion, at least according to many within the Udaipur Bhat community.

Ramu attended his job religiously, working from nine to five, at least six days a week. He was paid a fixed hourly wage, and thus earned a predictable monthly salary. He also had, as he often bragged to me, health insurance and a retirement package. He planned to open a bank account shortly, something other Bhats, though they advertised for state banks (e.g., putting on puppet shows teaching Indian peasants the nuts and bolts of tractor and water-buffalo loans, interest rates, and savings accounts), would not do. And although Ramu was occasionally docked for being late, he was told by his employers that, if he proved a steady worker, he could expect incremental raises. In our discussions together, Ramu frequently berated others within the community for having no "worry" (phikar). He told me worry was good for you, for in worrying, one was forced to bachat karna (to "make a budget"), and thus take responsibility for the future of one's children. Yet, Ramu seemed oddly isolated in his new job. Not only did he literally spend the entire day away from his family, but, financially, he chose to rely on the impersonal mechanism of his own salary and savings, rather than on the highly personal mechanism of mutual support. In Ramu's economy, that is, in his pursuit of the promises of the salary man, there are traces of what has been called the modern ethic of "possessive individualism"[1]—an idea I return to momentarily.

Most Udaipur Bhats crafted and performed puppets for the tourist industry. Their work was done within their own homes, and as they carved the heads and clothed the bodies of their wooden figures, they joked and drank with one another. Whole families also assisted with performances: fathers, hidden behind a curtained stage, danced the string puppets and whistled through a reed to create the puppets' voices; mothers sang, played a small double-sided drum referred to as a *dholak,* and narrated stories of brave Rajasthani kings like Amar Singh Rathor; and children helped out where needed. Most Udaipur Bhats, too, had developed relations with tourist hotels. This work, unlike Ramu's, was not salaried, though some drew a small stipend to cover transportation costs. Instead, Bhats performed for tips and the opportunity to sell their puppets to tourists. (See figure 17.) Bhats who engaged in these new kinds of labor did not work according to a regular schedule, but rather came and went as they pleased, and typically stayed for no more than two hours a day. In fact, they were known to disappear for the months of the wedding season when they returned to their villages to perform for their Bhambhi patrons. For these reasons, Bhats did not conceive of hotel managers as "bosses" (using the English word), as did Ramu, instead preferring to call them, if half-jokingly, jajmans (patrons), while recognizing that their new employers were not exactly equivalent to their traditional patrons. Hotel managers did not constantly watch over them and tell them what to do (if they were to try, Bhats would walk). Instead, according to Bhats, this was more a relationship of mutual dependence, in which managers were as much protectors as employers. Bhats had no health insurance or

FIGURE 17. These Bhat puppets will be sold in the market to foreign and domestic tourists and to local Rajasthanis. Photo by author.

retirement packages but, they told me, they did not need them because their community, and especially their own sons, were their insurance. They saw the appeal of a regular salary and the security it provided, but they were reluctant to exchange what they saw as their freedom for such security, and they looked with horror at having to work in a manner that would cut them off from friends and family for the entire day.

. . .

As these details reveal, Bedami was caught between two worlds, that of her husband, Ramu, and that of the rest of the Bhat community, to which her parents, natal relatives, and (perhaps most importantly) the devi belonged. Each of these worlds was associated with distinctive values that were expressed through particular social and economic relationships. Resolutely individual, self-contained, and self-concerned, Ramu located value in impersonal new economic mechanisms such as money, a wage regularized with the clock, life insurance, personal savings, and a retirement package, rather than in people and social relations. It could be said that Ramu, therefore, incarnated in some way these modern forces for the Bhat community. In similar terms, and again from many in the Bhat community's point of view, Bedami, as the devi, incarnated the traditional economy, with its emphasis on reciprocity, generosity, and the recognition of social others.

Ramu's Bhat neighbors explained his behavior toward the devi as the consequence of the thinking of a salary man, with its implicit individualism and isolation. Ramu did not want to spend on communal pujas because he preferred to invest in his own future rather than "wasting" his hard-earned money on others. He tried to possess the spirit that possessed his wife because he did not see her as a communal resource, as did others, but as private property that could be controlled as part of his household. We can even understand why, after it was established that Bedami was indeed the goddess, Ramu proposed she should only be called on Sundays, at a fixed hour and—in the name of efficiency—only when the entire community was assembled. Fearing that too many requests would drain her power, he treated her much like he did his salary, as a scarce resource that should be rationally managed.

For many Bhats, Ramu and his way of life symbolized the exploitative forces of the new economy. Ramu was believed to be taking the caste secrets of his community—not only the skill of making and dancing puppets, but also the old stories about the kings of Rajasthan—and selling them directly to the Bhats' competitors. The Bhats saw the indigenous persons Ramu trained, as well as the folklore institute itself with its museums and daily performances, as a menace. By his actions, Ramu was in fact threatening the livelihood of others and was frequently referred to as a traitor who had turned against his own brethren. Just as he wanted to exploit the devi for his own use, so was he exploiting the other Bhats by taking their traditional caste knowledge and putting it to use for himself—or, at least, this is how I was led by some in the community to see Ramu.

In these terms, when Ramu placed rupee coins and notes on his altar as an offering to the devi, he was making use of money that did not entirely belong to him. In part, this money was an expression of his own labor at his new job, but it also belonged to the Bhat community, given that Ramu's salary was predicated on his exploitation of the Bhat's traditional knowledge. I am thus not surprised that printed and graven images of the devi that sat on the altar next to the money, a divine symbol of economic productivity (and thus akin to the Hindu goddess of wealth Lakshmi), jumped to life—seeming to Bhats to spring into the very body of Bedami. For the money on the altar, like the other objects offered to the devi, was filled with the life of the Bhat community, and thus, within the Bhats' religious worldview, it took on a character akin to that of a dangerous god. Nor was it surprising that the goddess herself seemed to condemn Ramu as immoral, presumably because he, being a wage laborer, located in money rather than in people the source of value. His wife's possession, then, is seemingly a straightforward spiritual response to such greed: the goddess rides in on her charger (ghorala), Bedami, like a Bollywood film heroine, to reprimand Ramu for his miserliness and to remind him that people are more valuable than money.

To the Bhat community, and to Bedami (as the devi) seemingly as well, Ramu appeared to be an almost supernaturally evil personification of new economic relations—a ghost and a demon. This explained the supernatural labels that were applied to Ramu, as mentioned in the book's earlier background chapter: he was called a ghost (bhut), a demon (raksas), or simply, wicked (setan). In refusing to take part in the niceties that constituted social life, Ramu resembled a ghost, a lonely creature on the outskirts of society who was no longer fully human. Furthermore, the danger of evil spirits was said to reside in their tremendous appetites: they were described as devouring not only huge quantities of food but also human beings. Ramu, like the demonic middlemen who bought Bhat puppets for resale, was said to take more than he gave and was thus draining the very life out of members of his own society, robbing them of their daily bread (roji), and quite literally "eating" them.

Bedami's spiritual possession, then, can be said to have been predicated on her suffering. But her distress in turn resulted from tensions between her husband and the rest of the Bhat community, which reflected larger stresses and strains characteristic of the contemporary world. Unhappy in her marriage, Bedami found her voice in the devi, condemning Ramu and the new way of life he represented. Bedami's sterilization, the violation that seemed to precipitate her possession, exacerbated her anger both toward her modern husband as well as toward the Indian state. Her husband insisted on the operation, and the state agency performing the procedure reneged on its promise of a cash payment. These experiences seemed to be closely linked in

Bedami's mind: her betrayal by the modern Indian state evoked her husband's own inability to deliver the wealth promised by his new job and salary—an inability that in Ramu's view, necessitated Bedami's sterilization. Bedami's possession, then, seemed to be an angry outburst against her husband, and, more generally, against the corrupt, modern world. From this standpoint, her sterilization brought Bedami's suppressed emotions to the surface, which were then given form as a goddess—a divinely sanctioned stand-in for this young woman's own anger toward her husband's modern-inspired greed. Bedami, holding authority over her husband in the form of the devi, chased Ramu from his own home in response to his cheap pujas and, at another moment, attempted to circumvent his stinginess by demanding a costly new marble floor, while generally castigating him for failing to recognize his dependence on divine and communal powers.

It thus seems as if new economic relations and values were the "evil" that triggered Bedami's possession. Ramu's stinginess, the way he refused to spend on others, made him a pariah. Ramu's isolation, in turn, was painful to Bedami. Therefore, in the form of the devi, which could be interpreted as Bedami's disguised voice, she tried, if unconsciously, to force Ramu to behave more in line with Bhat communal values. To a large extent, she seemed to have succeeded. Within weeks of her initial transformation, Bedami's nuclear family, which had up to then been perceived as a drain on the community, takers and not givers, was able to give back in the form of the devi's power (sakti). Nevertheless, Ramu's stinginess, which was seen to have triggered the entire event in the first place, was no mere personal trait. Rather, the stingy and independent Ramu symbolized the dangerous aspects of the new economy, the fragmenting forces of private property, savings, and wages, and the terrible ethic of what C. B. Macpherson calls "possessive individualism." The goddess was thus a punishing force meant not only to fix Ramu's mind—a stand-in for Ramu's furious wife as well as for the furious Bhat community—but also more generally to do battle against an encroaching new way of life.

. . .

Stepping back a bit and thinking about these new ethnographic details in relation to the previous chapter's discussion, Bedami's dissociation into her second avatar identity allowed her to take a form that was superior in some way to her first self. As the devi, Bedami embodied a traditional Hindu ethic of generous reciprocity, with Bedami in her new form emphasizing the importance of prioritizing others over narrow self-interest. Further, in taking this form, Bedami seemed to correct in some way her experience of failure and limitation in her current familial and communal situation. That is, Bedami, in taking her new avatar identity, seemed intent on forging a new and more satisfying life, one premised on healthier relationships with *all* the important people in her life—her parents and natal family included, and thus not just with her husband alone. And that avatar-therapeutic process was most complete when Bedami's new identity allowed her to effectively bridge the social world of her parents with that of her husband. In these terms, criticizing her husband for his stinginess seemed to represent for Bedami an important first step toward eventually establishing healthier relationships not just with the rest of the Bhat community but with her husband Ramu as well.

In Edward Higgins's self-discrepancy theory (SDT) language, Bedami's incarnation as the devi, then, provided her with a superior, even ideal, second identity.[2] Further, in embodying a certain idealized Hindu morality, Bedami, as the devi, elevated her *social standing.* That is, she went from suffering, subordinated, and socially marginalized wife to a *goddess,* the very embodiment of a certain Hindu moral power. And in elevating her social status in this way, she takes steps toward reducing the stress in her life, which, as Michael Marmot and others have shown, can help to improve her overall health and well-being.[3]

Beyond my more *psychological* points about Bedami's dissociative experiences, highlighted in chapter 2, I emphasize in this chapter the eminently *psychosocial* nature of these events and how social context influences their trajectory and outcome. Bedami's dissociative experiences are framed in reference to Hindu spiritual norms, socially learned, and specifically in relation to ideas about the ability of ghosts and gods to take control of human agents. Without those spiritual beliefs, Bedami's experiences could have taken a very different course. Most importantly, without her experiences of being labeled divine as opposed to either demonic or simply insane, the course might have been much less positive, more illness than blessing. That is, the process of assuming a second avatar identity was a potentially therapeutic one for Bedami because of the social value attached to the devi, and the way such value was recognized and appreciated by meaningful others in the Bhat community. Without recognition from others in the group, Bedami would not have experienced her second self in the same superior and therapeutic way. And Bedami's experiences are thus *psychosocial,* rather than exclusively psychological or social, with me drawing on Higgins's and Marmot's work to frame these arguments.

. . .

In this chapter's next section, I develop these ideas about the psychosocial dynamics of avatar therapeutics in the context of *World of Warcraft* play in the Knights of Good, as described earlier, a *casual raiding guild*. In gaining and demonstrating to others WoW mastery, Lainey, Vern, and the other guild members develop in their online characters more highly accomplished and even idealized selves, alter egos of a kind, which provides them with elevated social standing in WoW's virtual world and this guild setting. As with Bedami, these processes too depend on how individuals in this setting embody group ideals, in this case related to skilled gaming rather than divinity. But as I further show, the extent that ideal avatar selves here relieve stress—rather than produce it—depends on the social context of play. The Knights of Good promotes play that respects members' offline lives. Other more *hardcore*—or seriously minded and competitive—guilds push their members in ways that can create conflicts with offline life and thus compromise rather than enhance members' well-being. Next, I return to spirit possession literature discussed earlier in the book—research by Gananath Obeyesekere, Aihwa Ong, Janice Boddy, and Rebecca Seligman— to expand the spiritual-avatar arguments beyond Bedami and Rajasthan. In the chapter's concluding integrative discussion, I draw on Higgins' and Marmot's work to draw parallels between spiritual and digital avatars, in ways that highlight the *psychosocial* rather than merely psychological nature of these therapeutic processes, thus extending the previous chapter's arguments.

A GUILD CULTURE OF CASUAL RAIDING ENHANCES AVATAR THERAPEUTICS

RL (Real Life) First

Emerging from their own negative experiences with their previous guild, Lainey and Vern promoted in the Knights of Good (KOG) an ethic of "real life comes first," which was repeated frequently to members of my research team. In part, as we learned from member Breezy, this meant relaxing raid schedules and attendance requirements, in recognition that members had other offline commitments, and not taking the game too seriously. As Breezy puts it, "I've changed some of my outlooks on life in general. I've become a bit more relaxed. Stuff that's not serious, you shouldn't take seriously. Just enjoy it and take it for what it is and move on." Reflecting such an ethic, KOG frequently made concessions for players' offline commitments, for example, adjusting raid schedules when one member, BlueFalcon, had affairs to attend to in Iraq, or stopping the raid progression when Vern or others, real-life students, had class projects to complete.[4]

Likewise, as we observed, raids themselves tended to be supportive endeavors, with Vern, as raid leader, and others as well, offering words of encouragement like, "Good job!," or advice on how to improve performance, rather than punishing or embarrassing members for mistakes. As Lainey puts it, on being asked about her guild by one of our research team members, Scarlett:

s: What kind of guild is KOG?

l: Where people aren't dicks to each other. If you've ever been in a real hardcore raid guild, they are not nice people.

s: So what do you do if somebody's not participating well?

l: We tend to be a little more forgiving of people, who have issues in real life. That's why we have class leaders [a *class* refers loosely to a gaming *profession* that includes a specific set of skills], we try to get people to work with their class leader. How they can get their gear better.

s: So it's more like training them, rather than punishing them?

l: Yes. But other guilds will just punish you. Have you ever been in a guild where like they're competing to be on the top-10 list on the server [i.e., with a raid progression performance ranked high relative to other groups]? The hardcore people are really ridiculous. They just want to do it as fast as they can. They call it "e-peen." Their *e-penis*. They stroke their e-penis by having the best gear, being number one. It's status, they have status, and they like to show it off.

Notice here that KOG has not abandoned their standards: they still strive for raiding mastery and success, checking on their members' performance. But KOG's senior members typically corrected others in a way that was helpful and supportive rather than punitive. They reasoned that in helping individual members improve they also helped the guild as a whole progress in the game.

To a large extent, these patterns reflected Lainey and Vern's own personal ethics, emerging from their life and game experiences. Lainey, the guild's "mom," and a mother of three now grown children in her offline life, prided herself on being a supportive and generous person: "I love the social aspect of it. I really love the people that I have in my guild too. I know a lot about them. I'm guild mom. So, if someone has a problem, I get dumped on for hours sometimes. But it's okay!" Lainey notes, too, how it is important to teach others to "behave like adults" and be "mindful" of others' needs (her words), especially during the potentially most contentious moments of the game, when distributing loot or gear won at the end of even months of pitched battles against a finally defeated tough raid boss. Indeed, Lainey conceptualizes her avatar Tessa as a generous patron of a kind who enjoyed helping others: "I see Tessa being a benefactor for a bunch of people, and I like to be able to do good things for people, in my real-world life and as much as I can in game." Although she and Vern had power and authority in the guild, she told us she did not like to order people around and "make anyone do anything," instead trying to motivate people to be better and aiming to be helpful instead of being "me-oriented" (her phrase). Lainey's main character, unsurprisingly, was a *healer* (i.e., one who restored others' *hit points* or life when they suffered damage from enemies), as this WoW class is known for attracting generally more supportive and generous personalities.

Likewise, Vern, too, strived to put others' needs and feelings above his own, promoting an ethic of generosity and humility rather than hardcore competitiveness. Here is the way the raid's main *tank* (i.e., the player-character who absorbs damage from enemies, thus protecting the group), Rayna, describes Vern and his avatar Steely:

> If you've met Steely, who is the guild leader, or Vern, he is an extremely charismatic guy, and that is one thing that I have never really mastered very well. He knows how to really pull people together, and they just love him. He's extremely humble. He's willing to sit himself [i.e., not participate in a particular raid event]. He'll always say that he's not performing, and someone else can take his spot. He's very altruistic and charitable, and those are features that I really don't possess very much.

Vern acknowledged that he could get frustrated sometimes with raid members' mistakes and a stalled game progression, but he prided himself on being a person who used his brains rather than his in-game brawn (he was a skilled player with a powerful avatar) to motivate others. Taking an analogy from youth soccer, of which he was also a coach, he told us, "You can yell at kids but not at adults."

Collaboration

One of my group's student researchers, Josh, observed in his field notes that "leadership" was not even the right word to describe the way Lainey, Vern, and the guild as a whole raided, echoing the observations of raid members themselves. As Josh noted in 2012:

> Overall, the raid seemed to be quite laid back as most of the players were still talking about news, sports, etc., while attacking the enemy. As one pointed out, there was little to no leadership within the guild about where to go, how to attack, etc. Everyone seemed to know, for the most part, what to do in order to beat the bosses.

Josh and others in fact documented how the raid members knew one another's style of play, strengths, and weaknesses, in part because they had played together for so long. As such, they were often able to coordinate even difficult raids in a relatively effortless manner, with few commands necessary, cloaking any obvious signs of raid hierarchy. When the raids were working as they should, according to KOG's members, they reflected true collective and supportive problem solving, with many to most members of the raid participating in not only the execution but also the strategizing, as documented by another in our research team.

> This week the raiders are finally trying Deathwing [a raid *boss*] on the *heroic* mode [a challenging setting], and I immediately notice a difference in the tone of their interactions. There is much more excitement and tons of talk about strategy before they begin . . . Sable, Breezy, Stee, and DocMartin are most involved in the planning. They begin the raid, and it becomes apparent to me that this is really a massive team problem-solving effort. Phrases like, "Does anyone understand the mechanics?" and "Let's divide into groups" are heard, as well as more detailed dissection of exactly what distance each player must be standing and who should be taking which hits, etc. They *wipe* [i.e., fail in their attempt to defeat the boss] almost immediately and then wipe again, but they seem to be encouraging each other. Breezy says "We've just got to be a little more aware overall" and jokes that they should "expect the unexpected." Emotions are definitely running higher than on the usual normal-level raids. Valissamunk begins to take a more prominent role in the strategizing. I had never heard him speak up this much.

The raid continued in an animated fashion, with raiders yelling things like, "No, no, no, dammit!" and "Good job!" After trying several new approaches and being defeated four or five times, they finally beat the boss, and the guild chatroom exploded with mad chatter, with the raid team and other observers congratulating one another and talking animatedly about the victory, reliving the action long after the actual event.

Doing Good, Promoting Tolerance

In addition to promoting positive feelings and cooperation during raids, KOG also aimed to promulgate a more general ethic of support, tolerance, and life balance, which would overall enhance, rather than compromise, guild members' offline lives. The guild once solicited donations and subsequently purchased a new wheelchair for one of its members, Hadley/Sapher (her real-life and character pseudonyms), who had lost a leg after being hit by a car. They even successfully gathered money for Hadley on another occasion, which paid for seven months of her game subscription. This helped her, as one member told us, "continue playing, because she's very confined in real life. She can't do much. So, she can run and jump and fly and do all kinds of really cool things she can't do in real life." Likewise, Lainey and Vern looked for members who were aiming to do good in the world, which they were asked to describe in KOG's guild application. And members were encouraged to donate time and money to social causes, including in the past, earthquake relief in Haiti and a local AIDS run. Additionally, the group's main raiding tank, Rayna, is a transgender woman, and her inclusion provides an example of KOG's respect and tolerance for diversity, of which many guild members prided themselves. Lainey often described to us how the guild helped Rayna get publicly more comfortable with expressing her female gender identity and "learn how to be a woman," by, for example, spending *"many* hours chatting with her, about what's going on with her life, just trying to offer her encouragement, giving her tips on nails and hair, all these things you wouldn't really think of as having anything to do with WoW."

In fact, Lainey, Vern, and others monitored the guild chat channels for examples of homophobia, racism, or excessive too angry words, which they quickly shut down, aiming to maintain an environment that remained friendly and supportive for all. Overall, the guild succeeded in maintaining its public ethic of respect and tolerance for diversity. To a large extent, this seemed to be because the guild members understood that Lainey, Vern, and others' hearts were in the right place. That is, they really cared for one another, we concluded, as we saw one day (April 9, 2012) when one raid member, Sable, was late and in fact had not been logged on for twenty hours (as they could see in the game's roster log). A long and somewhat worried conversation ensued before the raid, with everyone hoping he was okay.

Still (Somewhat) Competitive

Much of KOG's staying power and appeal to its members related to the fact that the guild was able to succeed in its promotion of the good, tolerance of diversity, and so forth, while also remaining competitive and successful as raiders. For example, Clark/Tracker described defeating a difficult boss as "a really good feeling, probably the best feeling I ever had in that game because it was something that not everybody could do."

Lainey, too, was driven by achievement motivations, though for her it was more about helping the guild succeed as a whole, rather than achieving individual success.

> Because I was a single mom, I dropped out of high school, I got a GED, and I took care of three kids and took a lot of crap from the welfare office for years, and a lot of crap from society for being the, you know, that which we consider a problem. So, it's been good for me as far as my self-worth to be able to be successful at running a guild in *World of Warcraft* and to have people respect me and look up to me, because I didn't get a lot of that in my real life until, until I started playing *World of Warcraft* and until I started running a guild.

Lainey continues:

> For me, what I want is for my guild to achieve things and for people to see us as being a good guild. I don't care what they think of me as a player. I'm more interested in the group, getting some kind of notoriety, I guess, because it means more that way.

In Lainey's words, we see the ethic of camaraderie, collaboration, and group effort that animates KOG's success: they succeed as a team together, rather than just as individuals. We see, too, KOG's emphasis on balance, on making sure that the guild succeeds in ways that do not eclipse or compromise life offline. As Lainey puts it, "Yeah, I wouldn't have been able to earn the degrees and stuff [laughs] if I didn't keep some kind of balance." Or, as guild member

BlueFalcon tells us: "Most people that display maturity are well balanced. Yeah, they get upset at times or are passionate about things, however they are not completely unreasonable, like 'I am going to spend all of my kids' college fund playing WoW' kind of thing." For BlueFalcon and others, KOG helps them regulate their play in just that manner, keeping them from doing "nothing but play WoW 24/7," as he and others have seen, even feeling at times such a pull within themselves.

KOG's Fragility

KOG's membership is in fact composed of many self-professed "recovering" hardcore raiders (their phrase), who joined KOG after experiencing WoW burnout. Still, sometimes KOG's more casual pace did not satisfy its members. One member, Stimpy, told us he frequently got bored during raids, which were often not challenging, and thus surfed the internet during them. Or, as DocMartin told us explicitly:

> I wanna say for me personally, and I can't speak for everyone, that there are times where I really would like to compete a little bit more. I think that we have a lot of good players, and I would like to see us push a little bit more. But I think that can very easily get out of control at times, and I would say that I can't fault us for maybe not pushing so hard, cause I would rather have a good experience and a little bit more fun playing than pushing five days a week for several hours and maybe killing like one boss or something. That's just not as much of a fun environment.

These somewhat conflicting desires led sometimes to guild tensions, as in one instance when a contingent of players suddenly and dramatically abandoned the guild to join groups progressing more quickly through the raid content. This left many group members perplexed as they logged into their WoW accounts to find the guild roster gutted.

This led to canceled raids over the coming nights. One member somewhat melodramatically declared to us, "This guild died." Another, Missy, *whispered* to a research team member (via a private in-game chat channel):

> [Missy whispers:] Where folks will come here and use them and their generous nature to gear up and then once they have what they need, move on to a more progressed guild. It is kind of sad, because the people in this guild that I do know actually really care about it and put in a lot of work

Another echoed this sentiment, telling us it was a shame when guilds like KOG put great effort into helping individual players advance in the game and then find its members using them more as a "stepping-stone" for gaining acceptance to a more hardcore raiding guild. Another described it as a "slap in the face" to the guild, when players benefitted from Vern/Steely's and Lainey/Tessa's kindness and then left in this manner. Eventually, the guild regrouped by concentrating on ten- rather than twenty-five-person raids (WoW has different raid modes), finding success at clearing tough groups of enemies from the game in the ten-person setting. Then, another core member left unexpectedly, which further challenged the guild's positive moral framework, as revealed by the following interview exchange:

> Breezy: And we slowly started to restructure it and we finally got back to a point where we could pretty much clear the place, and we did clear it, and that's when BlueFalcon left. And I was mad at him because we had put in a lot of extra time to get him his *legendary* weapon [a very high-status item that takes a lot of work and skill to acquire]. And that was what ticked me off the most, is that we had gotten him the legendary. We had gone on separate special *runs* [i.e., raid encounters] that weren't scheduled just to get him the legendary. [Interviewer: Who's "we"?] Myself and Stee[ly], especially Stee[ly], he put in a lot of extra time there, and other members of the guild. I mean it was all guild stuff. They had put it together and gotten him his weapon. And it was like, wow, so you're basically just taking that and ditching us now. That's really cool [sarcastically], especially since we had just got a group back together that could go in and clear the place. But he has always been that kind of person. He's like a child trapped in a thirty-seven-year-old man's body.

Beyond KOG—Guild Affiliation and Eustress/Distress

WoW raiding is a challenging activity, demanding precise coordination among a group of multiple players performing interrelated but distinctive in-game tasks, like dealing out damage to enemies, healing, and tanking. Expectations and in-game rewards are high during raids, and even small mistakes by a single player can lead the entire effort to fail, often necessitating starting over again from the beginning. As such, raids are stressful events, as evidenced in the following description by one of our interviewees:

> Everything else fades out. It's just you and your monitor and your headset. I get a little jittery when things are going really well cause I get nervous that

something's going to go wrong, and you're like, "Oh man, this could be it, this could be it." You know, we're doing really well, and nobody's saying anything, everybody's dead silent, except for whoever's calling out the things that need to be called out, like *adds* [additional enemies] coming or whatever, it's really quiet. Then, like I said, everything fades out except for what you're doing . . . it's intense.

Our interviewee describes the absorbed and focused attention, and the jittery nerves, characteristic of the stress that accompanies raiding. But, as we see, raiding is not just stressful in a negative way. Yes, raiders do experience nervousness and fear of failure. But they also experience positive anticipation of success and the rewards to be won: "Oh man, this could be it, this could be it." In fact, it is this complex mix of both the fear of failure and the anticipation of success that characterizes raids as potentially both, or either, eustressful or distressful activities.[5]

Importantly, we learned that the guild environment critically determines whether a raid is experienced as more *eustressful* or *distressful,* in Hans Selye's terms.[6] Hardcore guilds, we learned, often lead to raiding becoming experienced as distressful.

It's [WoW] always been a real-world stress reliever. It has also been a stress creator. When I was raiding in BC [the WoW expansion, *The Burning Crusade*], it was basically nothing but stress. You were constantly having to learn new fights, be at the bleeding edge of everything you could possibly be. The guilds I was in, there were always more people available than could raid, so you weren't always guaranteed a spot. So, you had to do your best performance, and just, "Okay, we want to bring him instead of this other guy because he knows his stuff." And then there were the two months of wiping [repeatedly failing], like that is incredibly stressful you know. I would never want to do that again, honestly.

Here, we see that pushing in a hardcore raiding guild to advance most quickly through the raid progression (the bosses are faced in stages) before other competitors do—being "at the bleeding edge of everything"—creates stress for this individual. Among other things, he had to ensure that his game remained at a very high level, stressing him, lest his raiding spot be taken by someone.

Hardcore progression guilds, as their name implies, aim to progress as quickly and efficiently as possible through raiding content (and through the defeat of successive bosses). As a result, they will keep at an in-game task for longer than they might have initially planned for or anticipated. This can give rise to particularly long gaming hours and frustration, as one interviewee told us.

> When I was in a progression guild, we were trying to kill him [the boss] for a very, very long time . . . I spent sixty hours a week playing this game, trying to get these items for myself in a very, very hard way. Going in and spending six to seven hours a night dying on the same boss, trying to figure out what to do, not making any progress, going in there seven days a week and taking two weeks to down one boss. Very, very frustrating . . .

Here, the long hours and pushing so hard can lead to eustress moments in such guilds, as when, to complete the first quote above, the player adds, "Very, very frustrating. But then when you get the gear off the boss, you're like, 'Aw, man this is sweet.'" Still, the daily grind is experienced more likely as distressful, with many players telling us the rewards, however prized, were often not worth it, leading many to leave their hardcore groups for more casual guilds. Indeed, some hardcore raiders seemed to cycle between distressful raiding and simple relief from tension, in the sense that it was now all over, rather than experiencing true eustress and thus spontaneous outpourings of joy, euphoria, or invigorating *fiero* after triumphing over adversity, as described by Jane McGonigal.[7]

Because the stakes are so high, hardcore raids also create particularly high-crisis situations, where players take the game very seriously, leading potentially to frustration and negative experiences.[8] With the stakes so elevated, raid leaders, along with those who successfully fulfill their roles, experience distressful frustration in the inability to control the raid in a manner that would allow the group to succeed, as another interviewee recounts.

> There's a boss a couple years ago where if you die during the encounter it pretty much can cost the raid to *wipe* entirely [again, fail in their attempt to defeat the boss]. It involves a lot of fire. And there were a couple of raid members that could not apparently notice that there was fire on them and would die repeatedly, which would cause us to wipe. And it was very frustrating to just not grasp that they couldn't just walk a few feet away from it.

Another raider echoed these sentiments, telling us, "I would have to say how many bad players there are. I mean, I hate to say it, people just don't know how to play, and they're dumb." Likewise, those who are responsible for the failed raid attempts feel distress, both because they can feel personal regret in that they are letting down all those who rely on them and because they can be treated with disdain and like incompetent subordinates. As another interviewee describes the situation:

> In the BC [*Burning Crusade,* a WoW expansion] guilds, the really hardcore ones I was in, people would get yelled at, people would get bitched out for screwing up and not so much now. Since I'm the guy in charge now, I'm very careful to not berate people, because I've been on the receiving end of that, and it sucks. You're trying, bad things happen, accidents happen. I've done it, everybody's done it. You just got to say, "Okay, so what happened there? Let's see what we can do to prevent that from happening again," and move one. You know, "Let's try it again. Let's see what happens." It's frustrating, but not as much as it used to be, because it's less of a big deal to me at this point. Like in our attempts on Wednesday, Bill and Edith sometimes have internet issues, and they disconnected a few times, [which] caused us to wipe. And I can be mad about that, but what's the point? It's not going to change anything, it's not going to magically fix their internet connection, you know. So, you just pick up and try again.

The latter interviewee explains his new more casual attitude toward raiding, where he is forgiving of player mistakes. But such an attitude was arrived at via earlier experiences in hardcore guilds, where even simple errors were not forgiven and could result in players getting yelled at or even removed from a raiding rotation. The combination of frustration from all sides—from the leaders and the more skilled players, and also from those making the mistakes—can result in a cycle of escalating distress, as the elevated stress levels might lead to even greater chance of silly errors, which one raider described to us as, "about as much fun as slamming my fingers in a drawer." More generally, such situations can lead to guild in-fighting—with accusations and counter-accusations—a form of guild *drama,* to take the insider's term, which can even lead some guilds to disband or at least to experience member loss.

Likewise, the distressful hardcore raiding experiences also get connected to potentially distressful offline experiences, given that hardcore raiders are much more willing to devote long hours to the game, even much of their lives, in order to succeed. As Sable describes it dramatically, on being asked by one of my team's interviewers about the potential benefit or harm to mental wellness received from WoW play:

> J: What about someone who plays in a hardcore raiding guild?
>
> S: It detracts from their wellness. For example, I am not exaggerating this at all. Let's say I'm in a very hardcore raiding guild. They raid four days a week, four hours a day. You need be there at the instance, on time. Let's

say I've raided for three months. Let's say my mom has a heart attack, and I go to the hospital and miss the raid obviously. I log on the next day and no longer have a raid spot. I cannot see how that would be fun, or how that much stress would be good on anybody. I just don't.

Hardcore raiders are expected to give all to the game. This includes putting WoW ahead of their offline lives, as we see in the following description, where Jane experiences problems with her ex-partner and family:

> With my ex, there were problems. I started raiding, and he would want me to go do something else and I'm like, "I'm raiding." And he's like, "So? Don't raid." One day, he's like, "I don't know why you play that game so much. I don't know why you don't spend time with me." And I'm like, "Why don't you try to be more interesting than *World of Warcraft* and maybe I will?" [interviewer and interviewee laugh] So, it has caused problems. And with my family too. If they want me to do something when I was more hardcore raiding, when you're spending twelve hours in the evening a week raiding, and you're working forty to fifty hours a week and what not, and you still have to do your laundry and grocery shop . . . take showers [laughs], you know, your own personal things that take time that you need to do. You don't have time for anything else. So, during the week I was off limits. And then I got even more involved. Then I would go to bed, get up and work eight to five, come home, eat dinner, whatever, make dinner, do whatever I had to do, and then I'd raid at night again. Then I got a second job where I worked like thirty-two hours [over] the weekend. So, all I did was work and *World of Warcraft,* and my family got jealous, because I wasn't there. And I was so burnt out on life that I wouldn't want to go do stuff.

As a result, hardcore raiders experience in-game distress during the raids themselves, due to the pressures to perform and resulting high emotions that can turn negative. In addition, the serious commitment to raiding can also lead to out-of-game distress, when players compromise their offline lives to give more to the game. So, hardcore raiding guilds seem to wed both in-game and out-of-game stress. Indeed, the two are irrevocably bound together, in that the first seems to lead to the second. But, likewise, when the second builds up, it can further magnify the first.

Online/Offline Social Standing, Guild "Micro-Cultures," and Avatar-Therapeutic Processes

In my team's web questionnaire, described in chapter 2, we tested relationships between individuals' self-reported *online* social standing—here, the

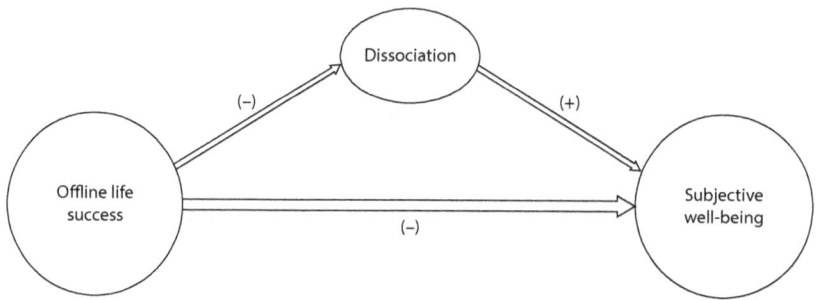

FIGURE 18. Conceptual model of the relationship between Offline Life Success and gaming-related Subjective Well-Being, as mediated by Dissociation.

extent to which WoW players perceived themselves as successful in online settings, with success defined according to gamer standards—and the same subjective well-being outcomes that featured in the previous chapter. Relying again on ordinal logistic regression techniques used in chapter 2 (and described in appendix A), we found that succeeding in WoW had a large positive relationship, adjusting for various control variables, with the perception that WoW increased both respondents' sense of happiness and their self-reported life satisfaction. Likewise, self-reported WoW gaming success was substantially positively associated with the report that WoW play helped players to relax in ways that combatted stress, with WoW success also having a small positive relationship with reporting that WoW play increased stress.[9]

With an eye toward the previous chapter's analysis, my research team and I also examined whether self-reported *offline* life success might affect *dissociative* experiences in ways that could improve well-being outcomes.[10] I anticipated that dissociative gaming experiences might function as a *mediator* variable between offline life success and positive subjective well-being outcomes. Specifically, I thought that having fewer successes in life might lead to deeper dissociative experiences, which in turn would produce increased self-reports of gaming-related happiness and stress relief. If so, dissociation would be said to *mediate* between—or connect via a causal pathway and thus reveal an important mechanism—experiences of life success and mental wellness. Analysis of the survey data revealed exactly that. It was the players who experienced less offline success—and thus the more psychosocially distressed individuals—who experienced the greatest gaming-related enhancements of their subjective well-being. And further, that process was mediated by deeper

TABLE 3 Selected Problem-Gaming Experience Items, Percent Distribution
(N = 253)

	Always (5)	Often (4)	Sometimes (3)	Rarely (2)	Never (1)
Others complain about amount of time playing.	8.3	16.2	30.0	22.1	23.3
Block disturbing thoughts about life with positive *WoW* thoughts.	6.3	9.5	16.2	20.6	47.4
Job performance or productivity suffers due to *WoW*.	5.2	8.7	17.4	30.4	38.3
Try to cut down amount of spent playing *WoW*.	10.7	13.8	16.6	28.5	30.4
	Strongly Agree (5)	Agree (4)	Neutral (3)	Disagree (2)	Strongly Disagree (1)
Feel addicted to *WoW*.	18.6	27.3	20.2	18.2	15.8

NOTE: Originally appeared in Snodgrass et al., 2011, *Culture, Medicine, and Psychiatry* 35 (1): 26–62.

forms of dissociative game play. Figure 18 graphically presents these postulated causal pathways and mechanisms. (In that figure, the negative signs on the pathways from offline life success to dissociation and subjective well-being mean that higher offline life-success scores are associated with lower dissociative and gaming-related subjective well-being experiences and, of most direct interest here, that *lower* life-success scores are linked to *higher* reports of dissociation and improved gaming-related mental well-being.)

Ethnographic observations such as those presented in this chapter also led me to wonder about the relationship between offline life success and *distressful* gaming, as could be experienced, for example, in hardcore raiding. For this, my team and I developed a WoW-specific *problem-gaming* measure. As seen in table 3, at least 30–50 percent of respondents on each of that measure's nineteen items acknowledged at least sometimes having the problem-gaming experiences described.[11] About the same percentage reported in a single-item response feeling "addicted" to WoW, further confirming these findings.

Moreover, as anticipated, self-reported offline success had a strong negative relation to the problem-gaming scale, a pattern replicated in relation to the single-item WoW *addiction* self-report. This showed that individuals reporting less life success were more vulnerable to problem-gaming experiences. Also, dissociation again functioned as a mediator variable between life success and problem play, which my team and I confirmed this time with *linear regression* techniques.[12]

. . .

Finally, I wanted to assess relationships between the social context of play—here, guild affiliation—and these well-being outcomes. Regarding guild affiliation, 29.4 percent of our sample in this smaller survey belonged to a friends-and-family guild, 46.8 percent to a casual raiding guild (such as KOG), 11.1 percent to a hardcore raiding guild, and the remaining 12.7 percent to no guild. Further, the mean score for problem play was highest, as might be expected, among members of hardcore guilds, though not remarkably so, while persons with other guild affiliations differed relatively little in reported problem experiences. Similarly, the mean for the importance of in-game achievement motivation was highest among hardcore raiding guild members. And hardcore raiding guild members also reported high levels of play in terms of hours per week.[13]

Using *linear regression* techniques, my team and I found that a player's level of achievement orientation within WoW, treated here as an important "control" variable—with the meaning of statistical controls described earlier in chapter 2—showed a small positive relation to problem play. Of more central interest here, we identified a substantial positive relationship between perceived in-game stress (i.e., lack of experienced control in online lives) and problem play. And incorporating into our analysis terms for guild affiliation–type interacting with WoW (in-game) stress showed that these two variables mutually conditioned each other's relations to problem play. This means that for both friends and family and casual raiding guilds (compared with hardcore raiding guilds) in-game stress was much less likely to translate into distress in the form of problem gaming. A visual representation of this relationship appears in figure 19, which shows how the relatively steeper slope of problem gaming with respect to in-game stress among hardcore raiding guild members stands out relative to those with other guild affiliations.[14] (See appendix B for a more detailed presentation of this chapter's survey results.)

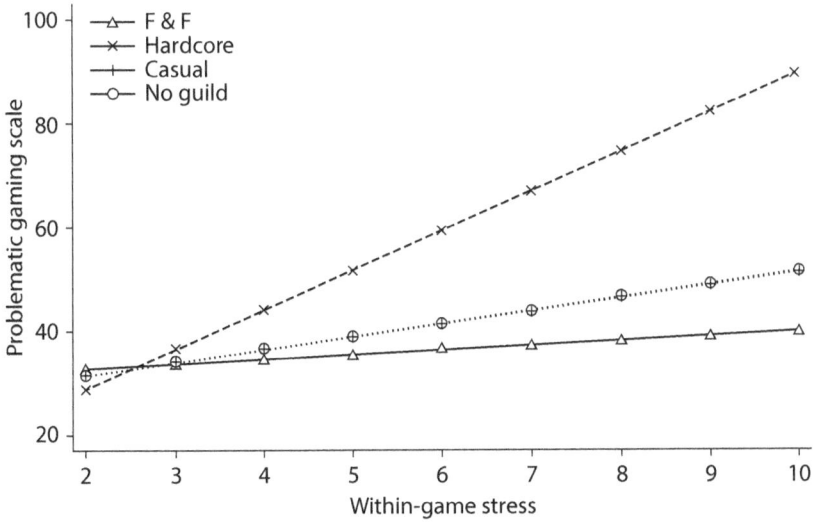

FIGURE 19. Predicted Value of Problematic Gaming Scale, by Game Stress ($N = 126$). Graph originally appeared in Snodgrass et al., 2016, *Ethos* 44 (1): 50–78.

WOMEN'S SPIRITUAL POSSESSIONS
ACROSS CULTURES

Bedami, as the devi's avatar, challenges Rajasthani gender norms related to women's speech and behavior. Kani Bai, who featured in chapter 2, in channeling the Saint of Kapasan, also speaks and behaves in a manner not appropriate to her status as a tribal woman, and in a voice impossible in other contexts. Ironically, Kani Bai takes on a male identity (the saint) to protest her community's patriarchal codes. I would add that Kani Bai takes on an identity that is at once both religiously sacrosanct (as a saint) and distinctly *not* Hindu (but Muslim). This may represent a further protest against dominant social mores, this time directed more toward upper-caste Hindus rather than toward men in her own community.

Cross-culturally, women, while spiritually possessed, frequently complain in ways that are not normally possible. For these reasons, I. M. Lewis interpreted women's spiritual possessions as protests against restrictive gender norms.[15] As an example of this, in another South Asian context, Gananath Obeyesekere investigated Buddhist-Hindu spiritual practices, which included possessions of female religious ascetics associated with the goddess

Pattini at the shrine of Kataragama in Sri Lanka.[16] These ascetics are known for their matted locks of hair and often painful devotional practices. In one of Obeyesekere's case studies, fifty-two-year-old Karunavati Maniyo was frequently possessed by Pattini, who symbolized for this woman (and for many other Sinhalese-speaking Sri Lankans) the ideal chaste wife and devoted mother. In becoming a devotee to and avatar of this goddess, Karunavati renounced the material world. This meant she refused to have sexual relations with her human husband, who was abusive, and instead married the god Kataragama. As Kataragama's priestess, Karunavati gave prophesies, for which she became known. Over time, Karunavati's matted locks grew, confirming and solidifying her new social status as a world-renouncing *sanyasin,* and divine avatar, which was quite different from her earlier one as an unhappy wife.

In Southeast Asia, Aihwa Ong drew connections between capitalist labor, gender relations, and spirit possession.[17] Specifically, Ong studied the spiritual attacks of women working in Malaysia's free-trade zones during the 1970s. These ordinarily quiescent Malay women, often unmarried migrants from rural areas, would sometimes explode into screaming and rage on the factory floor. The fits were interpreted locally as demonic attacks by angry spirits, who were commonplace in the local animistic cosmology, which was synthesized from Javanese, Hindu, and Muslim influences. The spiritual attacks were disruptive in ways that sometimes led to the normally relentlessly efficient factory assembly lines, supervised by foreign and local men working for largely Japanese, American, and European multinational corporations, to be temporarily shut down. Ong saw these possession experiences as women's critiques against factory work, with its long hours, unsafe working conditions, and frequent sexual harassment by male supervisors. That is, young women, in their new spiritual voices, rebelled against the harsh working conditions in covert ways that escaped punishment, since the women were not seen as responsible for their afflictions. This helped these women to renegotiate their new livelihoods to be more satisfying, or at least more tolerable. Male company managers might see these young women as cheap and easily controllable labor, with few rights and little voice, but, at least when possessed, the young Malay female employees were anything but that.

In her study of *zar* cults in the Sudan, Janice Boddy makes a similar argument, drawing attention to the fact that women there are more likely to find a voice through socially marginal spirit cults, which can be opposed to male-dominated, Islam.[18] In the village of Hofriyat, where Boddy worked, and all along the Nile River, many women—but very few men—are diagnosed at some point in their lives as being possessed by zar spirits, which is viewed by some as an illness. Boddy interprets these spiritual experiences in the context of Sudanese and Islamic concerns with women's sexuality and reproduction. Local custom includes genital operations performed on female children known as "pharaonic circumcision," where the labia and clitoris are removed, and the vaginal opening is almost completed closed. This procedure can cause severe bleeding and problems urinating, as well as complications with childbirth, and it can make women's sexual intercourse difficult, painful, and devoid of pleasure. The painful and dangerous surgery is justified locally by men and women alike as preparing girls for womanhood, by rendering their bodies clean, smooth, and pure, and by marking them as marriageable, fertile, and ready to bear children.

In her analysis, Boddy points out that some women in Hofriyat fail to have children, and of particular importance, fail to have *male* children. This is stressful for them, given the cultural expectations and ways that female identities are intricately bound to expectations around child-rearing and producing male heirs. And Boddy finds that zar illnesses most typically afflict women failing to live up to cultural expectations, often in and around concerns with giving birth to and raising children. Such women are known to fall ill, which is often interpreted as zar possession, believed to be an incurable, but manageable, condition. In curing rites, women communicate with the hedonistic zar spirits, learning their demands and forming contractual relationships with them, which is said to placate the spirits. Among other things, the hedonistic and willful zar spirits want to frolic and be entertained. To keep the spirits satisfied and thus at bay entails regular, even lifelong, participation in curing rites, where the zars, and their human trancing hosts, chant and dance with other spirits and similarly afflicted women. On exiting zar trances, which are often described as quite fun and like a "party," Hofriyat women say they "see things differently" and "feel well," pointing to the therapeutic benefits of these rites. Based on details such as these, Boddy says that participating in zar curing rites helps afflicted women learn to expand and regenerate their senses of self, even in ways that challenge patriarchal norms and expectations, e.g., by learning to become happier and even celebrate their childless conditions. Boddy's analysis thus follows the general lines of I. M. Lewis's argument, if challenging certain aspects of his thesis. As Boddy tells readers in a review of the spirit possession literature, she hopes to focus attention less on "instrumentalist" aims of the women in these cults—that is, how women explicitly and tactically use spirits to solve practical problems and redefine their social statuses, as Lewis's work suggests—and more on how zar-spirit cults, as alternative ways of performing femininity, implicitly challenge, often subtly and unconsciously, patriarchal meanings and naturalized realities.[19]

Finally, Rebecca Seligman researched the experiences of spirit mediums of African-derived Candomblé religion in Brazil.[20] Many of Seligman's study participants were poor women who led difficult lives. Her study participants' first spirit possession experiences were often precipitated by the sudden and unexpected onset of suffering, including distress related to sexual abuse and other forms of violence, deaths of loved ones, financial problems, and chronic illnesses, all of which were compounded by typically grinding daily poverty and experiences of racism. Afflicted in these ways, these individuals might seek diagnosis and relief in various medical or religious settings, of which Candomblé was but one example. At first, Seligman's research participants often recounted how they resisted the call of the spirits and the role of spirit medium, both being perceived as alien to their experiences, and oftentimes stigmatized by mainstream society. But slowly, these afflicted persons would find comforting the Candomblé community's healing rites, which could entail, among other things, dance, song, drink, frivolity, and ecstatic trance, alongside the general generosity, support, and warmth offered by the Candomblé community itself.

Thus, for example, the lively and warm sixty-two-year-old Dona Lucia had been a *filha de santo* (lit., "daughter of a saint," the term for initiated spirit mediums) for thirty years and was a respected senior member of the Candomblé community where Seligman worked. In her youth, Lucia was a political activist during Brazil's military dictatorship, which led her to greatly fear being caught by the police and jailed, raped, beaten, tortured, or killed. Her fear became so great, dominating her whole life, that she dropped out of college. Her anxiety was compounded by the death of her father, for which she felt partly responsible, having fallen asleep while caring for him after his stroke. Her father was hospitalized and died shortly thereafter. On a friend's suggestion, Lucia sought relief in Candomblé, eventually learning to channel, then, as a young woman, an ancient Candomblé deity, known locally as an *orixá*. The spirit was Oxalá, the oldest and wisest of the orixás, who, due to his old age, walked with a limp and a cane. Lucia learned to identify with the calmness, wisdom, kindness, and tranquility of Oxalá, learning to walk while channeling Oxala with his same stooped posture and slow and careful gait. After becoming a medium, and in this book's terminology, a divine avatar, Lucia felt less agitated, high-strung, and emotionally volatile. As Seligman sees it, Lucia found in her divine alter ego a healthier self. In becoming a medium, Lucia also gained a new elevated and powerful social standing, as the very vehicle of god, which contrasted strikingly with her daily more socially marginalized and agitated existence. And Lucia's prior weakness was reinterpreted by her as a test, a step on the path to her final spiritual-avatar identity, as a medium, and a now spiritually healed healer, who rather than ill and weak was able to help others.

DISCUSSION: ENHANCED SELF-IMAGE, ELEVATED SOCIAL STANDING, AND AVATAR THERAPEUTICS

As this and the prior chapter's ethnography show, Bedami's devi avatar provides her with a powerfully compelling second self. After all, Bedami's second self is interpreted as a Hindu goddess—in Bhat terms, an avatar of truth, goodness, and morality. Once the devi interpretation is cemented, Bedami becomes a spirit medium, a potent individual seen as capable of helping others solve their problems—again, quite a compelling, even *ideal,* second self, in Edward Higgins's terminology. As socially sanctioned by Bhat and more general Hindu religious norms, Bedami's avatar alter ego also is an *ought self,* again in Higgins's social discrepancy theory (SDT) language.[21] In allowing Bedami to act out her better self, in personal and social terms, the devi avatar identity would help Bedami, according to SDT theory, improve her mental well-being by minimizing depressed and anxious affect. That makes sense in this Rajasthani context, in the way that Bedami as the devi hopes to bring together and satisfy both her natal family and her husband, which would be felt as both personally uplifting and a relief.

The Bhat community is a grouping of like-minded individuals, who share in part common values and commitments, as well as context-specific rules, or social norms, to enforce shared values and commitments. Bedami's spiritual possession allows her to cement a new and improved social and moral standing within this community—eventually as a spirit medium, the devi's vehicle, which is appreciated and even celebrated by many other Bhats—that provides her with a healing path aimed at mending not only personal but also familial and communal disharmony. Further, Bedami's new divinely sanctioned status would potentially be experienced in a newly strengthened community. Bedami's "presence," identified as her husband Ramu's kuldevi, or clan deity, chastises Ramu for failing to respect and share with others in the community. Bedami as the devi, then, has something to communicate specifically to her husband, Ramu, which is meant to mend problems in their relationship, and thus help ensconce Bedami, her husband, and their children more firmly within the Bhat community as a whole. In these terms, Bedami's dissociative experiences are thus not only *psychological*, as presented in chapter 2, but rather eminently *psychosocial*. That is, they are at once mentally interior to Bedami but also shaped by spiritual norms particular to the Bhat community and Hinduism as a whole.

In Michael Marmot's analytical language, Bedami, as the devi, improves her *social status*. And as Marmot shows in an impressive body of work on what he calls the *status syndrome*, improvements of these kind can positively influence both mental and physical health.[22] In many respects, Bedami, as a woman and wife, is socially subordinate, and her nuclear family has become marginalized from the Udaipur Bhat community. But as the devi, Bedami improves her social standing in both these regards, no longer clearly subordinate to her husband and less isolated from other Bhats compared to before. Higgins clarifies the self-image processes associated with such health improvements. But Marmot's health-disparities analytical framework draws a finer point on the *social-status mechanisms* driving avatar-therapeutic health improvements of these kinds.

In fact, anthropologists have illuminated similar psychosocial processes in spirit possessions found around the world. In being possessed, women such as Karunavati Maniyo[23] and Lucia[24] reformulate their identities in ways that can improve their social relations and well-being. Like Bedami's experiences, such possessions are eminently *psychosocial,* both mental and interior to these women but also shaped by local religious and gender norms. In many cases, possessed women, whether working in Malaysian factories[25] or dancing in North African zar cults,[26] challenge patriarchal norms that would subordinate them, elevating their social standing in ways that concretely improve their lives and health.[27] However, in employing Higgins's and Marmot's more abstract analytical language, I hope to show in this chapter and more broadly in this book how similar avatar-therapeutic processes are characteristic not only of *religious* states of possession—which are typically the focus of anthropological case studies and comparative analyses such as those presented in this chapter—but also of a variety of other avatar experiences including contemporary *digital* ones.

This chapter's gaming material also illustrates the importance of social context to avatar-therapeutic processes, with a focus on WoW gaming guilds. Blizzard Entertainment, the makers of *World of Warcraft*, do provide WoW players with the possibility of creating and joining guilds, which operate according to programmed rules and principles. However, Blizzard never specifies the fervor with which guild members should pursue their goals, nor the informal norms and implicit and explicit guild ethics that might guide such pursuits. Instead, the guild types discussed in this chapter—like more *casual* as compared with *hardcore* raiding guilds—along with their often unique membership rules and regulations, emerge organically out of specific gamer practices and preferences.

Interdisciplinary research points to different types of gaming guilds defined by their goals, level of ambition, intensity of activity, and required expertise and time commitment—some driven by the desire for casual socializing, others by role-playing aims, and still others by varying degrees of zeal to defeat challenging WoW content or even other players.[28] As treated in this literature and also in this book, MMO guilds can be thought of as communities or organizations with distinctive cultures: worlds (guilds) within worlds (MMOs) within worlds (lives offline), so to speak, whose nested structures can be investigated ethnographically.[29]

This chapter's primary gaming case study is the Knights of Good (KOG), a self-dubbed casual raiding guild, located somewhere between a hardcore and friends-and-family organization. KOG takes an unusually relaxed attitude toward WoW gaming, organizing itself under the mantra of "real life comes first." The ethnography I presented shows how KOG's specific governance and management style—a more democratic team approach relying on the personal charisma and individual leadership skills of its two founders—works better for this guild's less hardcore membership. With Lainey and Vern as moral guides—and under the banners of real life and others first, leading by example, doing good, tolerance for diversity, and even social justice–KOG's members play in ways that model their founders' values and approach. Lainey and Vern's thought and practice infect the guild, so to speak, creating a distinctive culture of more relaxed raiding that furthered the well-being of KOG's members.

Again, in Higgins's SDT thinking, gaming avatars allow individuals in this context a chance to remake themselves into a potentially superior—even *ideal*—form, an *ideal elf* to reference a classic gaming study.[30] And inhabiting that new avatar identity can lead to subjective experiences, such as the feeling of having higher social standing, which, as Marmot and others have shown, can lead to improved health. But avatar identities in this context are *socially,* rather than simply personally, valued. Colloquially, Lainey and Vern are role models, as Rayna in fact describes them, who provide models of ideal behavior that are imitated by others, producing in the process KOG's distinctive patterns of play. KOG does have other more formal governance structures— for example, they experiment with *dragon kill points* (DKP) and other raid *loot* (treasure) distribution systems. (DKP offers a more formal way of keeping track of player participation and effort.[31]) But KOG's informal guild norms—a parallel and emergent form of governance relying largely on voluntary compliance—are particularly important in helping its members self-regulate, partially protecting raiders against even their own impulses to play harder and longer. Based in large part on these socially learned norms, KOG helps its members set reasonable limits on their hours played, thus protecting them from their sometimes own tendency "to care too much" (about raid progression), in one member's phrasing.

In these terms, KOG avatar identities also display dimensions of Higgins's *ought self,* in the sense that gamers enact guild standards and values in building their alternative digital lives, thus following not only their personal preferences but also social expectations. KOG provides its members with a second digital identity, which gives them a sense of belonging both in WoW and more generally in their lives. But importantly, that second identity is culturally defined in relation to KOG's guild values, its *ought* rules of behavior, or how one *should* be and behave from the point of view of social others. Specifically, within KOG, successful gaming is framed as progression through WoW's raid content in ways that help gamers respect the constraints posed by their offline lives. So-called *hardcore* raiding was generally not respected, or even tolerated, as such play had proved too psychosocially risky in the past for many KOG members. Being a KOG raider, then, could be conceptualized as a particular social identity, with the psychological benefits of that identity following from how well one personally embodied KOG commitments—that is, the extent to which one was *consonant* with KOG socially learned understandings or *cultural models*[32] of successful play, an analytical language that will play an important role in the next chapter.[33]

Further, offline settings play important roles in these digital-avatar therapeutic processes. For example, in the case of Lainey, KOG's guild mom, one hears how her WoW achievements helped her, a single mom, achieve a social standing within KOG not possible in the actual world. Being that group's respected leader clearly contributed positively to her sense of self and subjective well-being. Gaming identities and avatars, then, can approximate (in certain if not all ways) players' conceptions of their *ideal self* or *ought self*, potentially compensating gamers for slights and indignities they experience in their offline lives.[34] But Marmot's *health-disparities* framework helps capture the contribution of social inequality and power dynamics to our understanding of avatar-therapeutic processes. And I would further add that this analytical framework—combining as it does insights from SDT and health-disparities research—is useful for explaining relationships between avatar identities and health in both *spiritual* contexts—as in the cases of Bedami, Kani Bai, Karunavati Maniyo, and Lucia—and *digital* ones—like we find in KOG and with Lainey.

This chapter's first set of survey results allowed me to further confirm these ethnographic patterns. For example, those results demonstrate the tight relationship between WoW success and subjective well-being outcomes, such as gaming being perceived to contribute positively to players' happiness and life satisfaction. This is consistent with the idea that digital-avatar identities, in the way they embody gamers' WoW successes and relationships, represent for players *ideal* second selves (in Higgins' SDT terms) that contribute positively to mental well-being. But success in these instances is relative to WoW gamer understandings, which highlights the importance of normative and socially learned *ought* standards—and thus *ought selves,* as Higgins frames similar situations—to these avatar-therapeutic processes. Analysis also shows how players who experience less *offline* success—and thus are psychosocially distressed in some way—experienced the greatest gaming-related enhancements of their subjective well-being. Further, the mediation analysis highlights how *lower* life-success scores are linked to *higher* reports of dissociation and *improved* mental well-being. This points to potentially important health-disparities processes such as those described by Marmot—where in this context online avatars provide players with some form of psychosocial compensation for perceived offline shortcomings—while also drawing connections to chapter 2's findings. (See figure 18.)

Despite the health-promoting potential of digital-avatar second selves, some players of MMOs such as WoW game too hard and too long, creating for themselves psychological, interpersonal, work-related, and other problems.[35] (See table 3.) Here, stressful arousal such as was described in chapter 2 can play a role, with online hyperarousal over extended periods of time contributing to problem MMO play—or, what one scholar has referred to as *toxic immersion*.[36]

Indeed, *eustressful* and *distressful* gaming—to again use Selye's terminology[37] that features in chapter 2—are often linked, as it is the risk of losing and even losing big—having "skin in the game," so to speak—that leads to both positive arousal and also potential addiction, a fact long known in gambling studies.[38] Play that is simultaneously *achievement-* and *socially-*oriented, such as found in guild-directed collaborative raids, can influence the likelihood that players experience online gaming distress. And guilds' distinctive social patterns of play, as we have seen in this chapter, shape gamers' in-game avatar and offline identities and lead players to frame and thus experience arousing or stressful gaming in certain patterned manners—in Selye's terms, as alternately engaging and positive *eustress* or problematic *distress*—with implications for the psychological well-being of guild members. Raids and other WoW activities challenge players to succeed at difficult endeavors they have not yet mastered. These events can be thought of as posing challenges, which lead to "jittery" feelings of arousal and even imbalance, as if one is out of control, until the challenge is met and eventually defeated. As such, these activities are stress-inducing, with players experiencing some degree of loss of control and either fear of or actual failure. Researchers in a variety of fields commonly frame stress as negative and connected to poor mental and physical health. However, Hans Selye points out that stress itself is adrenaline- or cortisol-fueled arousal, relatively neutral in character, with context leading that arousal to be experienced as either pleasurable eustress or painful distress.

Theoretically, the schedule and structure provided by guilds facilitates the eustressful aspects of these experiences. One prosaic feature is that guilds provide a schedule around which players can organize their WoW lives, a point commented on by respondents, thus compartmentalizing stressful experience. However, in hardcore guilds, the opposite can occur, and substantial pressure from leaders and other members can expand the role and emotional intensity of WoW play in members' lives. Hardcore guilds strive to be at the edge of a given gaming progression, ahead of other teams on the server or in the game more generally, and members are thus under constant pressure to learn and master quickly new fights. Hardcore guilds also require that their members perform the oftentimes complicated coordinated maneuvers in high-pressure situations. Failure to do so can result not only in embarrassment and vocal criticism from guild leaders and other team members, but also in one's removal from a raiding team altogether. Not surprisingly, some interviewees describe raid and other guild leaders as "taskmasters," and more like one's work bosses than fellow players in a game.

Further, hardcore guilds also have not only regular but highly demanding schedules, typically four to five hours a night for three to four days a week for raids themselves, with additional days required to harvest or "farm" in-game resources to be sold for in-game currencies such as *gold* used to purchase raiding materials including *potions* to strengthen raiders' *armor*. (Farming, though tedious, is important in the way it allows a raid group to amass the resources necessary to help them defeat the bosses.) Players have to adhere to the strict time schedules. Hardcore guilds typically expect total commitment from their raider members, even asking them to put raiding at the center of their lives, ahead even of other offline commitments such as school, work, and family. Raiders thus frequently speak of the felt need to remain in the game even when they do not have time to, driven by their own desire to improve and even master the game, on the one hand, and by social obligation, in the sense of not wanting to let down their teammates, on the other. Raiders also know that not showing up on time can compromise their standing in the game-rewards queue.

As these details reveal, hardcore guilds fundamentally fuse in-game raiding arousal and even distress, on the one hand, with patterns of compulsive overplay that can interfere with offline commitments, on the other. In the stress language of fight or flight, hardcore raiders, when met with a challenge, choose not only to fight but also to continue to fight until the battle is won, which can lead to distress in those gamers' lives. By contrast, members of more casual easygoing guilds, such as in KOG, minimize both the distress associated with raiding or other gaming activities, as well as the secondary distress appearing when such activities become unduly intense and protracted and thus interfere with their offline lives. Instead of emphasizing relentless progression through gaming content, guilds such as KOG aim to create more enjoyable and supportive online experiences, serving more like informal social clubs than military units, which promote more mildly challenging *eustress* than overwhelming and compulsive *distress*. Indeed, there are more opportunities for flight from challenge in these gaming contexts, with these players and their guild-mates more likely to laugh off defeat and even move on to other challenges, or to simply stop playing, when the failure becomes too frustrating.

To further test these how avatar-therapeutic processes relate to guild affiliation, I again relied on an online survey in this chapter's second set of analyses, specifically examining patterns of association between in-game raiding stress and problematic gaming, as these were influenced by guild type. As anticipated, being a member of a hardcore raiding guild strengthened the relationship between online gaming stress and problematic online play. In other kinds of guilds, and among nonmembers, online gaming stress showed little if any relation to problematic gaming. (See figure 19.)

Overall, research presented in this chapter does not lead me to any singular judgment on the positive or negative character of online play. Rather, players' experiences depend in part on whether they belong to guilds that meet their needs and orientations. That is, the quality of players' gaming experiences depends on whether there is a *fit* between individual personalities and expectations, on the one hand, and guild structure and organization, on the other—which, in the next chapter, I frame as *cultural consonance*.

Placed within ethnographic understandings, this second set of survey analyses also has implications for the dissociative dimensions of avatar therapeutics, discussed in chapter 2. Although here, I would note that WoW raiding, as a distinctive set of social practices, promotes different forms of dissociation as compared with other forms of game play, which are also reflected in different forms of experienced stress. Specifically, raiding promotes more *absorptive* focus on collaborative social tasks, rather than on developing in-game character histories and full-blown alternative avatar identities. That is, WoW raiders *absorb* (in Seligman's, Kirmayer's, and Luhrmann's language[39]) rather than imaginatively *immerse* themselves in WoW (as games-studies researchers describe[40]): they feel deeply focused on in-game tasks, but perhaps not like they are really fully *in* an alternative reality. Nevertheless, raiders' unique states of consciousness—i.e., their deep focus and mental absorption—can promote *dissociative* breaks with the offline world, which can be experienced as discontinuities between life online and offline. But those dissociative breaks tend to be more perceptual than related to avatar identities.[41] The point is that even in raiding activities one still finds important relationships between dissociative gaming experiences, stress relief, and subjective well-being, with me focusing in this chapter on the role that social context plays in shaping the positive and negative tenor of those experiences.[42]

CONCLUSION

In this chapter, I take inspiration from Higgins's SDT thinking and Marmot's social-status approach to health disparities to analyze avatar-therapeutic processes in spiritual and digital settings. I show how avatar experiences, depending on the social context, can either therapeutically enhance mental well-being or, by contrast, hinder my Bhat and gamer respondents' ability to reach, according to their own assessments and frames of understanding, the good life. In the devi, Bedami finds a new social identity and standing, powerfully superior to her everyday existence, which has the potential to help resolve tensions between her and important people in her life and thus improve her health and mental well-being. But that process depends importantly on local Hindu interpretations of the nature of Bedami's dissociative experiences, e.g., whether they're divinely or demonically inspired. Likewise, in WoW, Lainey and other KOG guild members establish new digital identities and social standings, which can be far superior to those in their offline lives. But whether those online identities and statuses improve rather than compromise their lives overall depends importantly on the social context of their play, such as whether they belong to guilds such as KOG as opposed to more hardcore ones. Avatar therapeutics, then, are not only *psychological* processes, as argued in chapter 2, but also importantly *psychosocial* ones.

In my analysis, I suggest that spiritual and digital avatars possess characteristics of both *ideal* and *ought* selves, in Higgins's analytical language. My perspective is informed by what Roy D'Andrade,[43] and more recently Victor de Munck and Giovanni Bennardo,[44] refer to as "plural subjects"—that is, how a member of a group (as an *individual*) strives to think from the perspective of *what they see as shared by the collective group as a whole.* As I interpret Higgins's writing, the *ideal self,* as a simplified schema of an idealized lifeway, represents *individual*-level thinking—*How would I like to be?* The SDT *ought self* gets closer to "plural subject" thinking—*How should I behave, according to my understanding of group norms and expectations?* Nevertheless, the *ought self* in the SDT framework does not explicitly focus on what anthropologists such as D'Andrade, de Munck, and Bennardo call plural "we" thinking—*What do I think* we *as a group agree on constitutes reality?* As readers will see, that form of thinking is critical to anthropological frameworks such as cultural-consonance analysis, which features in the next chapter. Clarifying points such as those raised here will help researchers draw clearer connections between *psychological* frameworks such as Higgins's SDT and *psychological-anthropological* analyses such as those being developed in this book, with the latter aiming to capture culturally informed thinking that is at once individual *and* collective—again, how *I* individually imagine *we* think as a group.[45]

FOUR

Distinguishing Therapeutic from Toxic Avatar Experiences

NORM CONFLICTS AND FELT DISSONANCE

INTRODUCTION: THE CURSE OF COMMUNITY

Over the four years before Bedami's possession, Ramu suffered from splitting headaches which, like his wife's "feelings," came without warning and left as suddenly. The pain brought on by these headaches disoriented him, making it difficult for him to concentrate on even the simplest of tasks, much less carve statues and puppet heads. Such headaches necessitated Ramu's move to the folklore institute where he, as a teacher rather than as a full-time artist, was able to spend less time engaged in the actual art of carving; he gave up his forte, carving, to take up his new salaried employment. Ramu visited many doctors, even neurological specialists, but none of their treatments eliminated his suffering. During the first two years of his illness, Ramu lived in Bhopal with his patrilineal kin, where he collected a stipend from Union Carbide, his share of the damages awarded to the victims of the 1984 gas spill in Bhopal. Ramu ascribed his headaches to his toxic exposure at Bhopal, and periodically he would travel there to collect this money. Most Bhats I knew considered this a clever scam, suggesting that Ramu was nowhere near Bhopal during the gas spill. They also thought such a scam atypical of the straight (*siddha*—i.e., not clever or tricky) Ramu.

After two years of brain scans, doctors' fees, experimental drugs, and loan after loan, Ramu exhausted the good will of the Bhopal Bhats. At this point, Ramu's father-in-law, Bansi Lal, traveled to Bhopal and brought Ramu and his family to Udaipur. In settling in his wife's natal home and leaving his own patrilineage, Ramu placed himself in an unusual position, as evidenced by the following Rajasthani saying about the relations between a son-in-law and his in-laws (my loose, not literal, translation of this saying reflects Bhat comments on this poem's meaning):

Das kosh ka avan-javan
Bis kosh ka ghee gilavan
Pachis kosh ka mathe ka mor
Ghar ka jamai gandak ki thor

(When he lives ten kosh [~twenty miles] away, our son-in-law visits us as he pleases
At twenty kosh [~forty miles], our son-in-law, is fed ghee and treated with the utmost respect on his visits
At twenty-five kosh [~fifty miles] away, our son-in-law is given a fine turban when we see him—even more respect!
But a son-in-law who lives in our house is beaten like a dog! [An archaic unit of measurement used in India, a kosh is equivalent to approximately two miles.])

This lack of respect based on his living situation was compounded by the fact that Bedami's parents had invested thousands of rupees in Ramu's treatment, as well as in the feeding and clothing of his family. Bansi Lal did not complain about the fact that Ramu had never repaid them, nor that he and his wife had to care for two of Ramu and Bedami's four children. But he did complain that Ramu did not seem grateful for his kindness, even though he had surely saved his son-in-law's life. "I did his service for years, and now he has forgotten me," Bansi Lal told me.

In fact, most of the Udaipur Bhats had some story about how they had helped Ramu—whether it was taking him to the hospital late at night, letting him sleep in their homes when Bedami's terrifying "feelings" arrived, or lending him money. Ramu rarely repaid their loans or kindnesses, instead "eating them." Yet he remained proud, thinking himself superior to them, from their point of view. They, like Ramu's father-in-law, complained that he lacked memory (yad), a quality centrally important to a community of historians and genealogists. As Ramu's debts increased, and his pride showed no sign of waning, the Bhats even suggested that he suffered only from worry (phikar), suspicion (avishwas), and "tension" (they used the English word)—a coward's (*darpok's*) disease. They insinuated that he was consuming their wealth for an expensive treatment that was neither necessary nor effective. And the devi echoed these sentiments, arriving at one point just as Ramu was taking his pills, knocking them savagely from his hands, raking him with her nails, and screaming, "Stop eating those tablets! You have no sickness! All you have is *bhem* [fear]!"

This only begins to touch on the "tensions"—again, Bhats used the English word here—between Ramu and his wife's natal kin. As an example, in the year before Bedami's possession, a fight had been brewing over the marriage of Bedami's younger sister. Bedami's parents had already engaged the girl to a boy in Jaipur, but Ramu, disapproving of the match, and wanting to marry her to a boy from his own clan, argued with them. This dumbfounded Bansi Lal, who was amazed at the arrogance of his young son-in-law, and who told me, not mincing words, "As her father, I can marry her to whom I want." Koshila, Bedami's mother, even insinuated to me that Ramu was not really interested in marrying the girl into his own patrilineage, but simply wanted to sabotage the engagement, making her and Bansi Lal look bad when they went back on their word.

In a similar manner, on the very day that Chavanda Mata first entered Bedami's body, Ramu was bickering with the rest of the community over whether Ramu's niece (his brother's daughter), Kamal, who was married to Bedami's first cousin, should be allowed to visit her mother in Bombay for Raki. Ramu, siding with his brother, who was visiting Udaipur, vehemently argued that she should be allowed to visit Bombay, especially because her mother had just been injured in a scooter accident. Bedami's relatives, however, did not trust Ramu's brother to send Kamal back and pointed out that it would be costly for her husband personally to have to fetch her from Bombay. (The trip would be expensive not only because of the bus ticket but also because her husband would be "forced" to stay, during which time he would spend a lot of money on food and drink, borrowing if he must, from his in-laws.) Then, the second arrival of the devi came right at the moment that Ramu's brother—against the wishes of the Udaipur community—was forcefully dragging his daughter Kamal away from her husband.

Bedami's repeated possession by Chavanda Mata—although potentially a font of spiritual power and wealth and thus the answer to Ramu's problems—added to his stress. Once the pandit's authoritative diagnosis on Bedami's condition was made—or authoritative as any brahmanic opinion can ever be for Bhats, who were generally suspicious of those in power—the Udaipur Bhats immediately tried to put Bedami's power to use. Whenever Bedami entered an altered state of consciousness, the word would spread quickly. Dropping whatever they were doing, whether carving a puppet head or mending a tent, Bedami's kin sprinted to her location—typically, Ramu's house—and swarmed around her in a tight circle, which grew ever tighter as the Bhats struggled to get close to, even touch, divinity. All the while Bedami's relatives would shout a confusing mix of questions, requests, opinions, and demands, which invariably concerned money: "Will that merchant [baniya] give me the loan I requested?" "That other baniya who loaned me the money, Komal, he doesn't have his *goondas* [thugs] after me does he?" "How will I pay for my daughter's wedding?" "How much dowry might Shanti Lal pay?" Or, more directly, "I've hit hard times, could you hide some cash under a rock just outside my house?" Ramu's house had been invaded first by the raging devi and now by his wife's roiling relatives.

Ramu frequently complained to me that these chaotic talks with god were making him much like his wife: insane (pagal). To combat the disorder, as mentioned, he demanded that the goddess be summoned according to a regular schedule. The other Bhats, who rarely listened to Ramu anymore, refused to abide by his timetables, instead calling her haphazardly and frequently when Ramu was away at work. If anything, after the implementation of his rules, the devi appeared more, rather than less, often. These summonings— which the furious Ramu called "pesterings" (*satana,* "to pester") because Bhats called the devi for even the most minor of ailments—exhausted Bedami. As Ramu put it, his wife's relatives would spend all their money on alcohol and expensive feasts, and then summon the deity and ask her why the gods had cursed them with poverty. On one occasion, he discussed with me his brother-in-law (Bedami's sister's husband), who spent Rs50,000 on a funeral feast (mosar) for his father, telling me: "He could have had a scooter and a new house for that," adding, "These people earn well, but they appear dirt poor, with not even enough money for medicine or decent clothing. They feed guests alcohol and meat, and then go hungry for three days." He continued, "They eat and drink their lives away, and then when they fall on hard times, they cry like children to the devi. How can the devi possibly approve of this?" Furthermore, Ramu was not only furious and dumbfounded by Bhat spending practices that he saw as "crazy," but frightened by the other Bhats' seeming lack of respect for the goddess, telling me, "If we continue to call her whenever we have some little problem, then she may get angry and leave, not coming anymore." Then, pausing for a moment to consider his words, he added, "She may kill one of us—maybe me!"

In an idyllic construction of community, living in a small, face-to-face, primarily kin-based settlement might be seen to offer a respite from the many vicissitudes of modern life. At first, this seems apropos to Ramu's situation. He got sick and the community, first his patrilineage and then his wife's relatives, rallied to his defense, supporting him financially and emotionally in a time of need. But before long, because of the loans that he could never hope to pay back and the respect he lost in the process, the small face-to-face community became the very source of his problems. His wife's relatives' continual demands for money, ridicule of him as an outsider unable to support his own family, opposition to the interests of his own close kin, constant demands for reciprocal entertaining and feasting, love of argument and revelry, inappropriate invasion of his home, and overall seemingly irresponsible attitudes toward money only exacerbated Ramu's headaches. Whether because of his own bad manners or the chasm between his values and those of the Udaipur Bhats, Ramu's symbolic and financial capital with his wife's relatives dried up, and the Udaipur Bhats became merely a drain, or more appropriately, a "headache."

New forms of wage labor, then, seemed to have had a very different meaning for Ramu than they did for other Bhats. Ramu admitted that his new job could be stressful. His labor was constantly scrutinized by the authorities at the institute where he worked. He had to report on time, and if he was late or took time off, then his salary was cut. His work was also clearly *work,* time-consuming and labor-intensive, and his salary was less—in many cases much less—than what I calculated as the average Bhat income. (At the time of these events, around 1994, Ramu earned Rs1,300 in monthly salary, plus Rs300 more in filling private orders. The average Bhat in Udaipur, as I calculated it, averaged Rs2,500 per month.) Such limits on their freedom, financial and other, were intolerable for most Bhats, as was frequently explained to me by my seminomadic informants. But for Ramu, the wild demands for reciprocity that were characteristic of traditional Bhat society were terrifying, and the new economy's steady wage, life insurance, and bank accounts—that is, its seeming restrictions, from other Bhat points of view—were precisely what appealed to him. In his new job, Ramu imagined a life free from the unpredictable demands of his community; he saw the promise of debt-free ownership of his own life and thus the opportunity to be his own man.

In these terms, certain economic forms such as wage labor were not a source of destructive evil for Ramu, as it seemed to be for other Bhats, but a balm that Ramu applied to his malady. Likewise, if for many Bhats, the goddess represented the old economy and its reciprocal and mutually beneficial social relations, she did not mean the same thing to Ramu. For him, the devi pointed not to the good of traditional relations of exchange but to the dangerous and unpredictable horror that pulsed within them and that threatened to rob Ramu of his peace of mind. Or, at other moments, Ramu saw her as a reward for his new economic values. As Ramu explained to me, ancestors and ghosts frequently entered the bodies of Bhats, but a lineage goddess was a real boon. Her choosing Bedami as a vessel represented divine approval, the devi wanting to bestow on him and his family a steady and assured source of financial productivity.

Ramu did indeed turn his back on traditional Bhat morality and notions of community. But, in their stead, he substituted a new morality and sense of social relations that seemed equally compelling to him. Specifically, he located himself within an ethic of saving and planning for his family's future, as well as within the social spaces of his nuclear family and his new place of work. Such changes did not lead, however, at least not in his mind, to the denigration of his person. If anything, landing such a job instilled in him a newfound confidence in his talents as a teacher and craftsman. His turn to the new economy, then, did not seem to reflect an inherent immorality or lack of sociality on his part, as some members of the Bhat community implied, but an alternative morality and sociality.

In fact, Ramu viewed his new work at the folklore institute, despite its restrictions, as liberating in another important respect. As mentioned, most Udaipur Bhats maintained ties with their traditional Bhambi patrons. Bhats used their praise and insult poetry to inculcate in their patrons values such as unrestrained generosity. It could be argued that Bhats were thus curators of a traditional gift economy. Nevertheless, as Ramu frequently pointed out, Bhambis were still considered untouchable by most Rajasthanis. And Ramu thus saw his new employment as providing an escape from a traditional patron-client relationship that marked him and his community as the "lowest of the low," to take the words of the Rajasthani folklorist Komal Kothari (this was not his perspective, but how he summarized the views of others).[1]

Bedami's spiritual possession, then, inflected as it was by conflicting Bhat ideas on domesticity, clan, and money, exposed the multifarious and even contradictory views Bhats held on new economic relations. To simplify, I would point to two Bhat narratives about money. In the first, the new economy, with its terrible power to disrupt local moral communities, was associated with lonely ghosts and punishing goddesses. In the second (Ramu's version of the story), the meaning was neatly reversed. In Ramu's telling, the traditional community was depicted as a source of evil and instability, and the new wage-labor economy a source of comfort and stability. I would add that each of these stories differently construed the goddess Chavanda Mata. In the first, Ramu's kuldevi was interpreted as an enraged defender of traditional values. But, in the second, Bhats other than Ramu also asked this goddess all manner of questions related to their new livelihoods, for example, if she could help them go to "foreign" (using the English word), that is, land a lucrative performing gig in a foreign country. Here, rather than a protector of traditional relations of exchange, the goddess facilitated the Bhats' smooth entrance into the new economy.

. . .

In the previous chapter, I explain Bedami's spiritual condition, and thus these events' avatar-therapeutic mechanisms, in relation to a story in which members of the Bhat community appeared to be helpless victims, and the new economy a disruptive intruder, and in which Bhats were staunch moralists and Ramu a dangerous player. My informants clearly enjoyed condemning Ramu as an agent of an outsider worldview, a threat to their harmonious (extended) family values. It also made sense that Bhats would defend the value of generosity. After all, as praise-singers, Bhats served as curators of a moral economy based on flamboyant spending, and their livelihood depended to a large extent on the gifts they received from their Bhambi patrons. My Bhat informants' portrayal of Bedami's situation would even seem to validate accounts that view spiritual possessions as modes of social and political *resistance*—disguised forms of protest, typically culturally and historically sensitive, against unjust institutions such as gender inequality, as discussed in the prior chapter's spiritual interlude.[2]

However, as this chapter's new details reveal, this interpretation tells at best half of the story. Bedami herself, during the years preceding her sterilization and transformation into the devi, did sometimes criticize her husband's stinginess, usually through friendly jokes, both to her Bhat relatives and to me. But this was atypical of Bedami, who did not usually display overt antagonism toward either her husband or the changing contemporary world. Bedami also frequently, and quite lovingly, praised Ramu in my presence. And such praise was inextricably bound up with Bedami's perception of her husband's ostensible modern outlook on work, family, and life more generally: Ramu's long hours at work demonstrated his love for their children and desire for their advancement; his stint in the Indian Army, which no other Bhats in the Udaipur community had experienced, demonstrated his patriotism and bravery; even his written poems, and most Bhats including Bedami were illiterate, revealed both the power of his mind and the depth of his soul. All in all, Bedami found it difficult simply to condemn Ramu's new ways. This was, in part, out of her feelings of love and loyalty for her husband, but it also seemed due to the fact that Bedami, too, shared in the dream that she and her family would be raised up, even saved, by Ramu's new employment, bank account, pension, and, in an unfortunate emergency, life insurance.

Even Bedami's possession, in many ways, demonstrated a warmth and sympathy for Ramu. This was most clear in the manner that Bedami repeatedly insisted, in as forceful terms as was possible for this generally mild-mannered young woman, that Ramu be included in any summonings of the goddess and communal feasts held in Chavanda Mata's honor. On numerous occasions, Bedami stood firm against the wishes of her patriline, insisting that the goddess not be called or feted until her husband returned from work, no small feat for the soft-spoken Bedami. Similarly, Bedami, in her second-self form as the goddess's avatar, never gave up on Ramu despite his recidivist stinginess— offering Ramu opportunity after opportunity to redeem himself in the eyes of the community. The goddess even criticized many Bhats for thinking in terms of *tere-mere* (yours and mine). This phrase, as previously mentioned, was applied to persons such as Ramu, who refused to share economic resources. But the goddess also used the phrase to criticize gossips and backbiters in the Bhat community—that is, those who, in a perverse spirit of sharing, took what was not theirs, such as a secret, and shared it with others with whom they should not. Here, the goddess (and thus Bedami) intended to protect Ramu from those who spoke negatively of him behind his back. Bedami, in both her conscious and possessed avatar states, therefore seemed ambivalent toward Ramu—though Bedami's devi form surely allowed for more overt expression of hostility toward him, or at least on certain, if not all, occasions.

Bedami, then, was caught between the demands of the Udaipur Bhat community and the demands of her husband. The conflict between her natal family and her husband, centering around Ramu's debts, made it impossible for her to take sides. Living near and sometimes in her parents' home only exacerbated Bedami's already difficult situation, making it difficult for her to minimize the centrality of this dispute in her life. Bedami's relatives might celebrate community and condemn the modern economy, but Bedami herself, out of duty toward her husband, could not do so fully. Ramu might embrace the new economy's ethic of individualism, especially given his distance from his own patrilineage and thus from legitimate demands that could be placed on his money, but again, Bedami, immersed as she was in the communal space of her childhood, could not. As I interpret Bedami's feelings—both generally and in relation to her specific possession "feelings" or bhav—the new economy, as perceived through her husband's new work, seemed to be alternately demonic and divine, dislocating and comforting, exploitative and just.

Bedami's possession might be thought of as an attempt to forge a third story somewhere between a condemnation and celebration of the new economy and its associated way of life. Bedami, in the form of the goddess, did condemn those who failed to respect community. She did not, however, treat money earned in the new economy as intrinsically evil, but rather as potentially the very means to demonstrate loyalty to community. Ramu, simply by channeling his wages into communal feasts, and thus allowing his outside earnings to be domesticated by the community, would have avoided most if not all of the devi's wrath. In fact, I often got the impression that Ramu's cash infusions into communal feasts and the devi's gifts of healing were read by Bedami as mutually convertible currencies. Transformed into a goddess, a source of power from which her relatives could draw, Bedami compensated for her husband's stinginess.

Bedami's possession, then, unlike what might be suggested by the first two narratives, was neither a condemnation of her greedy husband nor of her own backbiting relatives. Rather, it represented an attempt to fuse old and new worlds and thus reintegrate her husband back into the community. The goddess's replies to questions put to her by the community, with Bedami the devi's medium, demonstrated this point, given they inevitably emphasized unity and harmony: the devi's most common responses were, "Everything will be alright," "Don't worry," "There is nothing to fear," "I am with everyone," "I will take care of everyone," "I will bring everyone happiness," and "You have no enemies here" (the latter responding to accusations of black magic within the community). If Bedami the goddess emphasized harmony over conflict, Bedami the person clearly enjoyed those festive periods following her possession. I am thinking in particular of a puja honoring Chavanda Mata, sponsored by Ramu, in which communal exuberance was particularly pronounced. Bedami, for the first time since her husband's protracted illness, seemed truly happy, as she watched her husband laughing and carousing with the other Bhats, enjoying himself with her relatives as he used to when, as Bedami put it, "All were 'one' [ek]."

This chapter's new ethnographic details, when contextualized against what I presented in earlier chapters, leads me to the following conclusion about avatar therapeutics in this Bhat context: *for Bedami, taking form as the devi was simultaneously therapeutic and distressful, medicine and illness.* I say this because the source of the devi's healing power for Bedami, as argued in the prior chapter, was the way that the goddess (avatar) form allowed her to improve her self-image and moral standing in relation to her natal family and with the Udaipur Bhat community as a whole. However, simultaneous with that, taking form as the devi, no matter how "superior" that identity seemed to be to many Bhats, even to Bedami herself, also placed this young woman in potential conflict with her husband. Or, to put it slightly differently, the general Bhat interpretation of the meaning of the devi's visit was contrary to Ramu's, and vice versa. And for Bedami, siding with the Bhat community's interpretation thus meant conflict with Ramu, and likewise, siding with Ramu's understandings created tension with her natal family and with the Bhat community. The therapeutic and distressful dimensions of this spiritual event were intertwined—inescapably so—meaning that Bedami's possession, I repeat, was experienced by her as *simultaneously* therapeutic *and* debilitating. Finally, and perhaps most importantly for this chapter's concerns: for Bedami's avatar experiences to be more purely therapeutic, she would need to embody the devi in ways that allowed her to successfully negotiate and balance Ramu's and the community's demands. That is, Bedami would need to find ways to embody the devi that simultaneously pleased Ramu and the other Bhats and thus forged that "third story" I suggest above. Successfully negotiating (at least to some extent) those different social demands would render Bedami's experience of her second avatar self on balance more pleasurable than distressful, more socially elevating, and thus more therapeutic in some sense—though such a balancing act was by no means straightforward, given the way Ramu and Bedami's other relatives seemed to inhabit conflictual social realities.

· · ·

In this chapter's analytical language, Bedami, in channeling the devi, becomes personally consistent with socially valued religious beliefs and practices, a process William Dressler refers to as *cultural consonance*.[3] As shown in chapter 3, enacting culturally valued principles in this way, whether through spiritual- or digital-avatar identities, can enhance individuals' self-image and social standing and thus also their mental well-being. Nevertheless, as seen in this chapter's ethnography, Bedami, in becoming personally consonant with certain values—Hindu religious ones and Bhat notions of community and generosity—also fails to enact other principles—like her husband's commitment to contemporary capitalist modes of living. Bedami tries to negotiate and even reconcile these alternative cultural systems, each situated within a competing moral universe, but suffers distress in the process. In reference to Leon Festinger's *cognitive dissonance* idea, Bedami suffers because she cannot eliminate incompatibilities in her conflicting beliefs and commitments.[4] However, in this chapter, I show how this is a *cultural*—rather than merely a psychological or *cognitive*—form of dissonance, given how Bedami's felt tension results from conflicts between competing socially learned and thus *cultural* systems of value.[5]

· · ·

In the next section, I present my 2016–2017 research on Udaipuri emerging adults[6] who play the video game *Counterstrike—Global Offensive* (CS-GO) in face-to-face internet parlors referred to locally as gaming zones. I follow this with further detail on spirit possessions, illustrating how the possessed around the world often feel pulled in different and conflicting directions, with their spiritual avatars alternately a source of wellness and distress, much as in the case with Bedami. Then, in this chapter's integrative discussion, I develop a similar argument for digital-avatar therapeutics in this Indian gaming context, as I just described in relation to Bedami's spiritual experiences. Specifically, I show that: *for these Udaipuri young adults, digital second-avatar selves are also often experienced as simultaneously therapeutic and distressful, and thus as cures for gamers' life problems but also the source of new problems.* More generally, I further develop in that culminating discussion the concept of *cultural dissonance*—building on Dressler's *cultural-consonance* idea and Festinger's *cognitive-dissonance* argument—to emphasize the way avatar therapeutics, whether spiritual or digital, depend on the extent that individuals successfully navigate between alternate and even competing sociocultural worlds where they locate their first and second lives.

CULTURAL DISSONANCE IN INDIAN GAMING ZONES

In my India gaming-zones research conducted in Udaipur, Rajasthan, in the summers of 2016 and 2017, I conducted observations and interviews to gauge how gamers there viewed and experienced divergent social expectations related to their online and offline lives. In the language of cultural consonance and dissonance, that ethnography helped me elicit the different components of a socially learned and widely shared "true-gamer" model of identity, as well as to understand how becoming consonant with such an identity might produce both pleasure and distress. After visiting cybercafes offering general internet services, I learned that only three gaming centers catered specifically to CS-GO players. These three *zones* or *lounges* and their regular players (around twelve to fifteen in each zone) became the focus of the research, with me typically visiting one of them during mornings for between one and a half and three hours, and another evenings, for roughly the same amount of time. For each visit, I took shorthand fieldnote jottings, which I expanded evenings into fuller scenes, documenting what I learned about play in these zones based on these observations and informal interviews. I also conducted more structured interviews with individuals and small groups of gamers about their lives outside of gaming, including about the pressures they felt from family and broader society regarding their careers and impending arranged marriages. This helped me understand Rajasthani social norms related to the proper trajectory of young men's lives. And I spoke with older individuals—for example, gaming and internet-center owners, parents, and other family members—about video games and the internet to further enhance my ethnographic understandings (see figures 20 and 21).

"Everybody Knows Everybody"

Though first drawn to Udaipur's gaming zones for the superior computers and stable internet connection, the friendships made these places special. One respondent told me that he did not have much in common with his other university friends, but his passion for games kept him close with the lounge's gamers. Others told me that the transition from high school to the local public university, Mohan Lal Sukhadia University (MLSU), was difficult. It was challenging to make new friends there, so they spent time in gaming lounges, with zones' core members becoming over time, in one's respondent's words, "like a family."[7]

Many gaming zone friendships were longstanding. For example, one group of gamers, now at Udaipur's private Pacific University, had studied together beforehand at the same prep school. In fact, this group had been close since childhood, growing up in the same neighborhood, and the

FIGURE 20. A screenshot from a first-person shooter (FPS) game, *Nuclear Dawn,* depicting the London based *Clocktower* map from a player's first-person perspective. *Nuclear Dawn* by InterWave Studios, https://interwavestudios.com/. No changes to the original image, "Nuclear Dawn—Clocktower FPS." License: https://creativecommons.org/licenses/by-sa/3.0/deed.en.

FIGURE 21. Udaipur gaming zones are darkened to enhance gaming focus and pleasure. Photo by author.

gaming zone allowed them to remain close as they transitioned to their next stage in life. Another group of MLSU friends had attended the same high school, but they did not know one another well then, only forging their "strong bonds" (as one of them described it) later at the zone, after they got more serious about video games. In both cases, "everybody knows everybody" in these gaming lounges—a mantra repeated 3–4 times by this interviewee, as he explained to me the social importance these places held for him.

On a typical Sunday, and even some weekdays, individuals might spend up to 6–7 hours in their preferred gaming zone. But they would only pay to play at a computer for maybe 2–3 hours, and typically only after their closest gaming friends had showed up. Half the time spent there was as a spectator. During a match, the atmosphere was animated. Gamers shouted out in Hinglish (a mix of Hindi and English) directions and instructions to one another, either to teammates, who were networked with them in the same zone, or to online friends, identifying enemies and the like with, "*Upar* [above], *piche aaye* [come back], left, right!", "*Dabbe ke niche!*" (below the box), "SSSS over here!," "Fuck you bro" (voiced quietly in English to an online opponent, who couldn't hear the taunt), "Oh *madar chod*" (mother-fucker), "Rush *karun bahen chod*" (rush them sisterfucker), "Restart *karo*" (restart the match), "*Last maro kare!*" (kill the last one). Such dialogue was interspersed with laughter, victory chants, and howls of defeat, the whole scene encircled by empty Pepsi bottles and chips wrappers. While waiting for a match, or after being killed in an earlier one, players sat and watched ongoing games, either calmly or just as animatedly as when playing. Outside of matches, the zones' clientele would hang out and chat with their friends, sip tea or colas, talk about gaming and sometimes their lives, and laugh. Others might take a smoke break in one of the zone's stairwells, or perhaps outside, discuss strategy, and then return to playing. In one zone, gamers smoked only either the Indian brand *Classic Regulars* or *Marlboro Lights,* with most keeping a pack with their names written in Sharpie in the lounge owner's desk drawer, with traded cigarettes and tea and snacks too forming an informal friendship currency.

To sum up what one gamer liked about playing in these lounges, I was told simply, "The ambiance is much better . . . [pause] Plus I can smoke cigs here." By this, this interviewee referred in part to the strong friendships he had forged there. But he also referenced how gamers interacted with one another in these spaces in ways that were frowned on in public. Here, all were free to get rowdy, within limits, celebrating victories and lamenting defeats with cussing, taunting, and raucous joy. I often saw players getting visibly upset on losing a close match and start hitting others, typically playfully, and frequently reciprocated in good spirits, and with laughter, though owners and others stepped in if things got out of control. Gamers teased one another, too. One group introduced their friend to me as a "playboy" and a "ladies' man," who "breaks ladies' hearts." The cussing and drinking was further fueled by smokes and power drinks, which boosted players' energy. Around lunch time, 1:30pm or a bit later, many players filtered out of the zones, going home to eat. But others stayed and ordered food, butter chicken, for example, or Domino's pizza (Udaipur had two of these).

Such are gaming zones' social bonds that they endured even after players were no longer actively gaming there. One individual going to Bangalore to study IT said, "I will have to play on a laptop there, but I plan to keep in touch with my buddies." Another doing a BA at Pacific University, with plans to pursue a MBA in London, told the owner of his zone, during a conversation we were having, "Don't let this place die if one of us leaves [the owner was also planning to move abroad], I really love it."

A Global "Gamer" Community

As an online game, CS-GO connected local Udaipuri players to a massive network of other gamers. *Steam,* the digital-distribution platform that provided access to this and other games, displayed the number of currently active players. At one point, over 400,000 players were networked online while I was watching. Each player had a chat window, which was typically filled with not only the directions, commands, and taunts described earlier, but also with texted encouragement from often geographically distant teammates. With servers typically in Delhi, Pune, Singapore, and other parts of Asia (the gaming computers connect thousands of regional players), CS-GO linked Udaipuri residents not only to these places but to many others. "Wherever there are students, there you'll find gaming zones and video games," I was told by one respondent, himself a university student. One Udaipuri gamer spoke of his "clan friend" who lived in Iraq working as a dentist, from whom he learned the fighting there had settled down recently. (CS-GO players create "clans" of friends and like-minded players with whom they collaborate.) Such sharing of personal experiences and stories brought this local gamer closer to online friends, whom he says he now knew well and were "true friends," with the others in his group from Singapore, Pune, the US, and also

Udaipur itself. Another gamer respondent told me, "I have a gaming friend in Delhi who I can really trust." ["More than real-life friends?", I asked.] "No, but like the same."

CS-GO helped Udaipuri gamers transcend what they often saw as narrow national and religious identities. Udaipuri Hindus and Muslims alike often gamed with Muslim players from Pakistan, telling me that they treated them the same as they did players from other parts of the world, in fact seeing them as "very friendly." Further, the Hindu players I knew told me they never thought much about one gaming zone owner's Muslim identity. And an owner explained to me that internet gamers interacted with so many different kinds of people from around the world, that tolerance became an almost innate quality. Indian players were gamers first, with affiliations related to caste, religion, geography, and so forth a distant second. In fact, some gamers I knew, when asked, described themselves as atheists, something I rarely heard in other Indian field projects. Another player agreed with others' assessments about the general lack of prejudice among gamers, though added that a group of four Indian players might more readily kick a Pakistani from their group, and that the Dubai players sometimes discriminated against Indians.

Typically, my gamer respondents displayed the same playfully competitive dynamic with online gamer friends as they did with local ones. When a player was killed, the game showed the name and image of the killer and the weapon used, a kind of programmed visual taunt. At one point, MrSexyyBoyz, a networked player on the opposing team, was getting the best of one of the locals, Ramu, with MrSexyyBoyz's avatar appearing in the middle of the screen repeatedly (that happens in CS-GO after a victory). After suffering a final loss, Ramu shot back in Hinglish text, "gg noobe sale" [good game you newb brother-in-law] ("newb" is slang for "newbie" or "new player"; the implication here is that Ramu was having sexual relations with his opponent's sister).

Though frequently initiating conversations in Hindi, I often found the register shifted to English or Hinglish, which were preferred by Udaipuri gamers. And English was the global language that typically connected gamers both from other parts of India and indeed from around the world to one another. Some gamers could be shy speaking English over headphones with non-Indians, preferring to listen rather than to speak, especially when internet "lags"—or delays—garbled communication. But more typically, my respondents relished showing off their English language skills and signaling their belonging, game knowledge, and prowess. And even those who did not speak, still enjoyed the conversations.

Respondents told me that gamers from around the world also smoked, chugged power drinks, and snacked on junk food. "Gamers are addicts," I was once told. In fact, it was these consumption patterns, along with the English and the passion for gaming, that set my respondents off from others as "true" or "real" gamers, which was how my respondents described themselves. Playing with gamers from around the world produced a sense of identity and belonging alongside the thrilling gaming experiences. Udaipur's gaming zones connected local players with one another. But what was critical here was the way that locals themselves connected to one another because of their shared aspirations to be "true gamers."

Digital Dreams

When asked about the positive benefits of video gaming, respondents told me in gaming they found their "passion" and "motivation" in life, using those English words. One said gaming instilled in him a "competitive spirit," which served him well in life. He and others also told me that in gaming "time flies," and "you forget about time." Or, as one respondent put it directly, "gaming is a good way to pass time." This was often implicitly, and sometimes explicitly, contrasted with school and work, which were not described similarly.

Part of the pleasure here was the way that my respondents experienced steady improvement in their play, posting their (ideally) ever-rising CS-GO ranks on gaming lounge whiteboards, with local players' names and associated ranks descending hierarchically from top to bottom. To improve their play, local CS-GO gamers watched internet videos and live-casts of matches between well-known teams, who sometimes took home prize pools grossing millions of US dollars. Likewise, players and zone owners alike organized local matches between rival lounges, where players further tested and honed their skills. I myself organized one of these matches between two of the local zones, which included snacks and drinks, and served as a 2016 farewell and thank you party to my respondents.

Given the competitive nature of the game, players searched for any edge they could find. The smokes and energy drinks were said to help focus and stamina, allowing them to stay awake and thus compete longer, and with better concentration. Some said that the brief cigarette breaks were more effective than the constant sipping of (expensive) energy drinks, which, producing the urge to pee, interfered with the sometimes hour plus long matches. By contrast, one cigarette, I was told, could carry a gamer energetically through a full hour of play. One individual even told me that "weed" (marijuana) served these same functions for him—"all things that put your mind in one place," he told me, were effective in this regard.

Surprisingly to me, most of Udaipur's serious gamers dreamed of "going pro." One explained that as a pro gamer, "I'd love the job. It's good to do something you love. Pays a lot too. But the best reason is you get to be a 'real gamer.' You get the title, 'real gamer,' 'pro.'" Locals took inspiration from professional Indian esports teams, such as the Indian Wolves in the game *Dota 2* (that's the name of a well-known Indian team of gamers; *Dota 2* belongs to a particular genre of games referred to as a "MOBAs," for "multiplayer online battle arenas"). They also spoke of a Pakistani gamer who won 1.5 million US dollars in the Asian *Dota 2* Championship. One of the gaming zone owner's friends had also gone to Paris and competed as the Indian representative in a one-on-one soccer video game championship.

Though dreaming in this way, my respondents did recognize the challenges they faced coming from a small Indian city such as Udaipur, where sponsors were limited, the internet relatively unstable, and with little public knowledge about video gaming, much less active support. (Well-known video game "e-athletes" can win lucrative sponsorships, scholarships, etc., though such opportunities were limited in Udaipur.) A place such as Udaipur, I was told in frustration by one owner, "has no scope." And local gamers needed to look toward going elsewhere in India or abroad to advance, which was unrealistic for most of them. Assessing this situation one evening with a research collaborator via Skype, I was reminded of the way that many young African American men dreamed of playing basketball professionally, with such dreams and invariable disappointments traced so memorably in the documentary *Hoop Dreams*.[8]

Gaming as Subcultural Escape

Central to gamer pleasure was how video-game activities ran counter to mainstream Indian norms, in that players in video-game zones could behave in ways not tolerated at home or elsewhere in polite society. As one owner put it, "Have you heard how they cuss? And celebrate when they win? All the *galis* [insults], the shouting. They could never do that at home." This same owner went on to describe how a group of players once celebrated for ten minutes after a victory that pushed one of their teammates into the next higher CS-GO rank (as in MMOs, CS-GO players gained levels or ranks as they advanced in experience): "They scrambled about madly for a marker to put the new rank on the whiteboard. They were really excited. They would never get that way at home." Outside the watchful purview of parents and other moral guardians, in this "boy's tree house"[9], gamers knew they could "shout abusive language," I was told, and also scream, fight, curse, be crude, eat and drink whatever they wanted, all permissible gaming-zone activities. By contrast, many said they did not have the *iccha* (desire) to play at home. One gamer said he did not feel comfortable in one of the gaming zones because it was located in the owner's home, preferring instead to play in another locale: "In a home, things don't feel right. Here, it feels like we are proper gamers. Plus, the owner here, he's a good man."

Many gamers told me that they found in gaming zones an escape from life's problems. As one put it simply: "I can escape from the real world, forget about my problems." Another told me in gaming, which were described as "no-*chinta*" (no-worry) places: "all your frustrations leave." When asked for more detail, gamers described the pressure to get good grades and perform well on exams, which was particularly intense in the twelfth year of high school, right before university (i.e., those exams determined their university placements and thus potentially their career trajectories). Likewise, they spoke of how many young Indians, even those studying high-prestige subjects such as engineering felt they had "no future." There was too much competition from many other educated Indians, and Udaipur's unemployment rates were sky-high.

These details show how Udaipuri gaming needs to be put in the context of emerging adults' broader lives. As typically students in their late teens and early twenties, my respondents found needed stress relief in a particularly tense period of their lives when their futures would be determined. As stated in chapter 1, most Udaipuri young adults would have arranged marriages, and the pressure to earn a proper living that would allow them to support their families was keenly felt. Gaming, I was told directly, provided relief from such pressures. Demonstrating the almost one-to-one relationship between gaming and such familial expectations and pressures, I was told, and also witnessed firsthand, how marriage invariably ended gaming as a hobby. As one respondent put it, "Once you have a real job and family, you get 'stuck' there, and can't make time to play anymore."

One of my respondents told me that he liked CS-GO compared with other games because of its realism. By this he referred to the in-game maps' resemblance to actual real-world battlegrounds, such as the way the map *Dust 2* (a CS-GO map where players battled one another as *terrorists* and *counter-terrorists*) resembled actual Middle Eastern—rather than mythological and Tolkienesque, for example—places to do battle. But I would propose that gamers' avatars in Udaipur—with names such as MaYYnYa (mania), DeltaForce1stAlways, MrSexyyBoyy, JJ Loner, DacTicColdZebraGBoy—provided fantastic escape from actual-world pressures, as did the way my respondents, none of them soldiers themselves, used military-speak to callout enemy locations. These were "magic-circle" places partially set apart from the actual-world, which in their assumed identities and social networks provided temporary cultural alternatives to real-world society and its pressures, thus ironically also remaining importantly connected to actual-world spaces and concerns.[10]

Societal Moral Panics: A Technological "Addiction"

Despite the psychosocial benefits gamers experienced from their play, many outsiders to the hobby framed gaming differently. As mentioned, looming large in these gamers' lives was the need for careers to make them suitable for marriage. In the Hindu *brahmacharya* discourse referred to in chapter 1, gaming was typically condemned as an overstimulating and thus intemperate waste of this important life stage. Gamers were seen to cater to their base impulses, rather than learning to control and master (niyantran) them.

In Udaipur, parents often restricted mobile phone and computer access during the month of school exams. Although some were sympathetic to their sons' passions, they typically agreed with the "no-scope" assessment of gaming. They saw gaming as "too high risk" of a career option for their children and instead wanted more of "a sure, safe thing," to take one respondent's phrasing. Even if they were sympathetic to their sons' aspirations, and some were, they knew that future in-laws might not be, not wanting to place daughters in homes with uncertain futures. So, despite their sons' views on the matter, gaming was viewed from a parental perspective primarily as a "distraction" from the studies and exams that provided a clearer career path.

Coming from a traditional Brahmin background, one of my long-term research collaborators, Chakrapani Upadhyay, himself was uncomfortable with the intemperate chain smoking and cussing he witnessed with me during a 2016 play session. He was also surprised to learn that one of the gamers he met planned on attending medical school, and that others had similar aspirations. In his experience, serious students, and especially those seeking to win government scholarships, he told me, would not waste time that might be spent studying, a perspective shared by many he knew. A member of his own family, for example, was studying eighteen hours a day in preparation for the rigorous medical school board exams.

From a similar perspective, a local cybercafe I knew, the Advanced Academy, represented a more productive use of the internet. There, students were trained in software and digital-communication technologies in preparation for exams that would grant them a RSCIT (Rajasthan State Certificate in Information Technology), which was vital to both government and private-sector employment. In contrast to the all-male gaming zones, this academy was gender integrated, with young men and women working energetically in front of computers, learning tasks that would form the foundation of their future careers. Not surprisingly, this industrious Jain academy owner, Alok, spoke disparagingly of youth who were "addicted" to games and the internet. For him, they had developed a "taste and ardent desire" (chaska) for technologies that felt good but did not lead anywhere. Such habits (aadats) were not that different from tea, cigarettes, chewing tobacco, and other *nasha* (stimulants): in his words, they provided "highs" that eventually took over and "closed the mind," distracting from more important tasks. Even his teenage son, he lamented, was a "*nashi-wale*" (addict) when it came to games and the internet.

Clearly, this condemnation of certain forms of technology use was generational. One cybercafe owner (not a gaming-zone proprietor), a middle-class Hindu of forty-five years, openly acknowledged this: "Ask any youth and they'll say the internet's good. Ask most older adults, and they'll talk about the bad." Continuing, without irony, he said:

> Let me speak frankly, the internet is mainly horseshit things. Shit things. 90 percent horseshit things. 90 percent of young people are addicts [aadii]. The rest, 10 percent, use the internet for education and valuable things. All kids do is look and see who's online. They don't do anything worth anything. They spoil their lives. The internet is not good for Indian society.

Of note, this condemnation was applied most strongly to the internet generally. Though some adults saw the benefit of the internet for learning and for promoting Hinduism, many older Hindus I knew were particularly sensitive to the way that the internet had disrupted gender relations, putting young men and women into new and inappropriate contact with one another, and fueling young men's lust for sex through pornography, which, at the extreme, produced a Western lifestyle–inspired epidemic of premarital sex and also rape. This rhetoric's application to online gaming was more muted, largely because the hobby was new and poorly understood. It was only when their sons' grades plummeted, for example, that the "waste-of-time" rhetoric was applied to video gaming, coupled with restrictions on internet use and parental panic about their sons' futures.

Felt Distress

Many gamers acknowledged that they and others they knew had problems with compulsive play. One group spoke to me about a gamer they knew, whom I had met and watched play: "He went one hunderd hours straight without a break. He did not eat or sleep much, just a few short breaks here and there." Others spoke of their own experience: "I have been seriously addicted at different times. I played CS-GO and other games all the time and couldn't stop." Most acknowledged that gaming was a nasha (stimulant) that provided forms of excitement much like other intoxicating highs, which, if not properly controlled could take over one's life. Another gamer pursuing a MBBS (Bachelor of Medicine, Bachelor of Surgery), with dreams of attending medical school, told me: "I once played CS-GO for three days and two nights, around seventy-two hours total. I just kept gaming day and night. I was a complete addict." He said he had recovered, but was nonetheless gaming even the day we spoke, when he acknowledged he should have been studying for the next day's upcoming exam.

In fact, most gamers I knew spoke of how gaming could interfere even dramatically with their studies. One gamer said he only went to about "2 percent" of his classes, preferring to spend his time gaming with friends. Another said his university professor asked him to stop coming to classes, because his continued success and low attendance was "setting a bad example." Putting it simply, another young gamer said, "Yes, you can sometimes play too much, then your grades suffer. My grades did suffer. I did not study for four years straight, just video games, my grades plummeted." A friend of his chimed in, patting him on the back: "His parents just banned him again from gaming! No more play until his grades improve." I noted that though banned from playing, this individual still regularly visited the gaming zone and watched others play, joining in all the regular activities except the gaming itself. He also temporarily carried a "dumb" rather than "smart" phone, which was the only one his parents now let him use.

I asked my respondents if they were "addicted" or just "passionate" about gaming. One said: "Because you come one time, then another, then another. You have to keep playing. You keep coming back to play, and you can't stop. That's an addiction." Another told me: "It's an addiction when you need it." Interestingly, most of my respondents acknowledged that they were "addicted" in some form or another, even in a "big way," according to many. Then they'd invariably list exactly that symptom of compulsivity, speaking both for themselves and also often for others they knew: "We have to do it (karna to hai). Sometimes all we do is play video games." In fact, many respondents were quick to label themselves and friends as being addicted, with several reporting that "more than 90 percent" of young adults are addicted to the internet. Another respondent answered my addiction/passion question more philosophically:

> Beauty is in the eye of the beholder. And all things in moderation are fine. Smoking, drinking, gaming. They can all be good. But you can crash and reach saturation. That's not good. You need moderation. Three to four hours is a good max stretch for a gaming session. Anything more is too much.

．　．　．

This study's survey allowed me to confirm the qualitative research findings. Of note, gamers in the Udaipur sample experienced overall more positive compared with negative experiences. I would also highlight that my respondents generally felt moderately socially connected to online communities and supported and not typically lonely in their offline lives (see figure 22).

Of more direct interest to my arguments, the survey allowed me to confirm the positive and substantive relationship between feeling that one was a *true gamer* and self-reported positive gaming experiences. Considering individually those survey items that compose the "true gamer" success model—e.g., reporting that one had close friends who were gamers, felt more online social support, and more strongly pursued competitive gaming—each was associated with an increase in reports of positive gaming experiences. I then repeated this analysis, but this time analyzing relationships between the *true-gamer* identity predictors and negative gaming experiences. In those analyses, having close friends who were gamers was also associated with higher reports of negative experiences, as was self-reported loneliness, more strongly pursuing competitive gaming, and the experience that video gaming conflicted

FIGURE 22. Udaipur gamers respond to the author's online questionnaire. Photo by author.

with Indian traditions and values. Finally, positive and negative gaming experiences were highly positively correlated—individuals who reported higher positive gaming experiences were more likely to also report higher negative experiences—pointing to the manner that pleasurable and problematic "addictive" gaming were intertwined in this Udaipuri context. (For more detail on these survey results, see appendix C.)

SPIRIT POSSESSION AS AFFLICTION OR MEDICINE

The English term *shaman* comes originally from the Tungus language, *saman,* which refers to a spiritual healer among the aboriginal people of Siberia.[11] Saman literally means "one who shakes," because the saman's *ecstatic*—that is, "out-of-current-state"—experiences involve trance and physical shaking. The trance states are framed locally in Siberia as magical flights or soul journeys to distant spiritual realities, where the shaman experiences things not perceived by others, which can help them become powerful and respected persons. Early anthropologists and others noted that spiritual specialists-cum-healers around the world shared experiences and behaviors with these Siberian samans. The term saman thus became a general one to refer to other spiritual healers around the world. In this book, for example, Bedami might eventually become something like a full-fledged shamanic healer—referred to locally in Rajasthan as a *bhopa* or an *ojha*—even though the devi is said to enter Bedami, rather than, say, Bedami's own spirit journeying outside her physical body. Bedami's becoming a divine avatar thus shares certain features with Siberian samans (ecstatic experiences, the power to heal) but not others (possession rather than soul journeying).

As noted earlier in the book, shamans, whether in Siberia or elsewhere, are often "healed healers" in the sense that overcoming their own spiritual crises and illnesses produced in them the power to cure others.[12] Shamanic power is said to derive to a large extent from the command of hidden forces such as *spirits,* agents who inhabit other planes of existence not easily perceptible to humans. Some of those spirits might have originally been tormenting and dangerous. But in the process of their own personal healing, shamans learn to control and manipulate those forces. In some important sense, shamans around the world might be considered spiritually and morally ambiguous or even amoral, with powers that can be used to both heal and hurt. On the one hand, shamans can compel even dangerous and "evil" spirits to heal others, thus using their power for good. On the other hand, there is a dark side to shamans: they can command spiritual servants to harm or even kill others, with some shamans also commonly believed to be powerful sorcerers and practitioners of the dark arts.[13] Shamans, then, control hidden forces such as spirits, both good or evil ones, which they wield in a variety of productive or destructive ways. Shamanic morality emerges from the manner they manipulate spirits—to heal or hurt—rather than from the essential nature of the shaman themselves or the spirits they control. Context and perspective matter too: wielding evil spirits to destroy enemies in a neighboring village might be judged locally as good and right, though the members of the neighboring village would surely see it differently.[14]

These details provide perspective on the previous chapter's spiritual descriptions, where I discussed women's spiritual possessions around the world. We might ask, Are those women's spiritual experiences essentially negative and destructive or positive and productive? Are they more affliction or medicine? As in the shamanic details just discussed, context and perspective matter in how we assess these experiences. From her husband's point of view, for example, Karunavati Maniyo's devotion in Sri Lanka to the goddess Pattini means the loss of his wife.[15] For Karunavati, by contrast, the possession provides her with an escape from an intolerable marriage and unhappy situation. In Malaysia, factory supervisors might see women workers' fits as destructive and "demonic," shutting down, as they do, the factories' assembly lines.[16] But for the possessed women, spiritual possessions provide a vehicle for expressing discontent, which even helps them negotiate better livelihoods and living conditions. Similarly, zar spirits are judged as demonic illness in North African patriarchal Islam, but more like a "party" from the perspective of the "afflicted" women themselves.[17] And while Candomblé might be labeled devil worship in some Brazilian sectors of society, it is joyous and liberating for poor, black women such as Lucia.[18]

In Catholicism, which may be closer to some readers' experiences, one finds similar gendered tensions in the way spiritual possessions are judged. From the perspective of male Catholic priests, possessing spirits might typically be deemed demonic and thus needing exorcism, while, for women (and some men), those spirits might be experienced in positive terms as emotionally cathartic.[19] Likewise, young Catholic women (and men) historically and contemporaneously are known to be visited by the Virgin Mary, who in her apparitions can bestow on those persons novel visions and special knowledge.[20] Here, too, male priests might judge the events differently from the oftentimes young women directly experiencing the visitations. For male Catholic priests, such visions might be seen as heretical and dangerous, even as witchcraft, in the way the visions represent heterodox knowledge that might challenge patriarchal scripture and church law. But for the young women involved, these visitations can signal new ways of practicing spirituality, which might be felt to be more deeply satisfying, featuring, as they do, feminine points of view.

Finally, what we might call *political* influences on judgments about spirit possession are not limited to gender relations. For a striking example of this, one need only examine the Hauka cult that appeared in West Africa in the early twentieth century, in a part of the world that was an epicenter of the slave trade and British and French colonialism, which has been interpreted by the anthropologist Paul Stoller.[21] Many Hauka spirits were viewed locally as the deceased souls of colonial administrators and other figures. So, for example, this new religion's gods, who were known to possess Hauka cult devotees in dramatic fashion, included the Governor of the Red Sea, Sam Kaki the Train Engineer, and Madame LoCotoro, the doctor's wife. And the cult's religious symbols were items such as fan belts representing colonial authorities' whips and a termite mound that stood for the colonial governor's mansion. For colonial officials, such practices were heretical and to be stamped out. In fact, one official who tried to eliminate the cult himself became an important divinity in this religion's pantheon, the Wicked Major. For the Hauka practitioners themselves, however, these spiritual forces were worshipped as deities. In the Songhay language, *hauka* literally means "craziness." As interpreted by Stoller, the Hauka spirits served as vehicles through which black Africans critiqued and mocked white colonial society and its seemingly arbitrary exercise of power. Hauka practitioners channeled the "craziness" of white colonialism, themselves becoming crazy in the process, as they channeled that insane power into their own bodies, becoming divine avatars of a sort.[22]

DISCUSSION: CULTURAL DISSONANCE AND
AVATAR THERAPEUTICS

Not surprisingly, Bhats encouraged Bedami to take on this second devi identity and thus mantle of spirit medium—to be *consonant* with those religious and cultural ideals, in Dressler's terms[23]—which cements this role and identity for her as well as the dissociative experiences and mental health benefits associated with it. By embodying such a religious ideal in her own life, Bedami elevates her social standing, which, broadly recognized and appreciated within the Bhat community, contributes to her personal experience of well-being, a *status-syndrome* pattern Marmot points to in other contexts.[24] But in the same breath, in finding personal consonance with certain Hindu and Bhat values, Bedami comes into conflict with others, such as those related to Ramu's livelihood. The inability to reconcile these conflicting commitments leads to Bedami's feeling of *dissonance,* in Festinger's terms.[25] In this case, the felt dissonance is *cultural*—rather than just cognitive or psychological—in the manner it emerges from conflicts between alternate socially learned lifeways. And Bedami's avatar experiences thus evidence what I refer to in this chapter as *cultural dissonance.*[26]

As demonstrated throughout the Bhat ethnography, the power of the devi's voice, in this case to forge unity from conflict, contrasts with Bedami's own personal difficulty in finding her voice. As mentioned, the people in Bedami's community usually described her as *bholi*—which implied a simplicity of disposition as well as a tendency to bow to the will of more clever others. Such difficulty in being heard was especially troubling to Bedami given the talents of the other members of her family. Bedami's father was the wise and very vocal leader of the Udaipur Bhats, and her mother was similarly renowned for her cleverness. Each of Bedami's four sisters—to the chagrin of her father, Bedami had no brothers—was also considered unusually bright and expressive. Her eldest sister, Gita, was seen as one of the most able voices within the community, the one whom people turned to in times of stress, and the true brains of her marriage. (Gita and her husband had also moved to Udaipur. But, perhaps because of Gita's husband's relative docility, they experienced none of the troubles of Bedami and Ramu.) Bedami's younger sister, Santosh, was also viewed as one of the cleverest of all Bhats despite her mere thirteen years of age at the time of these events and sure to be a Bhat leader one day. Bhats turned to her, given her literacy and volubility, for most of their letter-writing needs. And Bedami's youngest sister was considered equally precocious and beautiful—the latter quality particularly troubling for Bedami given that physical attractiveness was her primary claim to recognition, as Bedami's parents once pointed out to me.

Bedami's difficulty in being heard might relate to the relative value placed on men's and women's voices in this community, as seen for example in chapter 3's descriptions of women's spiritual possessions.[27] After all, women in north India are generally asked to demonstrate verbal and emotional restraint before fathers, husbands, and other men.[28] And in this context, possession itself was certainly a gendered phenomenon: Chavanda Mata herself was feminine, and women accounted for most of the goddess's supplicants; men, if they participated at all, lingered hesitatingly at the door waiting to ask a few terse questions. Similarly, the Bhat experience with the new economy was framed by ideas about the proper behavior of men and women—men earned money outside the home, and women, referred to as like the goddess Lakshmi, typically decided how such money was spent in the maintenance of the household. Nonetheless, such a construal, though surely partially correct, would ignore that Bedami's mother and sisters did not experience such a difficulty airing their opinions or having their voices heeded. Neither would it account for the fact that Bhats, unlike many Indian communities, recognized remarkable equality between the two sexes.

Whatever the origins of her difficulty with voice—whether gender expectations, personal difficulties, intrafamilial dynamics, or something else—Bedami, as the goddess, was endowed with a violently expressive manner of speaking and moving that contrasted with her typical calm when not possessed. Previously silent and even invisible, when possessed, Bedami became the focus of Bhat attention, heard and recognized in an unprecedented manner. Nowhere was this reversal more apparent to me than when Bedami's mother, among others, fell begging and whimpering before the "terrible and dangerous" (katharnak) divinity, who had settled into Bedami's flesh. According to an interpretation of spirit possession as a gendered critique, Bedami in this way seemed to find the voice and presence that so eluded her in everyday life.

But such a perspective, I feel, does not do justice to the confusion, disorder, and very literal *failure* of voice that also sometimes characterized Bedami's person when incarnated as the goddess. During her initial seizures, Bedami, for the most part, did not speak. Rather, she voicelessly tore at her clothes and rolled madly about. At this point, her movements and anger, unfocused as they were, were directed simultaneously at Ramu, whom she chased through the door of their home, at her relatives, who tried, often unsuccessfully, to restrain her, as well as at her own body, as when she beat her head angrily against the walls of her home. When Bedami uttered any sounds at all, they were usually screams, rants, and sighs of pain. When a word or two escaped her lips, the phrase was typically fragmentary or repetitive—for example, a passionate and perplexing repetition of the phrase, "Wrong! Wrong!"

Bedami's identification as Chavanda Mata's avatar did, in some sense, give her a firmer and more centered voice. And in the course of each episode, her violent fits became more ordered—after a while, she typically panted rhythmically in place and breathed staccato-like with her hands clasped above her head, rather than raging across the room. But, even after her initial seizures were finally identified as spiritual possession rather than insanity, Bedami still demonstrated, during the descent of the goddess into her earthly vehicle, mostly an almost impossible struggle to speak, to allow even the simplest of phrases to escape her lips. Bedami typically answered questions put to her in incomplete phrases, often incomprehensible, and always choked by a litany of gasps, sobs, gurgles, coughs, and moans. This explained why questions of a yes or no form—"Will I get that job in Sikkar?"—or at least questions that allowed for one-word answers—"Whose ghost is pursuing me?"—were typically put to her. Any response longer than a few words was next to impossible. And, in fact, such a fragmentary voice, or lack of voice, was typical of many forms of spiritual possession experienced by Rajasthani women, as referenced in chapter 2's descriptions of possessions in this Indian state.

Bedami's identification as the goddess, then, did not totally relieve her problem of voice and her problematic perspective on the changes around her. If anything, her possession exacerbated her already tremendous difficulty in articulating her experience. As the goddess, Bedami was pulled even more forcefully in different directions by diverse factions within the community who struggled to contain and control her power and meaning. Unable to take sides in this dispute, Bedami fell even more deeply into a structured kind of possession theater—at times, simply sitting and swaying and panting wordlessly, at other moments, lunging madly at unseen enemies and ranting incoherently—a performance that, despite its characteristically loud emotional outbursts, kept Bedami, once again, paradoxically silent.

Spiritual possessions such as Bedami's are sometimes interpreted as a protest against gendered and capitalist forms of oppression, often combined, as in Aihwa Ong's work in Malaysia discussed in chapter 3.[29] Bedami's spiritual experience, in effect, was a kind of protest both against her husband's demands and against the new economy; at certain moments, Bedami even seemed to experience it as such. But, for the greater part, one might question whether Bedami herself experienced her possession as a protest, conscious or unconscious—or, rather, largely as an inability to protest. Unable to articulate her experience through narratives that univocally condemned or celebrated her husband as an agent of change, Bedami, at times, multiplied herself so as to be two different persons—the loyal and loving wife and the demanding devi. But, I would also suggest that Bedami, at other moments of her possession, seemed to drop into a confused and typically speechless state that was not associated with any clearly defined person. Bedami's spiritual possession was not simply a multiplication of herself into a number of conflicting selves, though it was surely this in part, but a failure to locate herself exactly in any stable and coherent self. As the devi, and especially in those gasping speechless moments, Bedami seemed, at times, to be caught somewhere between her various possible selves.

In this sense, it is hard to distinguish clearly between Bedami's avatar experiences as a cure for her psychosocial afflictions or affliction in its own right. Therapy and illness are inextricably tied together. This is because the two were not experienced by Bedami as distinctive states of being, with the presence of therapeutic devi experiences—and indeed Bedami's new role as spirit medium—meaning the absence of ghost illness. Rather, Bedami experienced the positive and the negative—the devi's powerful, often comforting presence, the inability to articulate clear sentences—both simultaneously. Once again, Bedami's split consciousness, as I show throughout the book, emerged from the fact that she was torn between two social worlds—her husband's and her natal family's. And what was considered good, proper, and healthy by her husband Ramu—a steady job and salary, spending money to better one's own family—was seen as problematic by the broader Bhat community—who, referencing older systems of clan and socioeconomic interdependence, valued generosity in a broader sense. Thus, as in the digital cases, whether Bedami's avatar experiences were perceived as therapeutic or not, then, depended importantly in part on who was doing the perceiving and how those perceptions ultimately influenced the way Bedami herself made sense of her spiritual visitations.

Bedami, as the devi's avatar, then, did achieve, at least at times, a superior social identity and standing, which, as highlighted in this book's earlier discussions, could in turn promote positive experience and health. Following the classic shamanic healed-healer pattern, Bedami over time gained some modicum of control over her spiritual "sickness" in a manner that allowed her to improve her situation and indeed to help others do so, as their spiritual medium and guide.[30] Nevertheless, as this chapter's details reveal, Bedami, at least at the time my research concluded, had not totally controlled her spiritual visitations so that they were unequivocally a positive force in her life. Yes, she was lauded as the devi, the very embodiment of the goddess on earth.

And yes, too, in that role, she helped others. But she also could suffer during the devi's visits. And though Bedami, as the devi, aimed to "fix" her husband's mind and thus mend divisions within the Bhat community, bettering Bedami's own situation in the process, it was not yet clear that events would unfold as Bedami hoped. In fact, in some instances, the devi's visitation seemed to place *greater* strain on relations between Bedami and her husband, and between Ramu and the rest of the Bhats. In this sense, Bedami's avatar experiences were at once healing and debilitating.

The therapeutic nature of Bedami's avatar experiences depended on the extent to which she balanced and negotiated the demands from her various social worlds. This process was aided by psychosocial forces, such as Bedami valuing the presence she felt in her body, as god, rather than devaluing it, as just some troublesome spirit. Interpreting the presence as the devi enhanced Bedami's second self's status, potentially magnifying the health benefits of Bedami's avatar experiences. That interpretation also seemed to help bring Ramu closer to the other Bhats, given the way the whole community, Ramu included, saw a visitation by the devi as a blessing, though they interpreted its meaning differently. Valuing her felt presence in this way, then, seemed to allow Bedami to better reconcile herself with *all* the important people in her life, which could help relieve her felt tension and *dissonance*. Whether Bedami's avatar experiences could in the end be said to be more therapeutic than toxic depended again both on how much she gained compared with what she lost in her transformation, both in terms of her social standing and peace of mind, and also, most importantly, the extent to which her new spiritual form allowed her to successfully negotiate and mend the various tensions she experienced in her community and in her mind.

Overall, Bedami is torn between two alternate, and often competing, sociocultural (and in this case also economic) worlds. In Bedami's case, the first world was that of her husband Ramu, who was driven by a pursuit of money and seemingly by what has been called a modern ethic of possessive individualism. The second world was that of Bedami's natal family, and indeed the devi herself, who placed value on generosity and community. Further, Bedami feels tension between those two worlds, drawn alternately into each. It is Bedami's dissociation into her alternative devi identity and mediumship role, experienced as highly moral and thus superior, that seemed to partially bridge the distance between her husband Ramu and the rest of the Bhat community, thus improving Bedami's experience of well-being. Although in the process, Bedami, as the devi, also risked alienating herself further from her husband Ramu, who had his own moral justification for his "possessive" thinking and behavior. How Bedami personally embodies these cultural tensions in her own life, and seeks to resolve the felt incompatibilities, is what I call *cultural dissonance*.

This chapter's other spirit-possession descriptions point to similar cultural tensions. Karunavati Maniyo finds in her devotion to the goddess Pattini and marriage to the god Kataragama some relief from an unhappy prior earthly marriage. But Karunavati's husband and his relatives, as Obeyesekere shows in his ethnography, do not simply go away.[31] Women working on Malaysian assembly lines likewise lodge spiritual protests, which seem cathartic to them, even allowing them in some cases to improve their livelihoods and personal situations. But these possession experiences also bring risks, to these women's livelihoods and persons.[32] And dancing while possessed in a North African zar cult, however joyous, is also judged to be demonic from other cultural points of view,[33] with similar patterns seen in Brazilian Candomblé,[34] Catholic Marion visitations,[35] and the West African Hauka cult.[36] My ethnographic experience alongside the spirit possession literature would lead me to anticipate finding similar *cultural dissonance* patterns in each of these settings.

This chapter's gaming ethnography, carried out in the Indian town of Udaipur, unfolded primarily in face-to-face *gaming zones*. Ethnographically, I learned about the deep pleasures associated with play that was at once face to face and digitally networked. At the heart of such enjoyment were the local friendships. But the friendships had as their context gaming subculture, whose pleasures emerged from "enskillment," competition, connection to a larger global community, and cultivating a distinctive "gamer" style and pattern of consumption, which here opposed mainstream Indian norms. And alternative gaming identities—enacted through online avatars—provided my young-adult respondents needed therapeutic escapes from the pressures and expectations of their lives related to school, relationships, work, and their future careers and arranged marriages.

My gaming ethnographic data showcased moments of camaraderie and high emotion experienced by gamers in the three gaming zones where I worked. While the thrills of a well-fought victory would eventually diminish, requiring another successful match with teammates to bring about a new gaming high, the friendships that existed outside of the game were what fostered a true sense of community for these individuals. Gaming zones created spaces where gamers, committed to honing their craft and seeking the next rush from in-game dominance, could come together and experience highs and lows together, with shared communal feelings amplifying euphoric moments. The survey confirmed these ethnographic observations, demonstrating, for example, how having close gamer friends, more support from online others, a more competitive gaming spirit, and *less* support from society for gaming drove the positive gaming experiences. The latter finding highlighted the way these pleasures were tied to the experience of inhabiting a distinctive gaming subculture, which was in many ways opposed to mainstream Indian society.

Of interest to this chapter's cultural-consonance and dissonance arguments, Udaipuri gamers dissociated into their (oftentimes) superior second avatar selves, becoming personally *consonant* with gamer subcultural models of success and sociality in the process, in ways that helped to improve their lives. But in relation to felt *dissonance,* embodying values associated with a second digital life could sometimes mean rejecting, or at least seriously challenging, the social norms where one's first life unfolded. That is, being *consonant* with the values and norms shaping an avatar identity can mean being *dissonant,* or out of sync, with first-life society. As such, avatar processes in these digital contexts too can require serious psychosocial negotiations, as it is not simple for individuals to simply reject worlds where their primary identities unfold. And the outcome of those negotiations shape the extent to which avatar identities are therapeutic or, by contrast, detrimental to overall psychosocial well-being.

More specifically, I learned that many Udaipuris did not approve of online behavior such as gaming, judging it a potentially addictive distraction from young adults' more important cultivation of a lucrative career, which would position them better for marriage. Some of this condemnation of behaviors facilitated by the new technological innovation of the internet shared features of what has been described in another Chinese gaming context as *moral panic.*[37] But importantly, many of my gamer respondents themselves claimed to be dangerously addicted to online gaming, rendering incomplete societal moral panic theories of gaming addiction. This study's survey analysis confirmed that similar processes driving positive play experiences were also linked to negative ones. That is, having close friends who were gamers, lacking social support, playing more competitively, and feeling opposed to and in conflict with Indian society were each positively associated with higher self-reported negative gaming experiences. Importantly, survey analysis confirmed the ethnographic insight that positive and negative gaming experiences were strongly associated with each other in this Indian play context. That is, many of the *same* players reporting highly positive play also said they had strongly negative play experiences.

Prompted especially by that one respondent's "beauty is in the eye of the beholder" type-answer to my question about gaming as a passion or an addiction, I feel that my respondents' experiences of their play as simultaneously positive and negative were colored by the fact that they inhabited two different worlds. As committed gamers, they were passionate. Gaming was the center of their social and aspirational lives, and so they demonstrated deep commitment to the activity. But they were also young men with future aspirations of having a good job and happy marriage. From that second point of view, they acknowledged the risks inherent to spending all their time in this way, which could lead them to judge as addictive the very experiences that lent their current lives purpose and meaning. Neither they as gamers nor their parents as concerned caregivers were right or wrong. Each represented a valid cultural point of view, with gamers themselves inhabiting simultaneously both perspectives only with difficulty.

To understand the positive and negative feelings experienced by Udaipur gamers, I again employ the idea of *cultural dissonance:* a merging of Dressler's cultural consonance (adherence to cultural models) with Festinger's cognitive dissonance (the stress that results from holding incongruent thoughts or behaving in contrasting behaviors). In other work in the US, I found that WoW players experiencing higher levels of gaming compared with offline success could increasingly value their play in order to justify and validate the amount of time spent in Azeroth and thereby reduce their felt dissonance.[38] Udaipuri gamers, too, and particularly those who were experiencing greater CS-GO success, could also come to value online over offline achievements and social relations. However, in the Udaipur context, I cannot easily dismiss gamers' simultaneous commitment to mainstream Indian values. Arguably, for these Indian gamers, as compared with US gamers, conforming to mainstream norms were more socially monitored. And given how older Udaipuris condemned internet activities such as gaming as addictive, it is likely that my respondents partially internalized such a stigma in their own self-concept. Such an interpretation could help explain how gamers in this Rajasthani town simultaneously reported that video gaming was the basis of their happiness and satisfaction in life, as well as a potentially dangerously addictive form of recreation. As in Bedami's case, Udaipuri CS-GO gamers inhabited multiple cultural worlds. This led to my respondents' need to negotiate and minimize tensions between those two worlds—here, belonging to a global community of online gamers, and being marriageable-age Hindu sons needing to think of their future careers— to reduce their felt dissonance.

The dissonance experienced by these Indian gamers—resulting from being part of a gaming brotherhood and belonging to larger Indian society that had very distinct expectations of masculinity—left them in a difficult catch-22. The pressures to do well in school, to find a good job, and to marry were stressful. Gaming served as a magic circle to forget about such stressors, while forming meaningful and important social bonds. Yet, this very community distributed my informants' attention and energy across two incompatible cultural worlds, rendering their identity and consciousness double and divided. In one sense, my gamer respondents were digital denizens, connected via global mediascapes to larger internet culture through their "true-gamer" identities and e-sports aspirations, which placed them in an idealized imagined community of like-minded CS-GO players. But once they left these gaming zones and were no longer collaborating with clan mates and defusing digital bombs (the latter is one important in-game CS-GO action), they returned to the other reality of their lives, where their worth and futures were contingent on school test scores, entry into prestigious universities, and marriage to suitable partners. The digital escapades that they had spent hours honing were now from mainstream points of view just "horseshit things," a form of cheap escapism.

And gamers themselves sometimes referred to their play in similar terms, labeling their own play an addictive waste of time. As shown in the ethnography, my informants typically spoke of gaming in these negative terms in the context of pressures felt from society and their families related to their grades, careers, and future lives. Labeling their play as addictive was often followed by comments that they needed to study or work more, or to spend their time and money in more productive and socially acceptable ways, or to focus more on "serious" life concerns related to their careers and impending marriages. Speaking of their play in negative terms, then, though distressful in some sense, also helped realign my respondents more fully with dominant social norms. Further, such a realignment was necessary, given that I was told by all the gaming-center owners and gamers alike that a "true-gamer" lifestyle would *without exception* end after marriage. In these terms, framing their gaming as addictive—and thus by contrast their nongaming lives as superior in some sense—minimized the cognitive and emotional dissonance they might feel when imagining their necessary and impending futures as husbands and householders, compared with their current joyous and carefree existences. That is, speaking in the language of addiction helped my respondents transition to their next householder stage of life, by distancing themselves from their past addictions. When viewed through the lens of Festinger's theory of cognitive dissonance, this framing of their hobby as only a temporary addiction, one that would end after university and marriage—again, a sentiment expressed by zone owners and their clients alike—allowed these gamers to reduce the cognitive stress of inhabiting two competing cultural spheres. That this process involved attempts to minimize distress arising from commitment to conflicting cultural norms—related to true-gamer identity, and to local marriage and career expectations—explains why I refer to it as *cultural* rather than merely *cognitive* dissonance.

Based on these details, I hope readers will appreciate that there is no simple way to distinguish between therapeutic and toxic forms of immersion in this Indian gaming context. This is because the two are not distinctive states of mind, with the presence of therapeutic gaming experiences meaning the absence of toxic ones (and vice versa). Rather, therapeutic and toxic gaming are intricately intertwined, with Indian CS-GO players more typically experiencing them simultaneously. This is due to the fact that, as I show repeatedly in the last two chapters, gamers simultaneously inhabit two worlds, one online, and the other offline (and also in the Udaipur case, one in gaming zones, the other outside them). And what is often good, proper, and healthy in the online world—passionate, competitive, successful play—can be seen as problematic, addictive, and toxic in offline contexts—in the way too passionate video-game play can distract young adults in particular from other important life goals. Whether gaming is judged as therapeutic or toxic, then, depends on who is doing the judging and on whether that judgement is more influenced by online gaming or offline real-life (RL) points of view.

Or, to put it another way, I show in chapter 3 how achieving in-game success can provide gamers with a second superior self-concept and social standing, which in turn promote positive experience and health. *Achieving gaming success, then, is the heart of avatar therapeutics.* But likewise, as shown in earlier chapters and again here, achieving gaming success can mean investing less fully in offline RL goals, which can erode studies, careers, and actual-world relationships. *In these terms, achieving gaming success is also centrally implicated in toxic forms of gaming immersion.* The very source of therapeutic play, then, is also what produces toxic gaming. There is no way to avoid this, though, as I show in this chapter, some gamers better balance and negotiate demands associated with their two at-times conflictual lives. This can entail psychological processes—such as overvaluing WoW play, as some US gamers do,[39] or devaluing it, as we saw in the current Indian case—which can help relieve felt tension and dissonance. Whether video-game play can in the end be said to be more therapeutic as compared with toxic depends in part on the relative degree of gaming-related pleasure compared with distress, which in turn partially depends on gamers' relative success in their game-world of choice compared with their RL success. But, as more centrally argued in this chapter, this also depends on the extent to which gamers successfully negotiate tensions oftentimes felt to exist between their second avatar and first RL lives, thus pointing to utility of a cultural-dissonance—rather than a more direct-consonance—approach.

CONCLUSION

In this chapter's *cultural-dissonance* idea, I suggest that cultural norms discussed by William Dressler—in the form of socially learned frames of meaning to which individuals variably commit and embody in their lives—can be thought of as a particular form of the beliefs or ideas alluded to by Leon Festinger. Dressler tells us that individuals can be consonant or dissonant with a cultural frame of reference. Combining Dressler's framework with that of Festinger's, I point to a *double* process of consonance and dissonance. First, individuals can successfully embody, and thus be consonant or dissonant, with not one but several separate cultural norms. Consonance with each of the two norms, as Dressler tells us, can lead to positive feelings of happiness and satisfaction. Dissonance with one or both of the norms produces distress. Second, cultural norms or models can themselves be more or less consonant or dissonant *with one another*. Consonance between two or more norms, experienced initially or arrived at by changing or justifying one's beliefs or commitments, would produce feelings of harmony, satisfaction, and other positive sentiments. By contrast, dissonance between conflicting norms would lead to feelings of stress and anxiety as well as, potentially, to the attempt to eliminate or minimize such contradictions. Overall, the experience of psychological well-being would depend in these contexts on the extent to which individuals, first, more or less personally embody not one but several cultural norms and, second, manage to successfully reconcile the potentially conflicting frameworks of value and commitment established by these norms. This would especially be the case when embodying and negotiating competing normative models related to achieving the status of a successful person living the good life. Following this line of thinking, I have shown in this chapter how individuals in spiritual and gaming contexts alike negotiate between alternate socially transmitted cultural understandings, rather than between their purely personal ideals or commitments. These situations led me to rework Festinger's ideas, bringing them together with Dressler's, to speak of the importance to avatar-therapeutic processes of *cultural* rather than merely *cognitive* dissonance processes.

This chapter's analysis builds on and extends my earlier avatar-therapy arguments. For example, this chapter's reference to cultural norms helps explain why individuals are led to *dissociate*—in Krippner's, Lynn's, Seligman's, Kirmayer's and others' language[40]—into alternative avatar identities and realities, where they experience stress relief, chapter 2's focus. In part, this relates to the fact that those avatar identities are culturally—or *sub*culturally—valued and thus attractive. Human psychology is still at work but in the context of cultural valuations. Likewise, this chapter's analysis draws attention to how self-concepts are shaped in reference to mainstream or more alternative cultural norms, with those social standards helping to determine the experience of a primary or alternative self as more or less *ideal,* which is relevant to Higgins' SDT framework and my analysis in chapter 3.[41] As I use the term, *cultural consonance* is in part a *self-concept:* prompted by a researcher-observer, respondents step outside themselves and assess, report, and even claim a particular status in relation to a shared norm, whether for their avatar or for their actual-world self. Reconceptualizing cultural consonance in part as a self-concept highlights the manner that cultural dissonance might be especially relevant when individuals try to maintain coherence in an overarching self-concept informed by competing cultural norms. And forming a coherent concept of self that incorporates *both* avatar and RL identities has important implications for experiences of well-being in all the spiritual and digital case studies considered in this book.[42] Further, the cultural consonance/dissonance framework has allowed me to assess social status in spiritual- and digital-avatar contexts in culturally sensitive manners, thus extending Marmot's Whitehall ideas beyond that context with implications for chapter 3's *status-syndrome* analysis.[43] However, this chapter features that cultural "we"-thinking that I briefly referenced in chapter 3's conclusion.[44] In assessing and reporting their individual consonance or dissonance with a cultural standard, respondents step outside their personal point of view in order to think about their life success in relation to a group standard that presumably they and others know is important to the group and its members, whether they personally share that point of view or not. That is, they assess their congruence with that standard from the perspective of a cultural "we" rather than a purely personal one. In analyzing avatar therapeutics from a cultural consonance and dissonance perspective, then, this chapter focuses on processes that are not only *psychosocial,* such as those featuring in chapter 3, but also more fully psycho-socio-*cultural.*

This brings us close to the end of this book. The substantive analysis complete, there now remains the task of summing everything up and thinking a bit more about a few remaining topics, such as the future prospects for avatar-therapeutics research.

Conclusion

AS STATED IN THE BOOK'S introduction, my understandings of spiritual-avatar experiences, based largely on anthropological analyses of spirit possession, have shaped my interpretations of the digital-gaming experiences described in this book. The book is thus in some sense an *application* of insights developed in the anthropology of religion to new digital-internet realities. However, I also have drawn on other fields—including communication, psychology, and epidemiology—to draw out the more universal features of avatar experiences. My reference to digital-gaming immersion,[1] Higgins's self-discrepancy theory,[2] and Marmot's status-syndrome ideas[3] is thus aimed at developing a more abstract analytical language that makes sense of both spiritual- and digital-avatar therapeutic processes. In this sense, the book aims to *integrate* anthropological approaches to spirit possession with perspectives developed in other fields on psycho-socio-cultural processes in general. I hope in doing so I illuminate for readers how a general human capacity to inhabit avatar identities can shape well-being in positive or negative ways depending on the cultural context. This points to how avatar-therapeutic identities, though commonly found around the world in many different contexts, are not homogeneously enacted in those various settings. That is, avatar-therapeutic processes are *universal but not uniform,* to again reference cultural-psychologist Richard Shweder's idea.[4]

As shown in this book, Bedami Bhat experienced what anthropologists call "ecstasy"—that is, experiences that allowed her to step outside or transcend her current identity and situation, from the Greek *ekstasis,* which literally means "standing outside a current state."[5] Social scientists and clinicians alike refer to such states as *dissociative,* characterized as they are by a divided or partitioned consciousness, where part of the self becomes separated off—

dissociated—from the whole person.[6] In Bedami's case, that dissociated part of her person was eventually labeled the devi in that Hindu context. Here, a Hindu divinity, Chavanda Mata, was seen to project her consciousness into an earthly vehicle, Bedami, who served as her spiritual medium. In this book, I have described Bedami as a divine avatar.

In fact, avatar experiences such as Bedami's are common across cultures. Anthropologists typically describe them as spiritual possessions, where a god or spirit of some kind is understood to possess or gain control of the consciousness of a human being.[7] Clinicians are most likely to employ the language of dissociation, as in the case of dissociative identity disorder (DID), also referred to as multiple personality disorder (MPD).[8] For anthropologists, following local belief systems, such experiences are often treated as beneficial, helping individuals better manage and cope with life problems and even, in the case of spirit mediums, aid others.[9] Anthropologists note, for example, that many local medical systems—referred to as ethnomedicine— feature spirit mediums as healers.[10] By contrast, clinicians more typically identify dissociative conditions as illnesses or disorders—e.g., note how the term *disorder* features both in the labels DID and MPD.[11] Bridging the two perspectives in ways that remain sensitive to local culture, anthropologists do note that many spirit mediums follow the classic healed-healer pattern, where what was once an affliction, a ghost illness, is transformed over time into a source of power and good health.[12]

In this book, I focus on how Bedami's avatar experiences seem predicated on helping her positively address her life problems, such as her husband Ramu's alienation from the rest of the Bhat community, though it was not clear when my research ended how effective the devi's visitation was in that regard. Bedami, as the devi's avatar, did seem to parallel (at least in part) that common healed-healer pattern identified cross-culturally by anthropologists. Her early visitations were distressful: possessed as she was by a powerful feeling, she at first alternated between states in which she screamed and rolled madly about in the dust and others where she sat motionless and almost paralyzed, panting and incapable of speech. But over time, Bedami gained greater control over the devi. The goddess started visiting mainly when summoned in the context of community puja worship, which entailed offerings of incense, devotional chants, and sacred music. Over time, the devi rarely arrived uninvited into Bedami's body. Also, over time, when the devi was interpreted to have taken control of her earthly vehicle, Bedami appeared calmer, panting rhythmically, a sign of divinity, but generally sitting quietly and responding calmly to questions put to her, in ways that were seen to help others in the community.

I turn in this book to anthropological and interdisciplinary perspectives to help explain the avatar-therapeutic processes characteristic of Bedami's experiences. In Chapter 2, I focus on the positive benefits of those avatar experiences, such as how the devi provided Bedami with a second identity, a vehicle for potent dissociative episodes,[13] which allowed her to voice concerns she had in relation to her husband Ramu and thus partially relieve stress and suffering in her life.[14] In Chapter 3, drawing on Higgins's self-discrepancy theory,[15] I focus on how Bedami, in becoming the goddess, improved her self-image and elevated her social standing in the eyes of members of the Bhat community. To the Bhats, Bedami, when transformed into a Hindu goddess, was the very embodiment of sacred truth and morality, and a striking contrast to this young woman's more typical status as subordinate wife. Further, Bedami, as the devi's avatar, became the focus of Bhat attention during the puja ceremonies carried out in her honor. This also contrasted with Bedami's socially marginal position within Bhat society, given her marriage to the "troublesome" Ramu, whose actions had alienated him and his family from others within the group, relegating them to the social margins. All in all, such psychosocial transformations, I note, helped Bedami better manage her stress and improve her mental health and well-being, with my analysis framed in relation to health disparities research conducted by Marmot and others.[16]

However, in Chapter 4, I highlight the different ways Bedami's devi identity was interpreted by her husband. I show how Bedami, and the devi too, were pulled in conflicting directions by various Bhats, which created additional stress for Bedami. This created for Bedami *cultural dissonance*,[17] I suggest in that chapter's concluding discussion. I emphasize how Bedami's devi visitation was for her simultaneously therapeutic and distressful, boon and bane. And I argue that whether Bedami's avatar experiences ultimately were more positive and therapeutic rather than distressing depended on how well Bedami's new identity helped her manage and negotiate various strains she felt in her family and community. In the analytical language of this book, the avatar therapeutics of Bedami's situation depended on the extent she could maximize the benefits from her embodiment or *consonance*[18] with Hindu moral ideals (as manifested in her second devi self) and minimize the *dissonance*[19] she experienced, given the way her new avatar identity both solved some of her life problems but also created new ones for her (the devi meant different things to Ramu compared with other Bhats).

I would add one further detail about the social dynamics of Bedami's possession: Bedami, in her spirit-possession role, was also frequented by non-Bhats, including high-caste ones, living in the Udaipur shanty colony where I was doing field research. Once Bedami's spiritual visitor was identified (more or less consensually) to be a Hindu goddess, word quickly spread in this Bhat colony situated on the northern outskirts of Udaipur city, which was inhabited by poor families of diverse origins, including high-caste Brahmin and Rajput. It was particularly striking to me to see high-caste individuals, male and female alike, some elderly, some relatively wealthy, bowing, and in a few cases weeping, before the young Bedami, as they pleaded for their prayers to be answered. On these occasions, I noted to myself how standard Hindu social hierarchies—based on gender, age, wealth, and caste—were reversed. I have focused in this book on how Bedami's second avatar identity gave her a higher social standing relative to other Bhats within her community. However, the social ramifications of Bedami's avatar transformation were broader than this. Bedami, as the devi, experienced a more general elevation in her self-image and social status, which, following Higgins's, Marmot's, and Dressler's reasonings, could bring additional positive health benefits to her.[20]

In fact, many spiritual possessions around the world feature hierarchical reversals such as I describe here. Readers may recall my references to I. M. Lewis's famous *deprivation hypothesis* of religious trance.[21] Lewis shows how spirit possessions often allow subordinated individuals, such as women and the poor, to express themselves in new ways, providing them with novel opportunities for social recognition and emotional catharsis, with positive health and well-being implications. This idea resonates with Bedami's situation, further illustrating how her avatar transformation influenced her social standing, with that elevation potentially contributing not only to her individual well-being but also the well-being of her nuclear family and indeed to the Bhat community as a whole. After all, Bedami's family and the Bhat community now possessed a valuable spiritual resource, access to which was desired by others in their neighborhood.

I add these details to this culminating discussion of spiritual avatars to give readers more to think about regarding how Bedami's transformation was an eminently sociocultural one, with further implications for the importance of avatar therapeutics for health-disparities research. I have drawn attention in this book to internal Bhat societal hierarchies. But around the world, psychosocial avatar transformations such as Bedami's have even greater potential to positively influence the health and well-being of individuals belonging to low-status communities such as the Bhats, with those benefits not only generated according to the internal workings of local communities.

. . .

Research on spiritual avatars, including my own analysis of Bedami Bhat's situation, informs my thinking on digital-avatar therapeutics, which is the second substantive empirical focus of this book. Specifically, as I show throughout this book, anthropologists and others point to the positive benefits of dissociative experiences, how such temporary breaks from reality and leaps into alternative identities can reduce stress and improve health.[22] This book's central conceit is that spiritual avatars find their parallel in digital-gaming avatars, which serve as vehicles into which video game players project their consciousness and identity. Archaic ecstasy[23] has come online, so to speak. And forms of dissociation originally primarily facilitated by spiritual practices have contemporary corollaries in online gaming worlds such as *World of Warcraft*. Combining as they do persistent and immersive virtual realities and landscapes with engaging tasks and challenges related to character creation and advancement, games such as WoW help players to escape ordinary reality. Easily accessible and popular as it was, WoW's lands of Azeroth provided me with an ideal context to examine avatar therapeutics related to so-called normal (or "normative") dissociation[24] in a contemporary digital context. Overall, I found that psychological absorption-cum-dissociation, or what is sometimes referred to by media and communications scholars as *immersion*,[25] does promote positive health and is reminiscent in many ways of avatar-therapeutic processes characteristic of Bedami's devi experiences.

In chapter 2, I focus first on establishing that certain players immersed so fully in WoW that they felt like they really were *in* the game and sometimes *actually* their avatar-character, fully identifying with their WoW characters as a kind of second self. That is, I show how *World of Warcraft*—and more generally multiplayer online role-playing games (MMOs) of which WoW is but one example—promoted a partitioned[26] or dissociated consciousness. Further, I describe in some detail the form and frequency of WoW dissociative experiences, as well as how such experiences were connected to positive subjective well-being outcomes. I find that players of online video games such as WoW commonly reported reaching deeply immersive states of consciousness, losing themselves in computer-generated fantasy landscapes and attributing dimensions of self and experience to in-game characters. Imaginatively immersed in WoW, some players' psychological processes related to perception, memory, and identity could feel distorted, as compared with everyday reality. Some lost themselves so fully in the game that they became unaware of events happening around them in the rooms where they played. In losing themselves in the absorptive tasks and adventures provided by online games such as WoW, many players found stress relief by temporarily escaping into WoW's virtual sandboxes and tree houses.[27] Players dissociating more deeply in WoW also reported that such experiences enhanced their perception that this game contributed to their happiness and life satisfaction.

In chapter 3, I show how online gaming groups referred to as *guilds*[28]—in-game associations of like-minded players—could draw players into intensive online commitments. This was especially the case when gaming guilds organized players into achievement-oriented collaborative events such as WoW raids, where multiple players together tried to defeat challenging end-game content and powerful bosses. More casual raiding guilds such as the Knights of Good (KOG), a WoW group I knew well, balanced its in-game ambitions with a respect for offline life commitments and a moral imperative "to do good in the world." The KOG guild generally promoted positive play experiences for its members and protected them from over-play. By contrast, hardcore WoW raiding guilds strived to be the first to complete MMO end-game content, thereby satisfying members' ambitions. Failure and defeat were less acceptable in such contexts, and, to avoid them, such guilds could require members to give, in their own estimation, too much to the game, compromising their offline lives.

Overall, in chapter 3, I show how some guilds, such as KOG, better helped their members regulate the stressful arousal emerging from challenging gaming activities such as collaborative raids. Such guilds more positively contributed to members' subjective well-being, fomenting more eustress than distress. By contrast, hardcore raiding guilds pushed their members to more extreme forms of online gaming, linking in-game arousal with problematic patterns of play and transforming pleasurable gaming eustress into harmful distress. That research was particularly important in the way it allowed me to show how guilds, as emergent communities of play, helped individual members differentially self-regulate. As such, that study sharply illuminated the deeply social shaping of the stress process. Further, KOG's unique constellation of values and behaviors—such as "offline life comes first"—was not for everyone, as evidenced in that final study section highlighting the guild's sometimes vulnerability to losing its members to more hardcore player groups. This showed how the fit between group culture and individual proclivities—what Dressler calls cultural consonance, the following chapter's focus—importantly structured well-being in these digital environments.

In this chapter's analysis, I again draw explicitly on Higgins' self-discrepancy theory (SDT)[29] to show how some video-game players identified with their in-game avatars—that is, with those partitioned parts of themselves—as ideal selves of a kind, superior in certain ways to offline personas. I find that being in sync with shared gamer models related to what constituted superior WoW play was in fact associated with positive health outcomes, such as players' perceptions that WoW play contributed positively to their happiness, life satisfaction, and stress relief. I further demonstrate how gamers who were less congruent with real-life (RL) understandings of success—a social marginality of a kind—reported greater positive contributions of WoW game-play to their subjective well-being. Also, further linking this and the prior chapter's analysis, I show in a mediation analysis how survey data was consistent with the idea that less actual-world success might produce deeper levels of dissociation, which in turn resulted in greater gaming-related positive subjective well-being outcomes. This analysis points again to the utility of a *health-disparities* framework to explaining well-being in these digital contexts, framed in reference to the *status-syndrome* work of the epidemiologist Michael Marmot.[30]

However, in chapter 3, I also show how some players dissociated *too* deeply into WoW, to the point that they lost control of their game-play and were no longer able to effectively extricate themselves when they wished. Such players experienced the distressing symptoms of WoW addiction or toxic immersion.[31] Of most interest for this book's arguments, players who were less successful in their offline lives were the most likely to report WoW overplay, with that study's analysis consistent with the idea that such a process was mediated by those gamers' stronger reports of dissociative experiences. Possessing digital-avatar identities, then, is a double-edged sword, with benefits to be had but with risks as well, especially for the socially subordinate and marginal.

In both chapters 2 and 3, I avoid singular judgments on the purely positive or negative character of online social play. Critical was the way players found online communities that met their orientations and needs at a certain point in time. This theme guided chapter 4's analysis as well. There, I focus on how virtual-world frameworks of meaning, experiences, and behaviors intersected with Udaipuri young-adult gamers' actual-world lives. I found that to effectively address this book's gaming-related mental-health questions I needed to understand how gamers' playful selves—both their avatar identities and their gamer identities more generally—intersected with the actual-world. And whether gaming was experienced as wondrously restorative adventure or, by contrast, as highly addictive and thus disruptive to gamers' lives, depended critically on the extent that players achieved and successfully negotiated normative models of success, which were situated in potentially competing virtual- and actual-world moral universes and social networks. Only by understanding gamers' complex negotiations between virtual- and real-world identities—processes I again referred to as *cultural dissonance*—could I more fully understand patterns of wellness and stress in these gamers' lives. In earlier US gaming work of mine, this meant heeding how gamers there could sometimes overvalue their play identities in order to protect themselves from cultural dissonant patterns of thinking. By contrast, in India, gamers tended to eventually undervalue their CS-GO play—referring to it as highly addictive— to prepare themselves, I argued, for their inevitable transitions to marriage, career, and adulthood, and thus again minimize culturally dissonant ideas and feelings.

Finally, as readers have seen, my analysis of Bedami's spiritual-avatar experiences relies largely on ethnography in the form of participant-observation and informal interviews. Participant-observation and qualitative interviews also feature in this book's digital-avatar studies, though I complement those with quantitative-web questionnaires. These studies came at different periods in my career, as described in chapter 2. I carried out my fieldwork with the Bhats during my PhD studies in the 1990s and then as a new assistant professor of anthropology in the early 2000s, working as a broadly trained cultural anthropologist and ethnographer. I initiated my digital-avatar work later, in 2008, at which point I increasingly identified myself as a psychological anthropologist and mixed-methods ethnographer. The qualitative data, in both the religious and digital studies, provided the foundation for my analysis and, indeed, for my understanding of avatar-therapeutic processes described in this book. However, in the digital-gaming studies, I was able to further verify patterns of association between key variables that emerged from the qualitative research. This gave me the ability to check whether my data was consistent with causal explanations suggested by the ethnography— e.g., how low RL consonance led to deeper forms of dissociation, which in turn was more likely to produce both greater gaming satisfaction and more problem play. That extra quantitative phase of research, triangulated with qualitative data, gives me added confidence in the explanations I posited in the digital-avatar studies.

. . .

By recognizing both the therapeutic and distressful features of avatar experiences, and how the two are linked, I have tried in this book to provide a balanced portrait of spiritual possession and digital gaming alike. In the spiritual-avatar case, I have endeavored to show how understanding Bedami's dissociative experiences as alternately therapy or distress entailed placing those experiences in their relevant social contexts. In this case, that meant understanding the tensions in Bedami's life, pulled as she was between her husband's and the other Bhats' demands. The devi visited Bedami to address and ideally beneficially resolve those tensions, though, at the time my research concluded, it was not entirely clear how successful the devi would be in that regard. In the digital-avatar case, I appreciate how ethnographers of virtual worlds—such as Boellstorff in his study of *Second Life*[32]—decided to study them entirely from *within* the persistent virtual world in question, as cultures in their own right, and not mere expressions of the offline world. Still, to address patterns of wellness and distress in WoW and CS-GO gamers' lives, I hope readers now have a greater appreciation for how understanding those processes entailed analyzing how gamers' digital experiences intersected with RL ones. Research presented in this book shows that both pleasurable and problematic play emerged when gamers felt themselves to be better psychosocially positioned in an online compared with offline social world and indeed came to believe—either rightly through a realistic assessment of less-than-desirable offline opportunities, or wrongly through misplaced rationalization—that online life offered more fulfilling possibilities. That is, the research presented in this book suggests that an individual's position relative to online compared with offline group norms—rather than any game per se, which should not be pathologized—could be better understood as a more ultimate source of gaming-related well-being.

I realize that some readers may be dissatisfied with what I say, wanting a clearer answer to whether the spiritual- and digital-avatar experiences described in this book are in the end better construed as therapeutic or toxic, or cure or illness. But I hope readers will understand that the inherently sociocultural nature of the avatar experiences I describe render challenging such clear distinctions. This is because the therapeutic power of avatars rests on their ability to transport the spiritually possessed and gamers alike into alternative social worlds, where identities and social standings can be improved in some important sense. But that transportation can be associated with costs as well, with second avatar identities potentially coming into conflict with first selves, in ways that toxically erode those primary identities. The therapeutic and toxic dimensions of avatar experiences are thus inextricably bound together, in ways that cannot be easily uncoupled.

．．．

The strength of this book, I believe, is its cross-cultural comparative case-study approach. I aim to provide readers with richly descriptive portraits of both spiritual- and digital-avatar experiences. Bedami's spiritual-avatar life, described in detail, provides the foundational theory and logic for the digital-avatar analyses, pointing to plausible stress pathways that might connect dissociative experiences with health outcomes. In the digital avatar-therapeutic analyses, I used field surveys to further confirm patterns of association characteristic of avatar-therapeutic processes, which had been suggested by the participant-observation and qualitative interviews. The field surveys also allowed me to sample a moderately large number of respondents, modeling with statistical precision relationships between, for example, dissociative experiences, stress, and wellness in digital contexts. In turn, the participant-observation and interviews, and indeed my own play experiences, lent sense and meaning to the processes behind the numbers provided by the surveys. That back-and-forth between the qualitative and quantitative data, and what researchers refer to as *triangulation* between multiple data sources, gave me greater confidence in the validity of the health mechanisms I identified to be associated with games such as *World of Warcraft,* which I see as a contemporary technology of absorption, extending as it does more archaic avatar-therapeutic processes.

Alongside these strengths, having reached the end of this book, I am also aware of the limitations of my research. By way of offering readers a proper conclusion, I would like to sketch future prospects for avatar-therapeutic research, which could importantly extend this book's analysis and findings.

First, it is important to study the role avatars play in other spiritual and digital contexts. In the spiritual cases, it was appropriate, I believe, to start with Hinduism, as I did in this book, given the historical roots of the notion of "avatar." However, other traditions promote analogous processes. For example, I mention in chapter 1 how the idea of the Christian *messiah* parallels what I refer to as avatars, as do, I think, being filled with the Holy Spirit or perhaps even embodying Christ in one's daily life.[33] Also, in Christian and other faiths, the notion of *fate* or *destiny* seems similar to the idea of the Hindu avatar, in the sense of carrying a greater purpose, if not necessarily one animated by an alternative consciousness, as avatars entail. Being fated in a spiritual sense is experienced by a larger number of individuals in a healthy and normal manner, I would think, whereas claiming to be a or even *the* messiah is more likely to be deemed a mental illness. Likewise, this book has focused on digital-gaming avatars. But as readers are well aware, there are many other forms of digital avatars, in the sense of graphical representations of a user in digital environments. In fact, any graphical image that serves as a focal point for digital conversations with other users—whether on older internet bulletin boards, on contemporary social networking sites such as Facebook, or in nongaming virtual worlds such as *Second Life*—are commonly referred to as *avatars*. And these other digital avatars share principles with the spiritual and gaming second selves discussed in this book, such as the ability to represent a user's social standing within a virtual community. It would thus be interesting to trace avatar-therapeutic processes in these other digital environments, especially given the wide recognition of the positive (and negative) ways that social networks, for example, can affect health.[34]

Second, I wonder how distinctive avatar-therapeutic processes are from more general ones related to, say, ritual, play, pretend, theatre, and the like. In this book, an avatar entails the projection of a first agent's consciousness into a second agent, who serves as the material vehicle or vessel for that first consciousness. But it is worth asking: What are the truly important features of the therapeutic processes described in this book? Is it the projection of one consciousness into another? Is it the projecting of a consciousness into an external material vehicle? Or is it simply the power of play and pretend?[35]

Third, I focus primarily in this book on avatars as *ideal* and *ought* second selves, drawing as I do from Higgins's self-discrepancy theory and from Dressler's cultural-consonance theory, which collectively examine how individuals embody personal and cultural ideals in their thought and behavior. But avatars need not be *idealized* or *normatively valued* second selves. Future research might investigate other user-avatar relationships, including what has been called an "alter ego" profile, where players might even enact their *worst* selves online, *trolling* and the like, with potential psychosocial benefits (and risks) to be had from that antisocial behavior.[36]

Fourth, I highlight in this book how stress processes feature in avatar therapeutics. The studies described in this book typically use respondent self-reports as proxies for psychosocial stress, whereas biomarkers, such as the stress-hormone cortisol, can sometimes provide more objective assessments of stress in these contexts. In fact, my lab has made some progress in this regard, identifying more favorable stress-related immune biology in gamers who were more intensively involved in online play. Those results are promising, and I invite readers to consult those studies of mine, though more work of this kind remains to be done.[37]

Likewise, and fifth, as stated above, I do believe that avatar-therapeutic research could benefit from looking at interactions between the sociocultural processes discussed in this book and processes working at the level of individual personality and biology, with such a project even informed by *dual inheritance* cultural and biological evolutionary perspectives.[38] Here, I would emphasize that I see sociocultural, personality, and biological processes as complementary, and potentially synergistic, rather than opposed.[39] For example, researchers might identify how underlying personality traits, even partially biologically based ones, contribute to an individual's likelihood to dissociate in a spiritual or digital context, or to game compulsively. But taking the latter case as an example, the extent to which compulsive gaming was deemed passion or addiction would still importantly depend, at least in part, on the social setting in which the gaming occurred. Among one's guildmates, compulsive gaming might be celebrated, whereas in a family of other non-gamers, it might be more likely to be condemned. In these terms, it would be some (potentially synergistic) combination of personality, biological, and sociocultural factors that shaped the relative eustress as compared with distress associated with gaming activity, a topic well-worth exploring in more depth.[40]

Finally, sixth, I simply encourage more rigorous research. Recently, I became aware of Judea Pearl's book on causal inference, *The Book of Why: The New Science of Cause and Effect.*[41] I see now how incorporating even more processual diagrams, and longitudinal and experimental research designs, would have further bolstered the causal arguments that feature in this book. I encourage other researchers in this regard, and blessings to this book's next avatar incarnation!

ACKNOWLEDGMENTS

This book would not have been possible without the support of many individuals and institutions. First, I would like to thank my research collaborators with whom I developed arguments featured in this book. They include François Dengah and Mike Lacy, and the many students who have participated in my virtual-worlds methods seminars and have been members of my joint research and teaching laboratory. I especially thank the student members of my original 2008 research methods seminar taught inside the *World of Warcraft* for that lightning-in-a-bottle experience. And I greatly appreciate students in my fall 2020 virtual worlds methods seminar for providing timely feedback on the book while still in manuscript form. The latter includes graduate students in that seminar who have stayed engaged with all things virtual-worlds as my student research assistants and collaborators: Shawna Bendeck, Seth Sagstetter, and Katya Zhao. I also thank student participants in those and other seminars who stay in touch via our Virtual Worldz Facebook group, which now includes over a hundred members. To my students in particular, thank you for helping me stay apprised of ever-evolving virtual-world, gaming, and avatar realities, trends, and forms of identity and social connection.

Likewise, I am extremely grateful to the research participants in my various projects. This means first and foremost members of the Bhat community, and especially my adopted Bhat family, Bansilal and Bedami Bhat and their five daughters, Gita, Kamla, Koshila, Krishna, and Santosh. It also includes many gamers from around the world, such as the members of the Knights of Good *World of Warcraft* guild and the *Counterstrike—Global Offensive* gamers I got to know more recently in Udaipur, Rajasthan. Bhats and gamers alike, you have inspired me with your serious approach to creativity and play, and with your playful approach to serious things. Thank you.

The spirit-possession parts of this book go back to my PhD dissertation research in the 1990s with the Bhat community. I thus again would like to express gratitude to my dissertation committee members, Roy D'Andrade, Freddy Bailey, Tanya Luhrmann, and Michael Meeker, for their wisdom and guidance. Roy and Freddy both passed away recently, a loss I feel keenly. I also thank Jean DeBernardi, who was my postdoctoral advisor while at the University of Alberta, Edmonton. Much appreciation also goes to my friends, colleagues, and mentors in India, but especially to N. K. Bhargava, Mohan Lal Advani, Chakrapani Upadhyay, and Yuvraj Singh Jhala. To Dr. Jhala and his entire family, thank you for giving me in Udaipur a home away from home.

For providing me the space to pursue my ideas, and for financial support, I thank the Department of Anthropology and Geography at Colorado State University. Likewise, for financial support of research featured in this book, I am grateful to the American Institute of Indian Studies, the Foundation for Psychocultural Research, the Izaak Walton Killam Foundation of the University of Alberta, the National Endowment for the Humanities, the National Science Foundation, the Spencer Foundation, and the University of California San Diego.

The Society for Psychological Anthropology, a section of the American Anthropological Association, has provided me with an intellectual home for many years now. For that, I thank its members, which includes researchers working on culture and dissociation: Laurence Kirmayer, Tanya Luhrmann, Chris Lynn, and Rebecca Seligman. Likewise, I appreciate the Foundation for Psychocultural Research's (the FPR's, https://thefpr.org/) integrative vision of psychological anthropology and for inviting me into its stimulating Culture, Mind, and Brain (CMB) research network conversations (see https://thefpr.org/cmb-network-main/), which have influenced my recent thinking and writing. I am especially grateful to the FPR's founder and president, Rob Lemelson, and to the codirectors of the CMB network, Connie Cummings and Carol Worthman. In a similar vein, I also appreciate Russ Bernard and Amber Wutich for the opportunity to serve as faculty in the new NSF-funded Cultural Anthropology Methods Program and Community of Practice (https://methods4all.org/). That group's members are pushing the frontiers of what synthetic anthropological research can and should be, and I feel privileged to be a part of the effort.

I thank Kate Marshall and Enrique Ochoa-Kaup at the University of California Press, who sagely shepherded this book through its various stages. For helpful feedback on key ideas featuring in this work and on the manuscript itself, my appreciation goes to Adrienne Cohen, François Dengah, Bill Dressler, Glenn Etter, Mike Lacy, Tanya Luhrmann, Mona Thapa, Jo Weaver, and Sammy Zahran. Likewise, I am grateful to the journal editors and reviewers of work that now appears in this book, if in somewhat different form.

I also thank Sri Komal Kothari for first introducing me to the Bhats and Gary Dmytryk for introducing me to William Gibson (and to The Pixies). Thank you to ArenaNet and to Blizzard Entertainment for making your games. I also thank the makers of tabletop roleplaying games (TTRPG) like *Dungeons & Dragons, Fate,* and *GURPS* (Generic Universal Roleplaying System), and my various TTRPG play groups, who have helped me over the years gain further insight into avatar identities and processes. I also express my gratitude to my brothers John and Tom and their families for many things, including for lending my life a sense of continuity.

Finally, I wrote this book in relative isolation during the COVID-19 crisis. That isolation, and crisis, made me acutely aware of the importance, and potential, of virtual worlds. In crises such as these, those internet connections, and avatar second selves, can be the main thing that keep some of us going, psychosocially speaking. And I greatly appreciate the support from my various digital quarters. Thank you. But likewise, I also became acutely aware during this crisis of my need for face-to-face contact with my actual-world friends, family, colleagues, students, and kindred spirits, which digital avatar experiences do not provide. I say this here to remind readers, and future researchers, of both the vast potential of virtual worlds and avatar second selves, and of their limitations as well.

Chapter 2 Supplemental Material

SURVEY METHODS AND RESULTS

For this chapter's survey analysis, my team and I used a technique referred to as ordinal logistic regression to identify relationships between dissociative gaming experiences and positive mental well-being.[1] For the reader unfamiliar with this technique: Like an ordinary least-squares (OLS) *linear regression* (described in appendix B), this analysis involves using an equation to produce a predictive model for an outcome variable. However, a special approach is taken that does not assume the outcome is measured as a continuous variable, instead treating it strictly as an ordinal variable. The model fitted is used to describe how the various predictor or explanatory variables are related to the odds that a respondent scores in category 2 or above as opposed to 1, category 3 or above as opposed to anything lower, category 4 or above as opposed to anything lower, and so forth. Thus, the coefficients I report here show how a one-unit change in an explanatory variable is predicted to multiplicatively increase the odds of being in the higher-versus-lower location of any category split. Odds ratios greater than one thus show positive relationships between an explanatory variable and the outcome, while those less than one indicate a negative association.

Of particular interest for this analysis, my collaborators and I developed ethnographic scales to measure individual players' levels of dissociative WoW experiences, modeled after two commonly used protocols to assess such experiences, the Tellegen Absorption Scale and the Dissociative Experiences Scale.[2] Here, gamers were asked to respond to WoW-specific questions related to the extent to which their play was associated with distortions in perception, memory, and identity seen to be typical of absorption and dissociation in other contexts. That scale measure included fourteen items, with respondents rating on an ordinal scale how much they had experienced each of the following:

WoW Dissociation (Cronbach's α = 0.90)

1. I can become so absorbed in the game of WoW that I am unaware of other events happening around me.
2. I find that I can sit in game, doing and thinking of nothing, and am not aware of the passage of time.
3. When I'm playing WoW, and someone in the real world is talking to me, I find that I do not remember all or part of what was said.
4. I find that I am able to ignore discomfort from ignoring bodily needs such as needing to use the bathroom, eat food, sleep or hygiene while playing the game.
5. I find that when I am playing the game that I talk out loud to myself.
6. I find that I bring elements of the game into my real-world experiences.
7. I find that I can become so involved in the game of WoW that it feels like it is really happening to me.
8. I find that events in WoW are more vivid or memorable than events in my real life.
9. I have the experience of remembering a past event (raid, quest, etc) so vividly that I feel like I am reliving the event.
10. I find that I act so differently in game compared to how I act in real life, so much so that I feel as if I am two different people.
11. I feel like I am my character.
12. I can confuse my own name with that of my characters.
13. I have the experience of not being sure if conversations or experiences happened in game or in real life.
14. I can feel as if I am looking at the real world as though I were in game.

We also asked survey respondents to assess their positive and negative mental wellness relative to gaming, for example, the extent players believed WoW or some other game added to their happiness and life satisfaction and alleviated or increased the stress in their lives. The web survey also included basic demographic data, intensity of gaming, self-rated accomplishment within gaming, motivation and styles of game-play, social interactions in the game, and numerous other topics, which here and in other analyses helped me better understand and isolate patterns connecting dissociative gaming, stress processes, and gamer well-being.

As noted in this chapter, my student collaborators and I posted our survey on gaming-related websites and extended invitations through our own personal play networks. We received 253 responses to our questionnaire, which included members of the Knights of Good gaming guild, who feature prominently in chapter 3.

Using ordinal logistic regression, my team and I identified substantial positive relationships between self-reports of WoW dissociative experiences (as a sum of an individual's self-reports of that scale's items) and WoW being perceived, first, to increase one's happiness and life satisfaction (two separate outcomes assessed with different single-question survey items) and, second, to provide for stress relief. For example, the relationship between dissociative experiences and WoW being perceived to increase one's happiness was strong and positive, with an odds ratio indicating that a one standard deviation increase in the dissociation scale score approximately doubled the odds of a respondent giving a higher rating on the happiness variable. In exact numerical terms, the odds ratios for relationships between WoW dissociative experiences, on the one hand, and the feeling that WoW positively influenced one's happiness, life satisfaction, and experience of life stress, on the other hand, while accounting for various control variables, were, respectively: 2.06, 1.82, and 1.66.

We also found that players who said WoW helped them relax were more likely to report that the game added to their life happiness and life satisfaction, with respective odds ratios of 2.55 and 2.79. And we found that players who experienced WoW as increasing their life stress were also more likely to report that WoW increased their life happiness, with an odds ratio of 1.3.

Results also indicated an interactive relationship between dissociative gaming experiences and relaxation in relation to both the experience that WoW increased one's life happiness and one's life satisfaction: the more a respondent experienced WoW as dissociative, the stronger the positive relationship was between the experience of gaming-related relaxation and reporting WoW as increasing one's happiness and life satisfaction. In both cases, dissociation considerably magnified the positive relationship of the experience of WoW play promoting relaxation to these mental well-being outcomes. For example, regarding the relaxation variable, the interaction is such that a respondent who was one standard deviation below the mean in dissociation (a score of −1.0), would have an odds ratio of 1.9 in relation to the happiness outcome variable. But for a respondent at one standard deviation above the mean on dissociation (a score of +1.0), the same odds ratio would be 3.4. The odds ratio for relaxation's relation to life satisfaction, through interactive with dissociation, is consistently positive, ranging from 2.0 when dissociation = −1 (one standard deviation below the mean), up to 3.9 for dissociation = +1 (one standard deviation above the mean).

Chapter 3 Supplemental Material

SURVEY METHODS AND RESULTS

In this chapter's first set of *social-identity and status* analyses, my team and I sought to identify associations between online/offline success and well-being, using both ordinal logistic regression, described in appendix A, and the most common form of regression analysis, referred to as *linear regression*.[1] Linear regression is a statistical method for describing the relationship between one or more predictor variables (like *offline success*) and some outcome of interest (such as *problem gaming*). In this form of analysis, researchers plot their pairs of values for their predictor and outcome variables, with the predictor on the X-axis and the outcome on the Y-axis. Then, they use regression analysis to see how well a straight line (or some other shape) describes this relationship. For example, as offline success gets larger, does problem gaming tend to get larger or smaller? Regression analysis does this in a detailed way, using a straight line to fit the plotted points. This makes it possible to take advantage of what is known about the equation of a straight line, as many readers would have studied in an algebra course. Regression analysis enables us to use the slope of the line fitting our plot of points to summarize how one variable (on average) changes as the other changes. So, here, regression would let us be able to talk about how much of a change in a respondent's problem gaming score is typically associated with (say) a one-point change in the offline social standing score (what is called a regression or slope coefficient).

For the mediation analyses, we conducted a formal test of mediation, using a publicly available Stata add-on program. The program is called –khb- and is documented in Karlson and Anders 2011.[2] These authors offer a new method that enables measuring mediation in both linear as well as logistic and other nonlinear probability regression models.

We used ethnography and specialized cognitive anthropological methods to develop the online/offline success measures sensitive to gamer respondents' experiences, with the specific scales and general approach described elsewhere.[3] The WoW success scale, an important predictor variable in this analysis, contained these seventeen items, with respondents rating on an ordinal scale how much they had experienced each of the following:

Online (WoW) Success (Cronbach's $\alpha = .90$)

1. I play my character, character class, and the game more generally with knowledge and skill.
2. I have succeeded, or will succeed, in some challenging game context—this could be "end-game" twenty-five-man raids, PvP arena competitions, or winning an exalted reputation with multiple factions.
3. I intelligently "spec" my characters, wisely distributing points in class-specific talent trees that help me meet my particular game goals.
4. I acquire good gear for my characters—this could include epic gear that allows my characters to excel in arena competitions or raids, epic mounts, or some other type of gear.
5. I am adaptable, flexible, and a quick learner—this could include possessing the ability to make wise decisions under pressure.
6. I am a cooperative, respectful, and responsible team player—this means being attentive and responsive to other players' goals and needs.
7. I am generous and helpful in ways that help my fellow players (such as those in my guild) meet their goals.
8. I excel at my chosen role, which I can play well in a variety of solo or cooperative group situations.
9. I demonstrate some degree of autonomy in the game—a good player of WoW is able and interested to independently solve some problems.
10. I am dedicated and committed to the game.
11. I play a lot, putting in the hours necessary to succeed in the game.
12. I play efficiently—a successful player uses their time in the game wisely so as to more efficiently achieve their goals.
13. I put in the necessary hours of out-of-game research in order to succeed in my goals—this could mean visiting game websites in order to prepare for challenging game content.
14. I display a healthy competitive spirit and a will to succeed.
15. I play with confidence.
16. I play with a positive attitude—this could mean remaining funny, courteous, and sociable in difficult game situations.
17. I enjoy the game.

The offline success scale, another predictor variable, contained these nineteen items, again rated ordinally based on self-perceptions:

Offline (Real-Life) Success (Cronbach's α = 0.91)

1. I am smart and knowledgeable.
2. I am well educated.
3. I am wealthy and materially prosperous.
4. I am economically secure.
5. I have a good job and a satisfying career path.
6. I am dedicated and determined in pursuing my life goals.
7. I am well liked and respected.
8. I have a good personality.
9. I have a good sense of humor.
10. I am generous.
11. I have satisfying family relationship.
12. I have a rich social life and network of friends.
13. I am responsible.
14. I am happy and satisfied with life.
15. I am healthy.
16. I am in good physical condition.
17. I enjoy a range of hobbies and leisure activities.
18. I find time to play and relax.
19. I live every day to its fullest.

Outcomes included the same subjective experiences considered in chapter 2's analyses, i.e., how respondents felt WoW contributed positively to mental well-being in the form of happiness, life satisfaction, and stress management. To assess problem play, we developed our own WoW-specific measure, adapted from Kimberly Young's commonly used Internet Addiction Test, itself adapted from measures used to assess other forms of addiction to drugs, alcohol, gambling, and the like.[4] That WoW-specific measure included nineteen items:

WoW Problem Gaming (Cronbach's α = 0.94)

1. How often do you neglect household chores to spend more time WoW?
2. How often do you prefer the excitement of WoW to intimacy with your partner?
3. How often do you form new relationships with fellow WoW users?
4. How often do others in your life complain to you about the amount of time you spend on WoW?

5. How often do your grades or schoolwork suffer because of the amount of time you spend on WoW?

6. How often do you regret the amount of time you spend on WoW?

7. How often does your job performance or productivity suffer because of WoW?

8. How often do you become defensive or secretive when anyone asks you about WoW?

9. How often do you block out disturbing thoughts about your life with positive thoughts related to WoW?

10. How often do you find yourself anticipating when you will go on WoW again?

11. How often do you fear that life without WoW would be boring, empty, and joyless?

12. How often do you snap, yell, or act annoyed if someone bothers you while you are playing WoW?

13. How often do you lose sleep due to late-night WoW playing?

14. How often do you feel preoccupied with WoW when off-line, or fantasize about being on WoW?

15. How often do you find yourself saying "just a few more minutes" when on WoW?

16. How often do you try to cut down the amount of time you spend on WoW and fail?

17. How often do you try to hide how long you are on WoW?

18. How often do you choose to spend more time on WoW over going out with others?

19. How often do you feel depressed, moody, or nervous when you are not playing WoW, which goes away once you are back online?

We also asked in a single item how much respondents felt they were "addicted" to WoW, which allowed us to check that item's correspondence with the full WoW problem-gaming scale.

We placed these experience items in the same survey described in chapter 2 and appendix A, receiving, as said earlier, 253 responses. I would again note that survey respondents included members of the Knights of Good gaming guild, who feature prominently in this chapter's ethnography.

Regarding results from this chapter's first set of analyses, for the happiness outcome, an odds ratio of 1.116 means that, for example, in standardized terms, a one-standard-deviation increase on the *online (WoW) success* scale measure corresponds to an odds ratio of 2.2, indicating that a respondent who was one standard deviation higher in WoW success had an odds of being in the next highest response "happiness" category that was 2.2 times larger. (Hereafter, I denote such standardized ratios as $OR_1\sigma$.) WoW success was also positively associated with the feeling that playing WoW added to respondents' life satisfaction, with an $OR_1\sigma$ of 2.0. Likewise, WoW success was substantially positively associated with the report that WoW play helped respondents to relax in ways that combatted stress ($OR_1\sigma = 1.8$), with WoW success also having a small positive relationship with reporting that WoW play increased stress ($OR_1\sigma = 1.2$).

Further, being higher on *offline success* was associated with modest somewhat lower odds of reporting that WoW increased respondents' happiness ($OR_1\sigma = 0.70$), life satisfaction ($OR_1\sigma = 0.79$), and positive or eustress ($OR_1\sigma = 0.56$). Further, using Karlson and Anders's approach, statistical analysis of our survey data was also consistent with the idea that lower offline success scores led to deeper dissociative experiences, which in turn produced increased self-reports of gaming related happiness and stress relief. A model with offline success by itself indicated that such forms of success had a weak negative relation to reporting that WoW increased happiness (nonsignificant odds ratio of 0.90 for a one standard deviation increase in offline success). Controlling for dissociation resulted in a positive but again small (odds-ratio 1.07) coefficient. However, the estimated mediation effect of offline success affecting perceived happiness through dissociation was negative and relatively strong (140% of the total effect, p < 0.01). For "helps relax/combat stress," the pattern was different. In the model with offline success as a predictor but without dissociation, offline success showed a weak and nonsignificant positive relation (odds ratio of 1.17) to reporting stress reduction. But when dissociation was introduced as a control, the relationship of offline success to stress reduction became stronger and statistically reliable (odds ratio 1.34, p < 0.05). The estimated mediated effect was negative and 150% of the size of the total effect (p < 0.01). This is precisely as would be expected if there were an indirect or mediated effect, with offline success affecting dissociation, which in turn affected these two outcomes.

Using linear regression methods, we also found that self-reported offline success had a strong negative relation to our problem gaming scale, with a slope of −0.44 on a standardized basis. This slope shows a predicted decrease of 6.05 points in problem gaming (1/3 standard deviation) for a one-standard-deviation increase in offline success: that is, persons who see themselves as successful in conventional (offline) society are *less* likely to report adverse consequences from their WoW play. This pattern was reproduced in relation to the single-item WoW addiction self-report, with an $OR_1\sigma = 0.51$.

Regarding the final mediation analysis in this first set of analyses, where the addiction scale was an outcome, the coefficient for offline success considered alone was smaller in absolute size than in models without dissociation as a covariate (−2.64 vs. −6.05). This is again as would be expected if there were an indirect or mediated effect, with offline success affecting dissociation, which in turn affected problem use. Using Karlson and Anders's approach, we found that the mediated or indirect effect of offline success was negative (-3.40) and 56% of the magnitude of the total effect, with $p < 0.01$.

This chapter's second sets of analyses concentrated on identifying relationships between guild affiliation—as online "microcultures" of a kind—and well-being.[5] Key to this analysis was a single-item question, where we asked respondents if they belonged to a guild, and if so what kind of guild, with possible responses including "a 'family' or 'social' guild," "a casual raiding guild," and "a hardcore raiding guild," or "no guild membership."

We also adapted two items from Cohen et al.'s item Perceived Stress Scale (PSS).[6] This index operationalizes *stress* as respondents' perceived level of control over their lives, with a higher score indicating a greater degree of perceived lack of control and thus higher stress. However, we changed this scale to instead ask about perceived control—or lack of control—experienced *in-game* rather than in life more generally.

WoW Perceived Stress

1. In the last month, how often have you felt that you were unable to control the important things in your virtual WoW life?
2. In the last month, how often have you felt virtual WoW-world difficulties were piling up so high that you could not overcome them?

Of note, this measure seemed to have ethnographic validity in the way that gamers often spoke of their gaming pleasures as being linked to *feelings of control:* e.g., they noted how they liked WoW because they felt they had more control there than in their offline lives, where they often felt out of control in a bad way.

To better distinguish individual achievement from guild-promoted behaviors, we included as a control a three-item index, where respondents reported the extent to which they were oriented to achieving instrumental goals within the game (advancing in level, gaining "gear," and competing successfully against other players), which we had used successfully in earlier research.[7]

WoW Achievement Motivation (Cronbach's Alpha = 0.67)

1. advancement
(like to meet goals, accumulate gear and other in-game symbols of wealth, and/or gain status and power)
2. mechanics
(driven by the desire to understand everything about how the game works)
3. competition
(play to challenge and compete with others)

Using linear regression techniques, we identified a substantial positive relationship between perceived in-game stress (i.e., lack of control in their online lives) and problematic play, with a regression coefficient (and thus slope) of 2.16. This means that a one-unit increase in perceived in-game stress (plotted on the X-axis) is associated with a 2.16 unit increase in problem gaming (Y-axis). None of the guild membership categories showed a significant relation to problematic play at conventional levels of statistical significance, although members of hardcore guilds had a relatively larger mean problematic play score than did persons in the friend and family guild used as the comparison category (4.47 higher).

Incorporating terms into the analysis for guild-affiliation type interacting with WoW (in-game) stress showed that these two variables mutually conditioned one another's relations to problematic play. For persons in the friends and family (reference) category of guild affiliation, the slope of problematic play with respect to WoW stress was quite small (0.95), with a large standard error. The estimated slopes for stress were larger, though not reliably so, for non-guild members or members of casual raiding guilds (e.g., for casual raiding, 2.35 (= 0.95 + 1.4)). However, among respondents affiliated with hardcore raiding guilds, the slope for stress was much larger and significantly so (7.46 (= 0.95 + 6.51)), indicating that a one-point increase on the stress index was associated with about a 7.5-point increase on the problematic play scale for these individuals.

Further, these patterns held even after controlling for a number of potential confounding variables, such as age, gender, and, perhaps most importantly, players' achievement motivation. One might imagine, for example, that the category affiliation of guild simply manifests one's own personal motivation, so that whether one joins a more casual or hardcore raiding guild depends on one's relative level of achievement motivation, which itself determines how in-game stress intertwines with problematic overplay. However, having controlled for players' relative achievement motivation, we found that guild affiliation shapes the relationship between in-game stress and problematic gaming *at each and every level of players' personal motivations*. Thus, the relationship of competitive guild affiliation to problematic gaming found here are not likely attributable to difference in competitive (achievement) orientation of guild members. There is something about guild affiliation that links in-game arousal and problematically compulsive play, as above and beyond other potentially confounding factors.

Chapter 4 Supplemental Material

SURVEY METHODS AND RESULTS

For this chapter's survey analysis, I used linear regression (described in appendix B) to identify associations between self-reports of being a *true gamer* and positive and negative gaming experiences.[1] Ethnographic observations and interviews led me to identity four prominent components of a *true-gamer* model of identity: *having close gamer friends, feeling connected to a global gamer community, dreaming of gaming professionally,* and *feeling part of a gamer subculture.* I used those *true-gamer* components of identity as survey questions—proxies to assess respondents' consonance with shared gamer models of what it meant to be a good and successful CS-GO player. Given that I did not use Dressler's formal cultural consonance procedures in this analysis, and thus did not have full-blown cultural-consonance scales, I analyzed cultural-dissonance processes in a different way.[2] Specifically, I examined whether being culturally consonant with that *true-gamer* model of identity (containing the above four components, ethnographically identified) might predict *both* positive and negative gaming-related experiences, including in the negative case addictive gaming. As I interpreted it, in concert with the ethnography, such a pattern would point to the way that identifying oneself as a gamer meant belonging to a distinctive subculture, a social standing that brought both positive mental-health gains and also incompatibility with mainstream Udaipuri culture and thus stress, leading to potentially felt *cultural dissonance.*

For this study, I used alternate gaming-related well-being measures: the WoW Problematic Use scale, described in appendix B, wasn't appropriate for this CS-GO context. Instead, I used two twenty-one-item measures for assessing in gamers' own terms their positive and negative play experiences, which I had developed in earlier work.[3] The negative gaming experiences scale assessed video game players' health in ways partly concordant with Western medical understandings, via eight gaming addiction items. But that scale further located addiction symptomology alongside other culturally salient positive and negative gaming experiences, with the latter including gaming-related distress and dysfunction items that were not framed in the Western clinical language of addiction.

Positive Gaming Experiences

1. I look forward to when I'll play next with anticipation and enthusiasm.
2. I find that gaming helps me relieve frustrations and improve my mood.
3. I feel that gaming can give me focus and even purpose in life.
4. I experience positive rushes of adrenaline and energy when I play, especially when defeating tough enemies and opponents.
5. I find it satisfying and even exhilarating to push my body by gaming long hours.
6. I feel calm, relaxed, and in control at certain points in the game.
7. I find that online games provide my life important regularity and structure.
8. I enjoy having my skills pushed to the limits.
9. I find it satisfying to repeat challenging gaming actions over and over again until they are nearly perfect and automatic.
10. I enjoy gaming for fun over other hobbies and habits.
11. I find that gaming takes my mind off problems I'm facing in my life.
12. I put effort into improving my game to grow and evolve as a player.
13. I experience an easy and sometimes instant connection with other gamers.
14. I find that connecting to diverse people via the internet expands my social circle and perspective on life.
15. I enjoy the sense of belonging that comes with being a part of a community of gamers.
16. I worry less about how my actions and words might be perceived by others because online gaming and the internet provide greater opportunities for anonymity.
17. I find that playing online games with offline friends and family strengthens those relationships.
18. I form strong bonds with other online gamers, feeling that I can rely on them and am willing to offer them help.
19. I feel satisfaction in sticking with a gaming goal until it is completed, even though this might entail a lot of hard work.
20. I find that overcoming difficult gaming challenges helps build my confidence to deal with life's problems.
21. I develop important skills through gaming that helps me advance in both careers and life.

Negative Gaming Consequences

1. I find it difficult to concentrate on other activities because I am thinking about gaming.

2. I feel frustrated and disappointed and get in a bad mood when I don't play well.

3. I feel that gaming isn't the best use of my time and often wish that I could have done something more productive or useful.

4. I feel mentally and even physically drained after long and intense gaming sessions.

5. I push my body too far, not eating or sleeping right, when I am gaming.

6. I get fidgety and irritable when I can't get online to play.

7. I get obsessed in a bad way about a game, even feeling like the game is taking over my life.

8. I find it difficult to control or limit my online play, gaming too much and at inappropriate times.

9. I often reach a point where gaming can be more of a boring routine than actual fun.

10. I find that gaming a lot makes it more difficult to enjoy other activities in my life.

11. I use gaming to avoid challenges in my life rather than deal with them directly.

12. I have to play more and more to get similar feelings of enjoyment and satisfaction.

13. I game so much that I find myself isolated and lonely.

14. I get too caught up in other gamers' opinions, perspectives, and demands.

15. I keep gaming even when I think other gamers are producing a "toxic" rather than supportive community.

16. I get annoyed and angry when anonymous players don't take responsibility for their words and actions.

17. I find that playing online games leads to conflicts with my friends and family.

18. I feel that I have to play for my online friends even when I don't want to.

19. I experience online gaming more like a draining job than something I love.

20. I get upset and even feel bad about myself and my abilities when I lose or don't play well.

21. I think I could be more successful in life if I didn't spend so much time and energy gaming.

Further, based on ethnography, I developed a series of twelve questions that asked whether respondents agreed that various persons and sectors of society supported gaming as a "positive and even healthy" activity. These questions were summed into a twelve-item Gaming-Related Social Norm Support scale. Here, higher scores on this scale would show gamers' feelings that their gaming was more fully socially supported by society. But more importantly for this study's cultural dissonance arguments, *lower* scores on this scale would reveal respondents' *greater* sense of belonging to a countercultural group, which, I anticipated, would be associated with the need for psychosocial negotiation. That is, individual respondents' lack of felt support for their hobby from mainstream society would indicate their enhanced feelings of belonging to a distinctive gamer community, with stronger feelings of opposition to mainstream society helping to explain respondents' greater sense of gaming pleasure, but also their felt distress.

Gaming-Related Social Norm Support Scale

"In my opinion, [each of the below] support gaming as a positive and even healthy activity."

1. Mainstream society
2. The media.
3. Non-gamers I know.
4. People in the town or city where I grew up.
5. People in the town or city where I currently live.
6. People I know or meet online.
7. Members of my family.
8. My friends.
9. People I know or have known at work and/or school.
10. The most important person in my life (e.g., spouse, partner, family member, friend, et al.).
11. Gamers I know (in gaming zones, etc.).
12. Devoutly religious people (e.g., Hindus, Muslims, Christians, etc.).

In addition to the measures just described, the survey also contained standard covariates, including age, education, caste and religious affiliations, socioeconomic status (SES), and average hours gamed per week

I presented all survey items in both Hindi and English, given the fact that respondents' first language was Hindi, though they often preferred to converse in English, especially about gaming-related matters. I distributed the survey to members of the three gaming zones where I worked. Coordinating with the gaming-zone owners, whom I by then knew well, I provided each gamer with several hours of free play time as an incentive to respond to the survey. Of note, I knew each of the (forty-eight) survey respondents by name, allowing me to connect observations and interviews with the survey data.

To give a sense of the size of effects, based on linear regression, in the first set of analyses, gamers who "Agreed" compared to those who "Disagreed" that their close friends were also gamers—as part of a *true gamer* identity experience—reported scores over twenty-six points or 1.35 standard deviations higher on the twenty-one-item positive experiences scale (sd = 19.48), which ranged from a minimum of 21 to a maximum of 105.

In the second set of analyses, a player who "Agreed" that video gaming conflicted with Indian traditions and values—and was thus not normatively valued there, experiences more likely to be associated with identifying as a *true gamer*—scored compared to the baseline "Disagree" respondent a little over seventeen points or almost a full standard deviation higher on the negative experiences scale (sd = 17.96).

Finally, positive and negative gaming experiences were highly positively correlated, with an R = 0.540, p = 0.0001. Controlling for SES and hours played per week, a one standard deviation rise in positive gaming experiences (again, sd = 19.48) was associated with an eight-and-a-half-point increase in negative experiences (19.48 X 0.435 = 8.47), which represented about a half of a standard deviation rise on this scale (sd = 17.96).

NOTES

INTRODUCTION

1. (Gibson 1986).

2. As I say in the preface, I generally italicize foreign terms the first time I substantively reference them and then subsequently only for emphasis or if there is a large gap since the term was last used.

3. *Material* may seem like an odd word when referring to digital realities. But digital avatars are material in the sense of allowing a user to take form and thus *materialize* or *embody* themselves in an alternative reality, in this case an electronic one. In cognitive science, an *agent,* roughly equivalent to *actor* (though not in the theatrical sense), is an entity with a will and a purpose who acts in ways that are meant to accomplish goals. See, e.g., (Boyer 2003).

4. For classic anthropological accounts of voodoo, see (Brown and Michel 2010; Métraux 2016).

5. (Cameron 2009).

6. (Morningstar 1986).

7. (*World of Warcraft* 2004).

8. Anthropologist Mel Spiro described the Buddha as "superhuman" (Spiro 1971).

9. On this history, see (de Wildt et al. 2019).

10. (Sterling 1986).

11. (Stephenson 1992).

12. (Wachowski and Wachowski 1999).

13. (ArenaNet 2012).

14. (Snodgrass, Lacy, Dengah II, Fagan, et al. 2011), which features in chapter 2.

15. (Bourguignon 2004).

16. On spiritual ecstasy, see, e.g., (Lewis 1971; Eliade 2020; Vitebsky 2001).

17. (Eliade 2020).

18. (Rosedale 2003).

19. On the notion of a "magic circle" of play, and also for critiques of that idea, see, e.g., (Castronova 2008; Consalvo 2009; Malaby 2007).

20. E.g., see (Snodgrass, Dengah II, et al. 2019).

21. E.g., see (Yee 2014).

22. On gaming relieving loneliness, see (Snodgrass, Bagwell, et al. 2018).

23. (Steinkuehler and Williams 2006).

24. (Jones et al. 2014, 3).

25. (Merkur 2014).

26. (Snodgrass, Lacy, Dengah II, and Fagan 2011).

27. (Lévi-Strauss 1963).

28. As noted in this book's preface, King's College researchers have developed novel clinical strategies for treating auditory hallucinations, which, though very different from the spiritual and gaming contexts described in this book, they also dub "avatar therapy" (Craig et al. 2018).

29. In all spiritual- and digital-avatar studies, names that appear in this book are pseudonyms.

30. The phrasing "toxic immersion" is Edward Castronova's (2008).

31. The Knights of Good is the name of the guild featured in Felicia Day's popular comedy web series, *The Guild* (*The Guild* 2007). The founder of the actual guild featured in my research suggested we use this fictitious name to better protect its members' identities.

32. (*Counter-Strike—Global Offensive* 2012).

33. (Seligman and Kirmayer 2008, 34).

34. (Seligman and Kirmayer 2008, 34).

35. (Krippner and Powers 2013).

36. As Lynn analogizes the situation, "Think of an office space comprising cubicles separated by partitions that can be moved around in a variety of configurations, interspersed with several dedicated offices that have more permanent walls. Information flows over, around, and through these separators, with various degrees of ease. The partitions can be unconsciously moved to divert or block streams of information" (Lynn 2005, 20).

37. See my discussion of this literature in (Snodgrass, Lacy, Dengah II, et al. 2011). See also (Lynn 2005; Seligman and Kirmayer 2008).

38. For a good case-study exploration of therapeutic trance, see (Seligman 2014).

39. For a classic anthropological account of spirit possession, see (Lewis 1971).

40. On immersion in video games, see, e.g., (Bartle 1996; Castronova 2008; Yee 2006b; 2014; Snodgrass et al. 2012).

41. E.g., see (Castronova 2008; Chen 2012; Nardi 2010; Yee 2014).

42. (Snodgrass, Bagwell, et al. 2018).

43. (Luhrmann 2006; Luhrmann, Nusbaum, and Thisted 2010).

44. (Csikszentmihalyi 2008).

45. (Seligman and Kirmayer 2008).

46. (Lynn 2005).

47. (American Psychiatric Association 2013).

48. (Williams et al. 2006).

49. Hans Selye conceptualized stress as psychosomatic arousal in response to environmental challenges, which has both positive *eustress* and negative *distress* dimensions, from the Greek roots, *eu-,* for well-being, and *dis-,* which connotes negative reversal (Selye 1975).

50. See, e.g., (Raz 2005).

51. (Benson and Klipper 1975).

52. (Davis 1984).

53. (Moerman et al. 1979; Moerman 2002; Kirmayer 2011).

54. (McClenon 2001).

55. (Brown 1974).

56. (Desjarlais 1992).

57. (Seligman and Kirmayer 2008, 33).

58. This case study analysis is adapted from (Snodgrass, Lacy, Dengah II, Fagan, et al. 2011). See that earlier writing for a fuller treatment of results and relevant scholarship.

59. (Higgins 1987; 1989).

60. (Lewis 1971, 31).

61. (Obeyesekere 1981).

62. (Ong 1988; 2010).

63. (Boddy 1988; 1989).

64. (Seligman 2005; 2010; 2014).

65. This study's results were previously reported in (Snodgrass, Batchelder, et al. 2017; Snodgrass et al. 2016).

66. For an overview of this research, see (Sibilla and Mancini 2018).

67. (Sibilla and Mancini 2018, 12).

68. (Mancini and Sibilla 2017).

69. E.g., see (Bessière, Seay, and Kiesler 2007; Mancini and Sibilla 2017; Dengah II and Snodgrass 2020).

70. On Marmot's work, see (Marmot 2004a; 2005; 2006). On the biology of stress disorders, as related to inequality and other factors, see (Sapolsky 1998).

71. (Dressler 2017, 82).

72. (Bennardo and de Munck 2014, 3).

73. Researchers have confirmed links between individual conformity to social norms and expectations—cultural consonance—and health in places as diverse as Amazonian Bolivia (among the indigenous Tsimane) (Reyes-García et al. 2010), China and Taiwan (Chick, Dong, and Iarmolenko 2014), and New England (Maltseva 2018), and in health outcomes in these and other studies as various as BMI, immune function, and positive psychological well-being, as well as cardiovascular health, depression, perceived stress, and other linked mental and physical health problems considered by Dressler himself (see chapter 7 in Dressler 2017 for a discussion of these and other studies).

74. (Festinger 1962).

75. For my early thinking on cultural dissonance, which I treat more fully in chapter 4, see (Snodgrass, Dengah, and Lacy 2014).

76. (Boellstorff 2008; Castronova 2008; Taylor 2009).

77. For an early version of this argument, see (Snodgrass, Lacy, Dengah II, and Fagan 2011).

78. (Luhrmann 2000).

79. For a step in this direction, see (Banks et al. 2019). See also (Banks and Bowman 2016; Downs, Bowman, and Banks 2019).

80. (Luhrmann 2006; Luhrmann, Nusbaum, and Thisted 2010; Lynn 2005; 2013).

81. (Dressler 2017).

82. (Banks 2015; Ratan 2013; Ratan and Dawson 2016).

83. (Banks and Bowman 2013).

84. (Castronova 2008; Yee 2014).

85. (Bessière, Seay, and Kiesler 2007).

86. See also (Mancini, Imperato, and Sibilla 2019).

87. On immersion in video games, see, e.g., (Bartle 1996; Castronova 2008; Yee 2006b; 2014; Snodgrass et al. 2012).

88. (Goodenough 1957, 167).

89. (Geertz 1973, 45).

90. (Geertz 1973, 362).

91. My *World of Warcraft* specific scale was modeled after two commonly used psychological protocols to assess such experiences, the Tellegen Absorption Scale and the Dissociative Experiences Scale (DES) (Tellegen and Atkinson 1974; Bernstein and Putnam 1986).

92. For more detail, see (Snodgrass, Lacy, Dengah II, Fagan, et al. 2011).

93. (Menon and Cassaniti 2017).

94. (Marmot 2004b).

95. On abstract human potentialities, see (Menon and Cassaniti 2017, 4).

96. (Shweder 2003).

97. (Shweder 1999).

98. (Lewis 1971; Eliade 2020; Bourguignon 1973).

99. (Eliade 2020).

100. For my mixed-methods approach to ethnographic research, see (Snodgrass 2014; 2016; Dengah II et al. 2020).

101. (D'Andrade 1995; 2008).

102. (Goodenough 1957).

103. For a recent collection of essays in this vein, see (Cassaniti and Menon 2017).

104. E.g., see (Johnson-Laird 1983; Mandler 1984; Schank and Abelson 2013).

105. (D'Andrade 1995; Strauss and Quinn 1997).

106. (Bennardo and de Munck 2014; D'Andrade 1995; Holland and Quinn 1987).

107. (Bourdieu 1977).

108. (Strauss and Quinn 1998).

109. (D'Andrade 1995; Hutchins 1995; Clark and Chalmers 1998; Rowlands 2010; Latour 2005; Menary 2010).

110. E.g., see (Snodgrass, Dengah II, and Lacy 2014; Snodgrass, Dengah II, et al. 2017; Dengah II et al. 2020).

111. (Romney, Weller, and Batchelder 1986).

112. (Lacy and Snodgrass 2016; Lacy et al. 2018).

113. See, e.g., (Cassaniti and Menon 2017; Schnegg and Lowe 2020). See also these cultural anthropological-methods handbooks, where these perspectives on culture are often employed (Bernard and Gravlee 2014; Hay 2016).

114. (Dengah II et al. 2020).

CHAPTER ONE: SACRED AND SECULAR SETTINGS

1. (de Wildt et al. 2019).

2. (Marriott 1955).

3. (Kothari 1982; Bharucha and Kothari 2003).

4. For more detailed descriptions of Rajasthani spirit possession, including a fuller engagement with scholarly sources on which my descriptions here are in part based, see (Snodgrass 2002b; 2004b).

5. (Kothari 1982, 25).

6. (Kothari 1982, 31).

7. (Gold 1988, 41).

8. (de Wildt et al. 2019).

9. This god is a local equivalent of the pan-Indian Bhairava, "the Destroyer," also referred to as Bhutesvara, "Lord of Ghosts," both "fierce" or "terrible" forms of Siva spoken of in ancient Sanskrit scriptures.

10. On Hindu auspiciousness beliefs, see (Snodgrass 2004c).

11. (Dwyer 1999, 113).

12. (Freed and Freed 1990, 405).

13. (Harlan 1992, 66).

14. (Freed and Freed 1990, 404).

15. (Seeberg 1994, 45).

16. (Lewis 1971).

17. E.g., see (Lewis 1971; Seligman 2014).

18. (Dwyer 1999, 123).

19. (Dwyer 1998).

20. (Kakar 1991).

21. (Freed and Freed 1990, 405)

22. (Castillo 1994a; 1994b).

23. (Obeyesekere 1981).

24. This case study, which frames chapters 2–4, was first described in (Snodgrass 2002a).

25. For a detailed portrait of this community, see (Snodgrass 1997; 2006).

26. *Dalit*—literally, "Oppressed Person"—is a preferred term of self-reference for persons previously referred to as "Untouchables" or Harijans. *Harijans*—literally, "Children of God"—is a Gandhian construct, meant to restore dignity to Untouchables, though which Dalits now find condescending.

27. (Tod 1914).

28. From *kath* or "wood" and *putli,* meaning "doll" or "figure."

29. Here, I cite R. P. Tomar's 1991 Census of India as it provides figures that coincide more closely with the period of my fieldwork with the Bhats in the early to mid-1990s.

30. (Maggs, Shapira, and Sides 1979).

31. (Adams, Albert, and Garriott 1985).

32. (de Wildt et al. 2019).

33. For more thoughts on these co-optation and techno-mysticism arguments, see (de Wildt et al. 2019).

34. (de Wildt et al. 2019).

35. For this statistic, and that early work of mine, see (Snodgrass et al. 2012).

36. (Tolkien 2012a; 2012b).

37. (Gygax and Arneson 1974).

38. (Nardi and Harris 2006).

39. (Castronova 2008).

40. In *World of Warcraft,* Azeroth refers to one of the three continents of the Eastern Kingdoms. It also sometimes refers generally to the planet as a whole on which this continent is found, as well as to the world as a whole that includes both Azeroth the planet and other planets like Outland.

41. On a theory of gaming fun, see (Koster 2013).

42. (McGonigal 2011).

43. For a good introduction to and overview of this research, by a leading specialist of gaming motivations, see (Yee 2014).

44. (Pontes et al. 2014).

45. E.g., (Pontes and Griffiths 2014; Rehbein et al. 2010; Turner et al. 2012).

46. One group of scholars define a behavioral addiction as "a repeated behaviour leading to significant harm or distress. The behaviour is not reduced by the person and persists over a significant period of time. The harm or distress is of a functionally impairing nature" (Kardefelt-Winther et al. 2017).

47. (World Health Organization 2018).

48. (American Psychiatric Association 2013).

49. E.g., see (Petry et al. 2014).

50. (Griffiths et al. 2016). For my review of these debates, see (Snodgrass, Zhao, et al. 2018; 2019).

51. For my thoughts on problem gaming as a response to life distress, and summary of those debates, see for example (Snodgrass et al. 2014; Snodgrass, Dengah II, et al. 2019; Snodgrass, Bagwell, et al. 2018).

52. E.g., see (Snodgrass et al. 2016; Snodgrass, Batchelder, et al. 2017).

53. Not surprisingly, felt loneliness is importantly associated with problematic internet use including problem gaming, and is even seen as a cause of such internet-related distress and dysfunction. For my review of this literature, see (Snodgrass, Bagwell, et al. 2018).

54. E.g., see (Castronova 2008; Yee 2014).

55. (Kardefelt-Winther 2014b; Snodgrass, Bagwell, et al. 2018).

56. (Huvila et al. 2010).

57. E.g., see (Chen 2012; Nardi 2010; Taylor 2009).

58. (Schiano et al. 2014; Shaw 2012).

59. (Snodgrass, Lacy, Francois Dengah II, et al. 2011).

60. (Kardefelt-Winther, 2014a, 2014b; Snodgrass, Lacy, et al., 2014; Snodgrass, Dengah, et al., 2014)

61. E.g., see (Ko et al. 2012).

62. (Snodgrass et al. 2014).

63. For a fuller description of my work with KOG, see (Snodgrass, Batchelder, et al. 2017).

64. At the time of our research in Fall 2011, KOG had switched to progressing through ten-man *heroic* raids, which were less ambitious than the twenty-five-man raids.

65. See C. Chandramouli and the Registrar General's 2011 Census of India.

66. For more on this work, which is the focus of chapter 4, see (Snodgrass et al. 2021).

67. (Arnett 2000).

68. (Subrahmanyam et al. 2008).

69. (Arnett 2000; Bessière, Seay, and Kiesler 2007; Turkle 2011).

CHAPTER TWO: THE PSYCHOLOGY OF
AVATAR THERAPEUTICS

1. Described in (Snodgrass 2002a), this case study was a part of my PhD dissertation research (Snodgrass 1997). I returned to the Udaipur Bhat community during the summer of 1998 while a Killam Postdoctoral Fellow at the University of Alberta. At that time, I investigated a form of possession in which women were "grabbed" by the spirits of still living men, with the women subsequently visiting a Sufi saint named Mastanna Baba to be cured, which is described in (Snodgrass 2002b; 2004b).

2. Other meanings of *bhav,* in a dictionary entry which reads like an extended metaphysical poem, are "sentiment," "idea," "existence," "being," "sense," "purport," "gist," "nature," "temperament," and interestingly enough for this context, as readers will see, "price" (Chaturvedi and Tiwari 1990).

3. As discussed in the preceding chapter, gods (devata) such as Kali, Hanuman, Bhairuji, and Tejaji (a god of snake bites) commonly seize human mounts. But Supreme Gods, such as the Hindu triumvirate of Brahma, Vishnu, and Shiva, do not possess Rajasthani persons, for it is believed that their overwhelming power (sakti) would cause a human vessel's head or body to explode.

4. Bhats referred to this exorcist as a *pandit.* Most North Indians refer to such persons as *bhopas* or *ojhas*—perhaps best translated "spirit medium"—distinguishing between Brahmin priests who would not deal with spirits (pandits) and spiritual specialists (bhopa*s*).

5. On this work, which discusses the theatrical dimensions of Rajasthani spirit possession, see (Snodgrass 2002b).

6. Again, on this point, see (Snodgrass 2002b).

7. (Snodgrass 1990).

8. See (Bharucha and Kothari 2003) for compelling conversations with Komal Kothari, which give deep insights into Rajasthani art and culture.

9. For alternatives to the lone-ethnographer model of research, see (Copeland and Dengah 2016).

10. Lila Abu-Lughod spoke of how her half-Egyptian (via her father) and half-anthropologist identity lent her a unique subject position (Abu-Lughod 1991). Riffing on the idea, Tanya Luhrmann described herself being a "halfie" in the sense of half psychiatrist (also her father) and half anthropologist (Luhrmann 2000). As an adolescent, I played *Dungeons & Dragons* with my brothers and close friends, but decided my school's D&D club wasn't for me. In high school, I actively played tabletop and sometimes role-playing games with my friends, but didn't typically speak about that outside my most intimate social circles. After returning from fieldwork in India, I played the Generic Universal Role-Playing System (GURPS) with some of my closest graduate student friends. Never fully embraced, even embarrassed at times by my own geekiness, games have nevertheless been integral to my life at its various stages.

11. These ideas appear in different form in (Snodgrass 2016). For more detailed descriptions of my virtual-worlds methods, see also (Snodgrass 2014).

12. On "mixed" qualitative-quantitative anthropological methods, see (Bernard 2011; Bernard and Gravlee 2014).

13. The lab now includes a large conference table and big-screen television for discussions and presentations, an extensive library on anthropology, virtual worlds, and research methods, five desktop computers outfitted with relevant software for interview transcription (StartStop, a pedal-driven system that frees up the hands for more efficient typing), qualitative data management and analysis (Maxqda), statistical analysis (Stata), social-network analysis (EgoNet, for ego-centered social-network software, and UCINET, with the latter also useful for cultural consensus and other statistical analysis), and games (*World of Warcraft* and *Guild Wars 2*).

14. These results and analysis first appeared in slightly different form in (Snodgrass, Lacy, Dengah II, Fagan, et al. 2011).

15. (Seligman and Kirmayer 2008).

16. E.g., see (Davis 1984).

17. The issue is slightly more complicated, and the pleasures of WoW stress emerge from the fact that monsters seem simultaneously real and fantasy. On some level, even when the monsters temporarily feel real, players know that WoW is after all only a game, fantasy and not real. Players surrender some degree of control over the game's fantasy dangers in order to be stimulated, but it is easy to snap back into a view of WoW as "only a game."

18. (Csikszentmihalyi 2008).

19. This table appeared originally in (Snodgrass, Lacy, Dengah II, Fagan, et al. 2011).

20. This table appeared originally in (Snodgrass, Lacy, Dengah II, Fagan, et al. 2011).

21. For more detail on these Rajasthani cases of spirit possession, see (Snodgrass 2002b), where these descriptions first appeared.

22. (Kothari 1982, 13).

23. I describe this ritual in (Snodgrass 2004a).

24. (Krippner and Powers 2013).

25. (Lynn 2005).

26. (American Psychiatric Association 2013).

27. (Lévi-Strauss 1963; Dwyer 1998; 1999; Seligman and Kirmayer 2008).

28. (Freed and Freed 1990).

29. (Bourguignon 2004).

30. For a classic account of the diversity of religious experiences, see (James 1902).

31. On immersion, see for example (Yee 2014).

32. (Lynn 2005).

33. (Luhrmann 2006; Luhrmann, Nusbaum, and Thisted 2010).

34. (Snodgrass, Lacy, Dengah II, Fagan, et al. 2011; Snodgrass et al. 2014; Yee 2006b; 2014).

35. (McGonigal 2011).

36. (Koster 2013; Yee 2006b; 2006a).

37. (Yee 2014).

38. (Csikszentmihalyi 2008).

39. E.g., see (Lynn 2005; Seligman and Kirmayer 2008; Luhrmann, Nusbaum, and Thisted 2010).

40. On gaming's promotion of human flourishing, see (Jones et al. 2014).

CHAPTER THREE: THE PSYCHOSOCIAL DYNAMICS OF
AVATAR THERAPEUTICS

1. (Macpherson 2011).

2. (Higgins 1987; 1989).

3. (Marmot 2004b).

4. These ethnographic descriptions were first published in (Snodgrass, Batchelder, et al. 2017).

5. These details and arguments appeared in different form in (Snodgrass et al. 2016).

6. (Selye 1975).

7. (McGonigal 2011).

8. (Yee 2006a).

9. For similar arguments, see (Snodgrass, Dengah II, and Lacy 2014).

10. I originally made this argument in (Snodgrass, Dengah II, Lacy, and Fagan 2011).

11. This table appeared originally in (Snodgrass, Lacy, Dengah II, Fagan, et al. 2011).

12. For more detail on this analysis, see (Snodgrass, Dengah II, Lacy, and Fagan 2011).

13. This analysis first appeared in (Snodgrass et al. 2016).

14. This figure appeared originally in (Snodgrass et al. 2016).

15. (Lewis 1971).

16. (Obeyesekere 1981).

17. (Ong 1988; 2010).

18. (Boddy 1988; 1989).

19. (Boddy 1994).

20. (Seligman 2005; 2010; 2014).

21. (Higgins 1987; 1989).

22. (Marmot 2004a; 2004b).

23. (Obeyesekere 1981).

24. (Seligman 2014).

25. (Ong 2010).

26. (Boddy 1988; 1989).

27. E.g., see (Lewis 1971; Bourguignon 1973; Boddy 1994).

28. E.g., see (Williams et al. 2006; Malone 2007; Cockshut 2012).

29. For a similar ethnographic approach to guilds, see (Chen 2012; Nardi 2010).

30. (Bessière, Seay, and Kiesler 2007).

31. (Malone 2009).

32. (Bennardo and de Munck 2014).

33. On cultural consonance, see (Dressler 2017).

34. On gaming as psychosocially compensatory, see (Kardefelt-Winther 2014a; Snodgrass, Bagwell, et al. 2018; Dengah II and Snodgrass 2020).

35. For these debates on this topic, see for example (Petry et al. 2014; Griffiths et al. 2016).

36. (Castronova 2008).

37. (Selye 1975).

38. (Coventry and Brown 1993).

39. (Seligman and Kirmayer 2008; Luhrmann, Nusbaum, and Thisted 2010).

40. (Castronova 2008; Yee 2006b; 2014).

41. For a description of WoW raiders' distinctive states of consciousness and mental absorption, see (Golub 2010).

42. I would remind readers that KOG raiders contributed importantly to this chapter's first survey as well, which also featured in chapter 2, answering those WoW-related dissociation, stress, and well-being questions, and thus influencing that study's conclusions.

43. (D'Andrade 2006).

44. (de Munck and Bennardo 2019).

45. On these points, see also (Gilbert 1979; Searle 1995), whom D'Andrade (2006) references.

CHAPTER FOUR: DISTINGUISHING THERAPEUTIC FROM TOXIC AVATAR EXPERIENCES

1. For more on Kothari's views of Rajasthan's folk artists and the contexts of their performances, see (Bharucha and Kothari 2003).

2. E.g., see (Lewis 1971).

3. (Dressler 2017).

4. (Festinger 1962).

5. For my original formulation of cultural dissonance, which was developed in a North American gaming context, see (Snodgrass, Dengah II, and Lacy 2014).

6. (Arnett 2000).

7. This description and analysis of Udaipuri gaming-zone experiences appeared first in somewhat different form in (Snodgrass et al. 2021).

8. (James 1994).

9. (Williams et al. 2006).

10. (Malaby 2007).

11. For classic accounts of shamanism, see (Howells 1950; Vitebsky 2001).

12. E.g., see (Lévi-Strauss 1963; Bourguignon 2004).

13. (Brown 1989).

14. See, for example, the film *Magical Death,* which concerns Yanomamo shamanism (Chagnon and Asch 1973).

15. (Obeyesekere 1981).

16. (Ong 1988; 2010).

17. (Boddy 1988; 1989).

18. (Seligman 2010; 2014).

19. (De Antoni 2017; Pietkiewicz et al. 2021).

20. On Marian visions, see, for example, (Horsfall 2000; Halemba 2015).

21. (Stoller 1984; 1989; 2014).

22. For a film featuring Hauka spirit possessions, see (Rouch 1955).

23. (Dressler 2017).

24. (Marmot 2004a; 2004b).

25. (Festinger 1962).

26. For an earlier version of this argument, see (Snodgrass, Dengah II, and Lacy 2014).

27. E.g., see (Lewis 1971; Bourguignon 2004; Boddy 1994).

28. E.g., see (Raheja and Gold 1994).

29. (Ong 1988; 2010).

30. (Bourguignon 2004).

31. (Obeyesekere 1981).
32. (Ong 1988; 2010).
33. (Boddy 1988; 1989).
34. (Seligman 2010; 2014).
35. (De Antoni 2017; Halemba 2015; Horsfall 2000; Pietkiewicz et al. 2021).
36. (Rouch 1955; Stoller 1984; 1989; 2014).
37. (Szablewicz 2010; Golub and Lingley 2008).
38. On this research, see (Snodgrass, Dengah II, and Lacy 2014).
39. (Snodgrass, Dengah II, and Lacy 2014).
40. (Krippner and Powers 2013; Lynn 2005; Seligman and Kirmayer 2008).
41. (Higgins 1987; 1989).
42. This idea has parallels in work on cognitive dissonance, which emphasizes how dissonant cognitions lead particularly to psychological discomfort and the desire for congruency when they threaten a coherent sense of self (Aronson 1999).
43. (Marmot 2004a; 2004b).
44. E.g., see (Searle 1995; Gilbert 1979; D'Andrade 2006; de Munck and Bennardo 2019).

CONCLUSION

1. E.g., see (Castronova 2008; Yee 2014).
2. (Higgins 1987; 1989).
3. (Marmot 2004a; 2004b).
4. (Shweder 2003).
5. (Lewis 1971; Eliade 2020; Vitebsky 2001).
6. (Krippner and Powers 2013; Lynn 2005; Seligman and Kirmayer 2008).
7. (Bourguignon 1973; Lewis 1971).
8. (American Psychiatric Association 2013).
9. E.g., see (Lynn 2005; Seligman and Kirmayer 2008; Luhrmann 2006; Luhrmann, Nusbaum, and Thisted 2010).
10. For a contemporary example, see (Seligman 2014).
11. (American Psychiatric Association 2013).
12. E.g., see (Bourguignon 2004).
13. (Krippner and Powers 2013).
14. (Seligman and Kirmayer 2008).
15. (Higgins 1987; 1989).
16. (Marmot 2005; 2006).
17. On cultural dissonance, see (Snodgrass, Dengah II, and Lacy 2014).
18. (Dressler 2017).
19. (Festinger 1962).
20. (Higgins 1989; Marmot 2004b; Dressler 2017).
21. (Lewis 1971).

22. E.g., see (Lynn 2005; Seligman and Kirmayer 2008).

23. (Eliade 2020).

24. (Lynn 2005).

25. E.g., see (Castronova 2008; Yee 2014).

26. (Lynn 2005).

27. (Williams et al. 2006).

28. (Williams et al. 2006).

29. (Higgins 1987; 1989).

30. (Marmot 2004a; 2004b).

31. (Castronova 2008).

32. (Boellstorff 2008).

33. Such a project would be importantly informed by an anthropology of Christianity, e.g., see (Bialecki, Haynes, and Robbins 2008).

34. For a recent debate on the harmful impact of social media and other forms of "screen time" on adolescent well-being, see (Orben and Przybylski 2019; Twenge et al. 2020; Orben and Przybylski 2020).

35. For anthropological analysis of the power of play, see, e.g., (Turner 1982).

36. (Mancini and Sibilla 2017, Sibilla and Mancini 2018).

37. (Snodgrass et al. 2018; Snodgrass, Lacy, et al. 2022; Snodgrass, Lacy, and Cole 2019).

38. E.g., see (Henrich 2017).

39. A perspective common in the field of social genomics, e.g., see (Cole 2014).

40. E.g., see (Weinstein and Lejoyeux 2015; Xiuqin et al. 2010).

41. (Pearl and Mackenzie 2018).

APPENDIX A

1. For the original analysis, see (Snodgrass, Lacy, Dengah II, Fagan, et al. 2011).

2. (Tellegen and Atkinson 1974; Bernstein and Putnam 1986).

APPENDIX B

1. See (Snodgrass, Dengah II, Lacy, and Fagan 2011) for the originally published analysis.

2. (Karlson and Holm 2011).

3. (Snodgrass, Dengah II, Lacy, and Fagan 2011; Snodgrass, Dengah II, and Lacy 2014; Snodgrass, Dengah II, et al. 2017; Dengah II et al. 2020).

4. (Young 1998; Young and Rogers 1998).

5. For more detail on this analysis, see (Snodgrass et al. 2016).

6. (Cohen, Kamarck, and Mermelstein 1983).

7. (Snodgrass et al. 2012).

1. This analysis was first presented in (Snodgrass et al. 2021).
2. For those procedures, see (Dressler 2017). For an application of formal cultural consonance/dissonance procedures to a North American gaming context, see my earlier work in (Snodgrass, Dengah II, and Lacy 2014).
3. (Snodgrass, Dengah II, et al. 2017).

GLOSSARY

ABSORPTION: a profound narrowing or concentration of attention

ALT: an alternate or secondary gaming character, distinguished from a player's *main,* or main gaming character

AVATAR (HINDI): an agent who is understood to be the vehicle or embodiment of another's consciousness; in the original Sanskrit, *avatar* literally means "descent"—joining *ava* (down or below) with the verb root *tr* (float or pass over something, such as a river)—and refers to the way that Hindu deities incarnate in earthly vehicles in order to combat evil and restore balance in the universe; contemporaneously, a digital self-object in a computer-generated environment

AZEROTH: the name of the world where core *World of Warcraft* events unfold

BHATS: low-status puppeteer performers originally from western Rajasthan (a region referred to as Marwar), but now also living in the city of Udaipur and throughout Rajasthan and India

BHAV A GAYA (HINDI): lit., "feelings have come," conventionally used by Rajasthanis to describe a state of spiritual possession

BHUT (HINDI): ghost

BHUT KI BIMARI (HINDI): ghost illness, a negatively experienced state of spiritual possession

BOSSES: powerful monsters or enemies found in games like *World of Warcraft*

CHAVANDA MATA: Ramu Bhat's lineage goddess, who was said to possess Bedami

COUNTERSTRIKE—GLOBAL OFFENSIVE: a multiplayer first-person shooter game (FPS) developed by Valve and Hidden Path Entertainment

CS-GO: *Counterstrike—Global Offensive*

CULTURAL CONSONANCE: defined by William Dressler as "the degree to which individuals approximate widely shared cultural models in their own beliefs and behaviors"

CULTURAL DISSONANCE: an extension of cultural consonance, refers to the stresses, strains, and psychological processes associated with embodying and negotiating potentially competing or conflictual cultural norms or models

CYBERPUNK: a subgenre of science fiction; stories set in typically dystopian near-futures, with emphases on street-smart characters, technology, and evil corporations often fomenting social disorder, or, as Bruce Sterling succinctly put it, a "combination of low-life and high tech"; examples of cyberpunk novels are William Gibson's *Count Zero* and Neal Stephenson's *Snow Crash*

DEVI (HINDI): goddess

DISSOCIATION: experiences and behaviors that seem to exist apart from the mainstream flow of one's conscious awareness and identity

DUNGEON: typically, five-player special events in games like *World of Warcraft,* where players battle powerful monsters (termed *bosses*) to win treasure and items like weapons and armor (called *gear*)

DASHAVATARA (SANSKRIT): Vishnu the preserver's ten primary forms; *das* literally means "ten," so, Vishnu's "ten avatars" or "ten incarnations"

DISSOCIATIVE IDENTITY DISORDER: a mental-health problem associated with extreme and dysfunctional discontinuities of experience; described in the American Psychiatric Association's DSM-5 (*Diagnostic and Statistical Manual of Mental Disorders,* 5th ed.); abbreviated DID, also referred to as Multiple Personality Disorder

ECSTASY: experiences that allow one to step outside or transcend a current identity and situation, from the Greek *ekstasis,* which literally means "standing outside a current state"

ERTL: the author's Ethnographic Research and Teaching Laboratory, at Colorado State University

ETHNOGRAPHY: case-study accounts of a group's practices and points of view, relying largely on qualitative field-based methods like participant observation

FARMING: in games like *World of Warcraft,* harvesting in-game resources to be sold for gold used to purchase important materials, such as raiding items including potions to strengthen raiders' armor, in order to more effectively battle powerful monsters termed *bosses*

FPS: first-person shooter games such as *Counterstrike—Global Offensive*

GAMING DISORDER: a mental health condition recently judged by the American Psychiatric Association (APA) and the World Health Organization (WHO) to warrant formal inclusion in their latest diagnostic manuals; sometimes glossed as *gaming addiction* and *toxic immersion*

GAMING ZONES: face-to-face gaming parlors found in Udaipur and throughout India; also referred to as *gaming lounges*

GEAR: gaming equipment like weapons and armor in MMOs, often won as a reward for completing difficult game content

GUILD: associations of like-minded players in games like *World of Warcraft*

GUILD WARS 2: A multiplayer online role-playing game produced by the company ArenaNet

GW2: *Guild Wars 2*

HARDCORE GAMING: serious and competitive gaming, opposed to more casual forms of play

HEALED HEALER: a term used to describe spiritual specialists such as mediums and shamans, who, in overcoming their own life problems, gain the ability to help others

HEALTH DISPARITIES: differential mortality and morbidity across social groups, related to, e.g., cardiovascular disease, cancer, and metabolic problems such as diabetes, which are understood to be driven importantly by factors such as poverty, educational attainment, and racism

IMMERSION: losing oneself in another reality such as a computer-generated gaming world, to the extent that one feels to be actually *in* that virtual world

INSTANCE: a new copy of an area in a game such as *World of Warcraft* generated for a particular group of players; dungeons and raids are examples of instances

KNIGHTS OF GOOD, a *World of Warcraft* guild founded by Lainey and Vern; also refers to a gaming guild in the popular web series, *The Guild*

KOG: The Knights of Good

KULDEVI (HINDI): lineage goddess

MAIN: a player's main or principal gaming character, distinguished from alternative or secondary gaming characters termed *alts*

MMORPG: massively multiplayer online role-playing games; examples are *World of Warcraft* and *Guild Wars 2;* also abbreviated MMO

PIR BABA (HINDI): a Muslim saint; Mastanna Baba is an example

PROGRESSION GUILD: in games such as *World of Warcraft,* groups of players that aim to systematically and often competitively progress through new gaming content such as raids

PSYCHOLOGICAL ANTHROPOLOGY: a field of study focused on the relationship between culture and mind

PVE: Player-vs-Environment, a play mode in games like *World of Warcraft,* where players test their skills against computer-generated challenges such as *bosses* found in *dungeons* and *raids*

PVP: Player-vs-Player, a play mode in games like *World of Warcraft,* where players test their skills against each other

RAID: special events in games like *World of Warcraft* typically involving more than five and up to forty players, where players battle powerful monsters (termed *bosses*) in order to win treasure and items like weapons and armor (called *gear*)

RL: real life, in gamer talk; sometimes also IRL, "in real life"

SAGASJI BAOJI: in Rajasthan, a class of spirits composed of the deceased souls of murdered kings

SAKTI (HINDI): in Hinduism, spiritual power or divine energy

SDT: Self-Discrepancy Theory, a framework developed by Edward Higgins, to examine how discrepancies between a person's perception of their actual and ideal selves can predict mental and emotional health

SHAMAN (ORIGINALLY TUNGUS): a spiritual specialist believed to have the ability to project his or her consciousness outside the physical body; from *saman,* lit., "one who shakes," referring to experiences involving trance and physical shaking

SPIRIT MEDIUM: a spiritual specialist believed to have the power to channel into their body outside spirits and deities, becoming the *medium* or *channel* through which spiritual agents communicate with humans; Bedami eventually transitioned into the role of spirit medium; Kani Bai, a tribal woman, is another example of a medium

SPIRIT POSSESSION: an altered state of consciousness associated with the feeling that one has become the vehicle of an intrusive spirit or deity

STATUS SYNDROME: Michael Marmot's idea that the social-health gradient was importantly driven by social-status differences, for example, via stress mechanisms and pathways

SUBJECTIVE WELL-BEING: the continuum of positive and negative experiences and emotions; a less clinical term than, for example, "mental health"

TRANCE: a termed used by anthropologists and others to refer to the altered states of consciousness experienced by shamans and spirit mediums

UDAIPUR: a city in the Indian state of Rajasthan

WHITEHALL: a road and area in London, where much of the UK's government employees work; in Michael Marmot's famous Whitehall study, he pointed to a social-health gradient in the civil service, with employee's differential health outcomes attributable in part to social-status differences across different service ranks

WORLD OF WARCRAFT: A multiplayer online role-playing game made by Blizzard Entertainment

WOW: *World of Warcraft*

REFERENCES

Abu-Lughod, Lila. 1991. "Writing against Culture." In *Recapturing Anthropology: Working in the Present*, edited by Richard G. Fox, 137–62. Santa Fe, NM: School of American Research Press.

Adams, Roe R., David Albert, and Richard Garriott. 1985. *Ultima IV: Quest of the Avatar*. Austin, TX: Origin Systems.

American Psychiatric Association. 2013. *DSM-5*. Washington, DC: American Psychiatric Association.

Aronson, Elliot. 1999. "Dissonance, Hypocrisy, and the Self-Concept." In *Cognitive Dissonance: Progress on a Pivotal Theory in Social Psychology*, edited by Eddie Harmon-Jones & Judson Mills, 103–26. Washington, DC: American Psychological Association.

Arnett, Jeffrey Jensen. 2000. "Emerging Adulthood: A Theory of Development from the Late Teens through the Twenties." *American Psychologist* 55 (5): 469–80.

Banks, Jaime. 2015. "Object, Me, Symbiote, Other: A Social Typology of Player-Avatar Relationships." *First Monday* 20 (2). https://doi.org/10.5210/fm.v20i2.5433.

Banks, Jaime, and Nicholas David Bowman. 2013. "Close Intimate Playthings? Understanding Player-Avatar Relationships as a Function of Attachment, Agency, and Intimacy." *AoIR Selected Papers of Internet Research* 14. https://journals.uic.edu/ojs/index.php/spir/article/view/8498.

———. 2016. "Emotion, Anthropomorphism, Realism, Control: Validation of a Merged Metric for Player–Avatar Interaction (PAX)." *Computers in Human Behavior* 54: 215–23.

Banks, Jaime, Nicholas David Bowman, Jih-Hsuan Tammy Lin, Daniel Pietschmann, and Joe A. Wasserman. 2019. "The Common Player-Avatar Interaction Scale (CPAX): Expansion and Cross-Language Validation." *International Journal of Human-Computer Studies* 129: 64–73.

Bartle, Richard. 1996. "Hearts, Clubs, Diamonds, Spades: Players Who Suit MUDs." *Journal of MUD Research* 1 (1): 1–28.

Bennardo, Giovanni, and Victor C. de Munck. 2014. *Cultural Models: Genesis, Methods, and Experiences.* New York: Oxford University Press.

Benson, Herbert, and Miriam Z. Klipper. 1975. *The Relaxation Response.* New York: Morrow.

Bernard, H. Russell. 2011. *Research Methods in Anthropology: Qualitative and Quantitative Approaches.* Rowman Altamira.

Bernard, H. Russell, and Clarence C. Gravlee. 2014. *Handbook of Methods in Cultural Anthropology.* Rowman & Littlefield.

Bernstein, Eve M., and Frank W. Putnam. 1986. "Development, Reliability, and Validity of a Dissociation Scale." *Journal of Nervous and Mental Disease* 174 (12): 727–35.

Bessière, Katherine, A. Fleming Seay, and Sara Kiesler. 2007. "The Ideal Elf: Identity Exploration in World of Warcraft." *Cyberpsychology & Behavior* 10 (4): 530–35.

Bharucha, Rustom, and Komal Kothari. 2003. *Rajasthan, an Oral History: Conversations with Komal Kothari.* Penguin Global.

Bialecki, Jon, Naomi Haynes, and Joel Robbins. 2008. "The Anthropology of Christianity." *Religion Compass* 2 (6): 1139–58.

Boddy, Janice. 1988. "Spirits and Selves in Northern Sudan: The Cultural Therapeutics of Possession and Trance." *American Ethnologist* 15 (1): 4–27.

———. 1989. *Wombs and Alien Spirits: Women, Men, and the Zar Cult in Northern Sudan.* Madison: University of Wisconsin Press.

———. 1994. "Spirit Possession Revisited: Beyond Instrumentality." *Annual Review of Anthropology* 23 (1): 407–34.

Boellstorff, Tom. 2008. *Coming of Age in Second Life: An Anthropologist Explores the Virtually Human.* Princeton, NJ: Princeton University Press.

Bourdieu, Pierre. 1977. *Outline of a Theory of Practice.* Translated by Richard Nice. Cambridge: Cambridge University Press.

Bourguignon, Erika. 1973. *Religion, Altered States of Consciousness, and Social Change.* Columbus: Ohio State University Press. https://kb.osu.edu/handle/1811/6294.

———. 2004. "Suffering and Healing, Subordination and Power: Women and Possession Trance." *Ethos* 32 (4): 557–74.

Boyer, Pascal. 2003. "Religious Thought and Behaviour as By-Products of Brain Function." *Trends in Cognitive Sciences* 7 (3): 119–24.

Brown, Barbara B. 1974. *New Mind, New Body: Bio-Feedback: New Directions for the Mind.* Harper & Row.

Brown, Karen McCarthy, and Claudine Michel. 2010. *Mama Lola: A Vodou Priestess in Brooklyn.* Berkeley: University of California Press.

Brown, Michael F. 1989. "Dark Side of the Shaman." *Natural History* 98 (11): 8–10.

Cameron, James, dir. 2009. *Avatar.* Century City, CA: 20th Century Fox.

Cassaniti, Julia L., and Usha Menon, eds. 2017. *Universalism without Uniformity: Explorations in Mind and Culture.* Chicago: University of Chicago Press.

Castillo, Richard J. 1994a. "Spirit Possession in South Asia, Dissociation or Hysteria?" *Culture, Medicine and Psychiatry* 18 (1): 1–21.

———. 1994b. "Spirit Possession in South Asia, Dissociation or Hysteria? Part 2: Case Histories." *Culture, Medicine and Psychiatry* 18 (2): 141–62.

Castronova, Edward. 2008. *Synthetic Worlds: The Business and Culture of Online Games.* Chicago: University of Chicago Press.

Chagnon, Napoleon, and Timothy Asch, dir. 1973. *Magical Death.* Watertown, MA: Documentary Educational Resources.

Chaturvedi, Mahendra, and Bholanath Tiwari. 1990. *A Practical Hindi-English Dictionary.* New Delhi: National Publishing House.

Chen, Mark G. 2012. *Leet Noobs: The Life and Death of an Expert Player Group in World of Warcraft.* Peter Lang.

Chandramouli, C., and the Registrar General. "Census of India." *Rural Urban Distribution of Population, Provisional Population Total.* New Delhi: Office of the Registrar General and Census Commissioner, India, 2011.

Chick, Garry, Erwei Dong, and Svitlana Iarmolenko. 2014. "Cultural Consonance in Leisure Activities and Self-Rated Health in Six Cities in China." *World Leisure Journal* 56 (2): 110–19.

Clark, Andy, and David Chalmers. 1998. "The Extended Mind." *Analysis* 58 (1): 7–19.

Cockshut, Tahirih Ladan. 2012. "The Way We Play: Exploring the Specifics of Formation, Action and Competition in Digital Gameplay among World of Warcraft Raiders." PhD diss., Durham University. http://etheses.dur.ac.uk/5931/.

Cohen, Sheldon, Tom Kamarck, and Robin Mermelstein. 1983. "A Global Measure of Perceived Stress." *Journal of Health and Social Behavior* 24 (4): 385–96.

Cole, Steven W. 2014. "Human Social Genomics." *PLoS Genetics* 10 (8): e1004601. https://doi.org/10.1371/journal.pgen.1004601.

Consalvo, Mia. 2009. "There Is No Magic Circle." *Games and Culture* 4 (4): 408–17.

Copeland, Toni J., and H.J. François Dengah. 2016. "'Involve Me and I Learn': Teaching and Applying Anthropology." *Annals of Anthropological Practice* 40 (2): 120–33.

Counter-Strike—Global Offensive. 2012. Bellevue, WA: Hidden Path Entertainment; Bellevue, WA: Valve.

Coventry, Kenny R., and R. Iain F. Brown. 1993. "Sensation Seeking, Gambling and Gambling Addictions." *Addiction* 88: 541–54.

Craig, Tom K.J., Mar Rus-Calafell, Thomas Ward, Julian P. Leff, Mark Huckvale, Elizabeth Howarth, Richard Emsley, and Philippa A. Garety. 2018. "AVATAR Therapy for Auditory Verbal Hallucinations in People with Psychosis: A Single-Blind, Randomised Controlled Trial." *Lancet Psychiatry* 5 (1): 31–40.

Csikszentmihalyi, Mihaly. 2008. *Flow: The Psychology of Optimal Experience.* New York: Harper Perennial Modern Classics.

D'Andrade, Roy G. 1995. *The Development of Cognitive Anthropology.* Cambridge: Cambridge University Press.

———. 2006. "Commentary on Searle's 'Social Ontology: Some Basic Principles' Culture and Institutions." *Anthropological Theory* 6 (1): 30–39.

———. 2008. *A Study of Personal and Cultural Values: American, Japanese, and Vietnamese*. New York: Springer.

Davis, Joel. 1984. *Endorphins: New Waves in Brain Chemistry*. New York: Doubleday.

De Antoni, Andrea. 2017. "Sympathy from the Devil Experiences, Movement and Affective Correspondences during a Roman Catholic Exorcism in Contemporary Italy." *Japanese Review of Cultural Anthropology* 18 (1): 143–57.

Dengah II, H. J. François, and Jeffrey G. Snodgrass. 2020. "Avatar Creation in Videogaming: Between Compensation and Constraint." *Games for Health Journal* 9 (4): 265–72. https://doi.org/DOI: 10.1089/g4h.2019.0118.

Dengah II, H. J. François, Jeffrey G. Snodgrass, Evan R. Polzer, and Cody Nixon. 2020. *Systematic Methods for Analyzing Culture: A Practical Guide*. Abingdon, UK: Routledge.

Desjarlais, Robert. 1992. *Body and Emotion: The Aesthetics of Illness and Healing in the Nepal Himalayas*. Philadelphia: University of Pennsylvania Press.

Downs, Edward, Nicholas D. Bowman, and Jaime Banks. 2019. "A Polythetic Model of Player-Avatar Identification: Synthesizing Multiple Mechanisms." *Psychology of Popular Media Culture* 8 (3): 269–79.

Dressler, William W. 2017. *Culture and the Individual: Theory and Method of Cultural Consonance*. New York: Routledge.

Dwyer, Graham. 1998. "The Phenomenology of Supernatural Malaise: Attribution, Vulnerability and the Patterns of Affliction at a Hindu Pilgrimage Centre in Rajasthan." *Social Analysis: The International Journal of Social and Cultural Practice* 42 (2): 3–23.

———. 1999. "Healing and the Transformation of Self in Exorcism at a Hindu Shrine in Rajasthan." *Social Analysis: The International Journal of Social and Cultural Practice* 43 (2): 108–37.

Eliade, Mircea. 2020. *Shamanism: Archaic Techniques of Ecstasy*. Princeton Classics. Princeton, NJ: Princeton University Press. First published in French in 1951.

Festinger, Leon. 1962. *A Theory of Cognitive Dissonance*. Stanford, CA: Stanford University Press.

Freed, Ruth S., and Stanley A. Freed. 1990. "Ghost Illness in a North Indian Village." *Social Science & Medicine* 30 (5): 617–23.

Geertz, Clifford. 1973. *The Interpretation of Cultures*. New York: Basic Books.

Gibson, William. 1986. *Count Zero*. New York: Ace Books.

Gilbert, Margaret. 1979. *On Social Facts*. London: Routledge.

Gold, Ann Grodzins. 1988. "Spirit Possession Perceived and Performed in Rural Rajasthan." *Contributions to Indian Sociology* 22 (1): 35–63.

Golub, Alex. 2010. "Being in the World (of Warcraft): Raiding, Realism, and Knowledge Production in a Massively Multiplayer Online Game." *Anthropological Quarterly* 83 (1): 17–45.

Golub, Alex, and Kate Lingley. 2008. "'Just Like the Qing Empire': Internet Addiction, MMOGs, and Moral Crisis in Contemporary China." *Games and Culture* 3 (1): 59–75.

Goodenough, W. H. 1957. "Cultural Anthropology and Linguistics." In *Report on the Seventh Annual Round Table Meeting on Linguistics and Language Study*, edited by P. L. Garvin, 167–73. Monograph Series on Language and Linguistics. Washington, DC: Georgetown University Press.

Griffiths, Mark D., Tony van Rooij, Daniel Kardefelt-Winther, Vladan Starcevic, Orsolya Király, Staale Pallesen, Kai Müller, Michael Dreier, Michelle Carras, Nicole Prause, Daniel L. King, Ellias Aboujaoude, Daria J. Kuss, Halley M. Pontes, Olatz Lopez Fernandez, Katalin Nagygyorgy, Sophia Achab, Joel Billieux, Thorsten Quandt, Xavier Carbonell, Christopher J. Ferguson, Rani A. Hoff, Jeffrey Derevensky, Maria C. Haagsma, Paul Delfabbro, Mark Coulson, Zaheer Hussain, and Zsolt Demetrovics. 2016. "Working towards an International Consensus on Criteria for Assessing Internet Gaming Disorder: A Critical Commentary on Petry et al. (2014)." *Addiction* 111 (1): 167–75.

Guild Wars 2. 2012. Bellevue, WA: ArenaNet.

Gygax, Gary, and Dave Arneson. 1974. *Dungeons and Dragons (D&D)*. Lake Geneva, WI: Tactical Studies Rules.

Halemba, Agnieszka. 2015. *Negotiating Marian Apparitions*. Budapest: Central European University Press.

Harlan, Lindsey. 1992. *Religion and Rajput Women: The Ethic of Protection in Contemporary Narratives*. Berkeley: University of California Press.

Hay, M. Cameron. 2016. *Methods That Matter: Integrating Mixed Methods for More Effective Social Science Research*. Chicago: University of Chicago Press.

Henrich, Joseph. 2017. *The Secret of Our Success: How Culture Is Driving Human Evolution, Domesticating Our Species, and Making Us Smarter*. Princeton, NJ: Princeton University Press.

Higgins, E. Tory. 1987. "Self-Discrepancy: A Theory Relating Self and Affect." *Psychological Review* 94 (3): 319–40.

———. 1989. "Self-Discrepancy Theory: What Patterns of Self-Beliefs Cause People to Suffer?" *Advances in Experimental Social Psychology* 22: 93–136.

Holland, Dorothy, and Naomi Quinn, eds. 1987. *Cultural Models in Language and Thought*. Cambridge: Cambridge University Press.

Horsfall, Sara. 2000. "The Experience of Marian Apparitions and the Mary Cult." *Social Science Journal* 37 (3): 375–84.

Howells, William. 1950. *The Heathens: Primitive Man and His Religions*. New York: Doubleday.

Hutchins, Edwin. 1995. *Cognition in the Wild*. Cambridge, MA: MIT Press.

Huvila, Isto, Kim Holmberg, Stefan Ek, and Gunilla Widén-Wulff. 2010. "Social Capital in Second Life." *Online Information Review* 34 (2): 295–316.

James, Steve, dir. 1994. *Hoop Dreams*. Burbank, CA: Fine Line Features.

James, William. 1902. *The Varieties of Religious Experience*. New York: Random House.

Johnson-Laird, Philip Nicholas. 1983. *Mental Models: Towards a Cognitive Science of Language, Inference, and Consciousness*. Cambridge, MA: Harvard University Press.

Jones, Christian, Laura Scholes, Daniel Johnson, Mary Katsikitis, and Michelle C. Carras. 2014. "Gaming Well: Links between Videogames and Flourishing Mental Health." *Frontiers in Psychology* 5: 1–8. https://doi.org/10.3389/fpsyg.2014.00260.

Kakar, Sudhir. 1991. *Shamans, Mystics and Doctors: A Psychological Inquiry into India and Its Healing Traditions.* Chicago: University of Chicago Press.

Kardefelt-Winther, Daniel. 2014a. "A Conceptual and Methodological Critique of Internet Addiction Research: Towards a Model of Compensatory Internet Use." *Computers in Human Behavior* 31: 351–54.

———. 2014b. "The Moderating Role of Psychosocial Well-Being on the Relationship between Escapism and Excessive Online Gaming." *Computers in Human Behavior* 38: 68–74.

Kardefelt-Winther, Daniel, Alexandre Heeren, Adriano Schimmenti, Antonius Rooij, Pierre Maurage, Michelle Carras, Johan Edman, Alexander Blaszczynski, Yasser Khazaal, and Joël Billieux. 2017. "How Can We Conceptualize Behavioural Addiction without Pathologizing Common Behaviours?" *Addiction* 112 (10): 1709–15.

Karlson, Kristian Bernt, and Anders Holm. 2011. "Decomposing Primary and Secondary Effects: A New Decomposition Method." *Research in Social Stratification and Mobility* 29 (2): 221–37.

Kirmayer, Laurence J. 2011. "Unpacking the Placebo Response: Insights from Ethnographic Studies of Healing." *Journal of Mind-Body Regulation* 1 (3): 112–24.

Ko, C. H., J. Y. Yen, C. F. Yen, C. S. Chen, and C. C. Chen. 2012. "The Association between Internet Addiction and Psychiatric Disorder: A Review of the Literature." *European Psychiatry* 27 (1): 1–8.

Koster, Raph. 2013. *Theory of Fun for Game Design.* Sebastopol, CA: O'Reilly Media.

Kothari, Komal. 1982. "The Shrine: An Expression of Social Needs." In *Gods of the Byways: Wayside Shrines of Rajasthan, Madya Pradesh and Gujarat,* edited by Julia Elliot and David Elliot, 5–31. Oxford: Museum of Modern Art.

Krippner, Stanley, and Susan Powers. 2013. "Dissociation in Many Times and Places." In *Broken Images, Broken Selves: Dissociative Narratives in Clinical Practice,* edited by Stanley Krippner and Susan Powers, 15–52. Abingdon-on-Thames, UK: Routledge.

Lacy, Michael G., and Jeffrey G. Snodgrass. 2016. "Analyzing Cultural Consensus with Proportional Reduction in Error (PRE) Beyond the Eigenvalue Ratio." *Field Methods* 28 (2): 153–69.

Lacy, Michael G., Jeffrey G. Snodgrass, Mary C. Meyer, H. J. Francois Dengah, and Noah Benedict. 2018. "A Formal Method for Detecting and Describing Cultural Complexity: Extending Classical Consensus Analysis." *Field Methods* 30 (3): 241–57.

Latour, Bruno. 2005. *Reassembling the Social: An Introduction to Actor-Network-Theory.* New York: Oxford University Press.

Lévi-Strauss, Claude. 1963. "The Effectiveness of Symbols." In *Structural Anthropology*, 186–205. Translated by Claire Jacobson and Brooke Grundfrest Shoepf. New York: Basic Books.

Lewis, I. M. 1971. *Ecstatic Religion: An Anthropological Study of Spirit Possession and Shamanism*. Harmondsworth, UK: Penguin.

Luhrmann, Tanya M. 2000. *Of Two Minds: The Growing Disorder in American Psychiatry*. Knopf.

———. 2006. "The Art of Hearing God: Absorption, Dissociation, and Contemporary American Spirituality." *Spiritus: A Journal of Christian Spirituality* 5 (2): 133–57.

Luhrmann, Tanya M., Howard Nusbaum, and Ronald Thisted. 2010. "The Absorption Hypothesis: Learning to Hear God in Evangelical Christianity." *American Anthropologist* 112 (1): 66–78.

Lynn, Christopher Dana. 2005. "Adaptive and Maladaptive Dissociation: An Epidemiological and Anthropological Comparison and Proposition for an Expanded Dissociation Model." *Anthropology of Consciousness* 16 (2): 16–49.

———. 2013. "'The Wrong Holy Ghost': Discerning the Apostolic Gift of Discernment Using a Signaling and Systems Theoretical Approach." *Ethos* 41 (2): 223–47.

Macpherson, C. B. 2011. *The Political Theory of Possessive Individualism: Hobbes to Locke*. Repr. ed. Oxford: Oxford University Press. First published in 1962.

Maggs, Bruce, Andrew Shapira, and David Sides. 1979. *Avatar*. University of Illinois' Control Data Corporation PLATO System.

Malaby, Thomas M. 2007. "Beyond Play: A New Approach to Games." *Games and Culture* 2 (2): 95–113.

Malone, Krista-Lee. 2007. "Governance and Economy in a Virtual World: Guild Organization in World of Warcraft." MS thesis, University of Wisconsin-Milwaukee.

———. 2009. "Dragon Kill Points: The Economics of Power Gamers." *Games and Culture* 4 (3): 296–316.

Maltseva, Kateryna. 2018. "Internalized Cultural Models, Congruity with Cultural Standards, and Mental Health." *Journal of Cross-Cultural Psychology* 49 (8): 1302–19.

Mancini, Tiziana, Chiara Imperato, and Federica Sibilla. 2019. "Does Avatar's Character and Emotional Bond Expose to Gaming Addiction? Two Studies on Virtual Self-Discrepancy, Avatar Identification and Gaming Addiction in Massively Multiplayer Online Role-Playing Game Players." *Computers in Human Behavior* 92: 297–305.

Mancini, Tiziana, and Federica Sibilla. 2017. "Offline Personality and Avatar Customisation: Discrepancy Profiles and Avatar Identification in a Sample of MMORPG Players." *Computers in Human Behavior* 69: 275–83.

Mandler, J. M. 1984. *Stories, Scripts, and Scenes: Aspects of Schema Theory*. Hillsdale, NJ: Erlbaum.

Marmot, Michael. 2004a. "Status Syndrome." *Significance* 1 (4): 150–54.

———. 2004b. *The Status Syndrome: How Social Standing Affects Our Health and Longevity*. New York: Owl Books.

————. 2005. "Social Determinants of Health Inequalities." *Lancet* 365: 1099–104.

————. 2006. "Health in an Unequal World." *Lancet* 368: 2081–94.

Marriott, McKim. 1955. "Little Communities in an Indigenous Civilization." In *Village India: Studies in the Little Community,* edited by McKim Marriott, 171–222. Chicago: University of Chicago Press.

McClenon, James. 2001. *Wondrous Healing: Shamanism, Human Evolution, and Origin of Religion.* DeKalb, IL: Northern Illinois University Press.

McGonigal, Jane. 2011. *Reality Is Broken: Why Games Make Us Better and How They Can Change the World.* New York: Penguin.

Menary, Richard. 2010. "Introduction to the Special Issue on 4E Cognition." *Phenomenology and the Cognitive Sciences* 9 (4): 459–63.

Menon, Usha, and Julia L. Cassaniti. 2017. "Introduction. Universalism without Uniformity." In *Universalism without Uniformity: Explorations in Mind and Culture,* edited by Julia L. Cassaniti, Julia L. and Usha Menon, 1–20. Chicago: University of Chicago Press.

Merkur, Daniel. 2014. *Becoming Half Hidden: Shamanism and Initiation among the Inuit.* Abingdon-on-Thames, UK: Routledge.

Métraux, Alfred. 2016. *Voodoo in Haiti.* Pickle Partners.

Moerman, Daniel E. 2002. *Meaning, Medicine, and the "Placebo Effect."* Cambridge: Cambridge University Press.

Moerman, Daniel E., Jean Benoist, Eugene B. Brody, Maureen Giovannini, Miguel F. Gracia, Edward T. Hall, H. K. Heggenhougen, Doris F. Jonas, Michael Kearney, and Dean Kedenburg. 1979. "Anthropology of Symbolic Healing [and Comments and Reply]." *Current Anthropology* 20 (1): 59–80.

Morningstar, Chip. 1986. *Habitat.* San Rafael, CA: Lucasfilm Games.

Munck, Victor C. de, and Giovanni Bennardo. 2019. "Disciplining Culture: A Sociocognitive Approach." *Current Anthropology* 60 (2): 174–93.

Nardi, Bonnie. 2010. *My Life as a Night Elf Priest: An Anthropological Account of World of Warcraft.* Ann Arbor: University of Michigan Press.

Nardi, Bonnie, and Justin Harris. 2006. "Strangers and Friends: Collaborative Play in World of Warcraft." In *Proceedings of the 2006 20th Anniversary Conference on Computer Supported Cooperative Work,* 149–58. CSCW '06, November 4–8, Banff, Alberta, Canada. ACM Digital Library. https://doi.org/10.1145/1180875.1180898.

Obeyesekere, Gananath. 1981. *Medusa's Hair: An Essay on Personal Symbols and Religious Experience.* Chicago: University of Chicago Press Chicago.

Ong, Aihwa. 1988. "The Production of Possession: Spirits and the Multinational Corporation in Malaysia." *American Ethnologist* 15 (1): 28–42.

————. 2010. *Spirits of Resistance and Capitalist Discipline: Factory Women in Malaysia.* Albany: State University of New York Press.

Orben, Amy, and Andrew K. Przybylski. 2019. "The Association between Adolescent Well-Being and Digital Technology Use." *Nature Human Behaviour* 3 (2): 173–82.

————. 2020. "Reply to: Underestimating Digital Media Harm." *Nature Human Behaviour* 4 (4): 349–51.

Pearl, Judea, and Dana Mackenzie. 2018. *The Book of Why: The New Science of Cause and Effect.* Basic Books.

Petry, Nancy M., Florian Rehbein, Douglas A. Gentile, Jeroen S. Lemmens, Hans-Jürgen Rumpf, Thomas Mössle, Gallus Bischof, Ran Tao, Daniel S. S. Fung, Guilherme Borges, Marc Auriacombe, Angels González Ibáñez, Philip Tam, and Charles P. O'Brien. 2014. "An International Consensus for Assessing Internet Gaming Disorder Using the New DSM-5 Approach." *Addiction* 109 (9): 1399–406.

Pietkiewicz, Igor J., Urszula Kłosińska, Radosław Tomalski, and Onno van der Hart. 2021. "Beyond Dissociative Disorders: A Qualitative Study of Polish Catholic Women Reporting Demonic Possession." *European Journal of Trauma & Dissociation* 5 (4): e100204. https://doi.org/10.1016/j.ejtd.2021.100204.

Pontes, Halley M., and Mark D. Griffiths. 2014. "Assessment of Internet Gaming Disorder in Clinical Research: Past and Present Perspectives." *Clinical Research and Regulatory Affairs* 31 (2–4): 35–48.

Pontes, Halley M., Orsolya Kiraly, Zsolt Demetrovics, and Mark D. Griffiths. 2014. "The Conceptualisation and Measurement of DSM-5 Internet Gaming Disorder: The Development of the IGD-20 Test." *PloS One* 9 (10): e110137.

Raheja, Gloria Goodwin, and Ann G. Gold. 1994. *Listen to the Heron's Words: Reimagining Gender and Kinship in North India.* Berkeley: University of California Press.

Ratan, Rabindra. 2013. "Self-Presence, Explicated: Body, Emotion, and Identity Extension into the Virtual Self." In *Handbook of Research on Technoself: Identity in a Technological Society,* edited by Rocci Luppicini, 322–36. Hershey, PA: Information Science Reference.

Ratan, Rabindra A., and Michael Dawson. 2016. "When Mii Is Me: A Psychophysiological Examination of Avatar Self-Relevance." *Communication Research* 43 (8): 1065–93.

Raz, Amir. 2005. "Attention and Hypnosis: Neural Substrates and Genetic Associations of Two Converging Processes." *International Journal of Clinical and Experimental Hypnosis* 53 (3): 237–58.

Rehbein, Florian, Grad Psych, Matthias Kleimann, Grad Mediasci, and Thomas Moble. 2010. "Prevalence and Risk Factors of Video Game Dependency in Adolescence: Results of a German Nationwide Survey." *Cyberpsychology, Behavior, and Social Networking* 13 (3): 269–77.

Reyes-García, Victoria, Clarence C. Gravlee, Thomas W. McDade, Tomás Huanca, William R. Leonard, and Susan Tanner. 2010. "Cultural Consonance and Psychological Well-Being. Estimates Using Longitudinal Data from an Amazonian Society." *Culture, Medicine and Psychiatry* 34 (1): 186–203.

Romney, A. K., S. C. Weller, and W. H. Batchelder. 1986. "Culture as Consensus: A Theory of Culture and Informant Accuracy." *American Anthropologist* 88 (2): 313–38.

Rosedale, Philip. 2003. *Second Life.* San Francisco: Linden Lab.

Rouch, Jean, dir. 1955. *Les Maîtres Fous.* Paris: Les Films de la Pléiade. http://www
.imdb.com/title/tt0048363/.

Rowlands, Mark J. 2010. *The New Science of the Mind: From Extended Mind to Embodied Phenomenology.* Cambridge, MA: MIT Press.

Sapolsky, Robert M. 1998. *Why Zebras Don't Get Ulcers—A Guide to Stress, Stress-Related Disorders and Coping.* New York: W. H. Freeman.

Schank, Roger C., and Robert P. Abelson. 2013. *Scripts, Plans, Goals, and Understanding: An Inquiry into Human Knowledge Structures.* London: Psychology Press.

Schiano, Diane J., Bonnie Nardi, Thomas Debeauvais, Nicolas Ducheneaut, and Nicholas Yee. 2014. "The 'Lonely Gamer' Revisited." *Entertainment Computing* 5 (1): 65–70.

Schnegg, Michael, and Edward D. Lowe. 2020. *Comparing Cultures: Innovations in Comparative Ethnography.* Cambridge: Cambridge University Press.

Searle, John R. 1995. *The Construction of Social Reality.* New York: Free Press.

Seeberg, Jens. 1994. "Spirits, Words, Goods and Money: Substance and Exchange at the Balaji Temple." *Folk* 36: 39–59.

Seligman, Rebecca. 2005. "Distress, Dissociation, and Embodied Experience: Reconsidering the Pathways to Mediumship and Mental Health." *Ethos* 33 (1): 71–99.

———. 2010. "The Unmaking and Making of Self: Embodied Suffering and Mind–Body Healing in Brazilian Candomblé." *Ethos* 38 (3): 297–320.

———. 2014. *Possessing Spirits and Healing Selves: Embodiment and Transformation in an Afro-Brazilian Religion.* New York: Palgrave Macmillan.

Seligman, Rebecca, and Laurence J. Kirmayer. 2008. "Dissociative Experience and Cultural Neuroscience: Narrative, Metaphor and Mechanism." *Culture, Medicine and Psychiatry* 32 (1): 31–64.

Selye, Hans. 1975. "Confusion and Controversy in the Stress Field." *Journal of Human Stress* 1 (2): 37–44.

Shaw, Adrienne. 2012. "Do You Identify as a Gamer? Gender, Race, Sexuality, and Gamer Identity." *New Media & Society* 14 (1): 28–44.

Shweder, Richard A. 1999. "Why Cultural Psychology?" *Ethos* 27 (1): 62–73.

———. 2003. *Why Do Men Barbecue? Recipes for Cultural Psychology.* Cambridge, MA: Harvard University Press.

Sibilla, Federica, and Tiziana Mancini. 2018. "I Am (Not) My Avatar: A Review of the User-Avatar Relationships in Massively Multiplayer Online Worlds." *Cyberpsychology: Journal of Psychosocial Research on Cyberspace* 12 (3), Article 4. https://doi.org/10.5817/CP2018-3-4.

Snodgrass, Jeffrey G. 1990. "Symbolic Curiosa." MA thesis, University of California, San Diego.

———. 1997. "Big Words, Little People: Cash and Ken in Modern Rajasthan." PhD diss., University of California, San Diego.

———. 2002a. "A Tale of Goddesses, Money, and Other Terribly Wonderful Things: Spirit Possession, Commodity Fetishism, and the Narrative of Capitalism in Rajasthan, India." *American Ethnologist* 29 (3): 602–36.

———. 2002b. "Imitation Is Far More than the Sincerest of Flattery: The Mimetic Power of Spirit Possession in Rajasthan, India." *Cultural Anthropology* 17 (1): 32–64.

———. 2004a. "Hail to the Chief? The Politics and Poetics of a Rajasthani 'Child Sacrifice.'" *Culture and Religion* 5 (1): 71–104.

———. 2004b. "Spirit Possession in Rajasthan." In *Shamanism: An Encyclopedia of World Beliefs, Practices, and Culture*, edited by Mariko Namba Walter and Evan Jane Neumann Fridman, vol. 2, 784–90. Santa Barbara, CA: ABC-CLIO.

———. 2004c. "The Future Is Not Ours to See: Puppetry and Modernity in Rajasthan." *Journal of Anthropology* 69 (1): 63–88.

———. 2006. *Casting Kings: Bards and Indian Modernity*. New York: Oxford University Press.

———. 2014. "Ethnography of Online Cultures." In *Handbook of Methods in Cultural Anthropology*, edited by H. Russell Bernard and Clarence C. Gravlee, 465–95. 2nd ed. Rowman & Littlefield.

———. 2016. "Online Virtual Worlds as Anthropological Field Sites: Ethnographic Methods Training via Collaborative Research of Internet Gaming Cultures." *Annals of Anthropological Practice* 40 (2): 134–47.

Snodgrass, Jeffrey G., Andrew Bagwell, Justin M. Patry, H.J. François Dengah II, Cheryl Smarr-Foster, Max Van Oostenburg, and Michael G. Lacy. 2018. "The Partial Truths of Compensatory and Poor-Get-Poorer Internet Use Theories: More Highly Involved Videogame Players Experience Greater Psychosocial Benefits." *Computers in Human Behavior* 78 (Supplement C): 10–25.

Snodgrass, Jeffrey G., Greg Batchelder, Scarlett Eisenhauer, Lahoma Howard, H.J. François Dengah II, Rory Sascha Thompson, Josh Bassarear, Robert J. Cookson, Peter Daniel Defouw, and Melanie Matteliano. 2017. "A Guild Culture of 'Casual Raiding' Enhances Its Members' Online Gaming Experiences: A Cognitive Anthropological and Ethnographic Approach to World of Warcraft." *New Media & Society* 19 (12): 1927–44.

Snodgrass, Jeffrey G., H.J. François Dengah II, and Michael G. Lacy. 2014. "'I Swear to God, I Only Want People Here Who Are Losers!' Cultural Dissonance and the (Problematic) Allure of Azeroth." *Medical Anthropology Quarterly* 28 (4): 480–501.

Snodgrass, Jeffrey G., H.J. François Dengah II, Michael G. Lacy, Andrew Bagwell, Max Van Oostenburg, and Daniel Lende. 2017. "Online Gaming Involvement and Its Positive and Negative Consequences: A Cognitive Anthropological 'Cultural Consensus' Approach to Psychiatric Measurement and Assessment." *Computers in Human Behavior* 66 (January): 291–302.

Snodgrass, Jeffrey G., H.J. François Dengah II, Michael G. Lacy, Robert J. Else, Evan R. Polzer, Jesusa MG Arevalo, and Steven W. Cole. 2018. "Social Genomics of Healthy and Disordered Internet Gaming." *American Journal of Human Biology* 30 (5): e23146.

Snodgrass, Jeffrey G., H.J. François Dengah II, Michael G. Lacy, and Jesse Fagan. 2011. "Cultural Consonance and Mental Wellness in the World of Warcraft:

Online Games as Cognitive Technologies of 'Absorption-Immersion.'" *Cognitive Technology* 16 (1): 11–23.

Snodgrass, Jeffrey G., H. J. François Dengah II, Michael G. Lacy, Jesse Fagan, David Most, Michael Blank, Lahoma Howard, Chad R. Kershner, Gregory Krambeer, and Alissa Leavitt-Reynolds. 2012. "Restorative Magical Adventure or Warcrack? Motivated MMO Play and the Pleasures and Perils of Online Experience." *Games and Culture* 7 (1): 3–28.

Snodgrass, Jeffrey G., H. J. François Dengah II, Evan R. Polzer, and Robert J. Else. 2019. "Intensive Online Videogame Involvement: A New Global Idiom of Wellness and Distress." *Transcultural Psychiatry* 56 (4): 748–74.

Snodgrass, Jeffrey G., H. J. François Dengah II, Chakrapani Upadhyay, Michael G. Lacy, Robert J. Else, and Evan R. Polzer. 2021. "Indian 'Gaming Zones' as Oppositional Subculture: A Norm Incongruity Approach to Internet Gaming Pleasure and Distress." *Current Anthropology* 62 (6): 771–97.

Snodgrass, Jeffrey G., Michael G. Lacy, and Steve W. Cole. 2022. "Internet Gaming, Embodied Distress, and Psychosocial Well-Being: A Syndemic-Syndaimonic Continuum." *Social Science & Medicine* 295: e112728. https://doi.org/10.1016/j.socscimed.2019.112728.

Snodgrass, Jeffrey G., Michael G. Lacy, H. J. François Dengah II, Greg Batchelder, Scarlett Eisenhauer, and Rory Thompson. 2016. "Culture and the Jitters: Guild Affiliation and Online Gaming Eustress/ Distress." *Ethos* 44 (1): 50–78.

Snodgrass, Jeffrey G., Michael G. Lacy, H. J. François Dengah II, Scarlett Eisenhauer, Greg Batchelder, and Robert J. Cookson. 2014. "A Vacation from Your Mind: Problematic Online Gaming Is a Stress Response." *Computers in Human Behavior* 38: 248–60.

Snodgrass, Jeffrey G., Michael G. Lacy, H. J. François Dengah II, and Jesse Fagan. 2011. "Enhancing One Life Rather than Living Two: Playing MMOs with Offline Friends." *Computers in Human Behavior* 27 (3): 1211–22.

Snodgrass, Jeffrey G., Michael G. Lacy, H. J. François Dengah II, Jesse Fagan, and David E. Most. 2011. "Magical Flight and Monstrous Stress: Technologies of Absorption and Mental Wellness in Azeroth." *Culture, Medicine, and Psychiatry* 35 (1): 26–62.

Snodgrass, Jeffrey G., Michael G. Lacy, H. J. François Dengah II, Evan R. Polzer, Robert J. Else, Jesusa M. G. Arevalo, and Steven W. Cole. 2019. "Positive Mental Well-Being and Immune Transcriptional Profiles in Highly Involved Videogame Players." *Brain, Behavior, and Immunity* 82: 84–92.

Snodgrass, Jeffrey G., Wen Zhao, Michael G. Lacy, Shaozeng Zhang, and Rachel Tate. 2018. "Distinguishing Core from Peripheral Psychiatric Symptoms: Addictive and Problematic Internet Gaming in North America, Europe, and China." *Culture, Medicine, and Psychiatry,* 1–30.

———. 2019. "The Cross-Cultural Expression of Internet Gaming Distress in North America, Europe, and China." *Addictive Behaviors Reports* 9: e100146. https://doi.org/10.1016/j.abrep.2018.100146.

Spiro, Melford E. 1971. "Religion: Problems of Definition and Explanation." In *Anthropological Approaches to the Study of Religion*, edited by M. Banton, 85–126. London: Tavistock.

Steinkuehler, Constance A., and Dmitri Williams. 2006. "Where Everybody Knows Your (Screen) Name: Online Games as 'Third Places.'" *Journal of Computer-Mediated Communication* 11 (4): 885–909.

Stephenson, Neal. 1992. *Snow Crash*. Bantam Books.

Sterling, Bruce. 1986. "Preface." In *Burning Chrome*, by William Gibson. City: Harper Collins.

Stoller, Paul. 1984. "Horrific Comedy: Cultural Resistance and the Hauka Movement in Niger." *Ethos* 12 (2): 165–88.

———. 1989. *Fusion of the Worlds: An Ethnography of Possession among the Songhay of Niger*. Chicago: University of Chicago Press.

———. 2014. *Embodying Colonial Memories: Spirit Possession, Power, and the Hauka in West Africa*. Abingdon-on-Thames, UK: Routledge.

Strauss, Claudia, and Naomi Quinn. 1997. *A Cognitive Theory of Cultural Meaning*. Cambridge: Cambridge University Press.

———. 1998. *A Cognitive Theory of Cultural Meaning*. Cambridge: Cambridge University Press.

Subrahmanyam, Kaveri, Stephanie M. Reich, Natalia Waechter, and Guadalupe Espinoza. 2008. "Online and Offline Social Networks: Use of Social Networking Sites by Emerging Adults." *Journal of Applied Developmental Psychology* 29 (6): 420–33.

Szablewicz, Marcella. 2010. "The Ill Effects of 'Opium for the Spirit': A Critical Cultural Analysis of China's Internet Addiction Moral Panic." *Chinese Journal of Communication* 3 (4): 453–70.

Taylor, Tina L. 2009. *Play between Worlds*. Cambridge, MA: MIT Press.

Tellegen, Auke, and Gilbert Atkinson. 1974. "Openness to Absorbing and Self-Altering Experiences ('Absorption'), a Trait Related to Hypnotic Susceptibility." *Journal of Abnormal Psychology* 83 (3): 268.

The Guild. 2007–13. Los Angeles: RobotKittenGigglebus Entertainment.

Tod, James. 1914. *Annals and Antiquities of Rajast'han, Or, the Central and Western Rajpoot States of India*. Vol. 1. London: Routledge. First published in 1829.

Tolkien, J. R. R. 2012a. *The Hobbit*. Boston: Houghton Mifflin Harcourt. First published in 1937.

———. 2012b. *The Lord of the Rings: One Volume*. Boston: Houghton Mifflin Harcourt. First published in 1954–55.

Tomar, R. P.. 1994. *India—District Census Handbook, Udaipur, Part XII-A & B, Series-21, Rajasthan—Census 1991*. Posted online on May 28, 2021. Census Digital Library. https://censusindia.gov.in/nada/index.php/catalog/29912.

Turkle, Sherry. 2011. *Life on the Screen*. New York: Simon & Schuster.

Turner, Nigel E., Angela Paglia-Boak, Bruce Ballon, Joyce T. W. Cheung, Edward M. Adlaf, Joanna Henderson, Vincy Chan, Jürgen Rehm, Hayley Hamilton, and

Robert E. Mann. 2012. "Prevalence of Problematic Video Gaming among Ontario Adolescents." *International Journal of Mental Health and Addiction* 10 (6): 877–89.

Turner, Victor. 1982. *From Ritual to Theatre: The Human Seriousness of Play*. New York: PAJ Publications.

Twenge, Jean M., Jonathan Haidt, Thomas E. Joiner, and W. Keith Campbell. 2020. "Underestimating Digital Media Harm." *Nature Human Behaviour* 4 (4): 346–48.

Vitebsky, Piers. 2001. *Shamanism*. Norman: University of Oklahoma Press.

Wachowski, Lana, and Lilly Wachowski, dir. 1999. *The Matrix*. Burbank, CA: Warner Bros.

Weinstein, Aviv, and Michel Lejoyeux. 2015. "New Developments on the Neurobiological and Pharmaco-Genetic Mechanisms Underlying Internet and Videogame Addiction." *American Journal on Addictions* 24 (2): 117–25.

Wildt, Lars de, Thomas H. Apperley, Justin Clemens, Robbie Fordyce, and Souvik Mukherjee. 2020. "(Re)Orienting the Video Game Avatar." *Games and Culture* 15 (8): 962–81.

Williams, Dmitri, Nicolas Ducheneaut, Li Xiong, Yuanyuan Zhang, Nick Yee, and Eric Nickell. 2006. "From Tree House to Barracks the Social Life of Guilds in World of Warcraft." *Games and Culture* 1 (4): 338–61.

World Health Organization. 2018. "6C51 Gaming Disorder." ICD-11—Mortality and Morbidity Statistics. Version 02/2022. 2018. https://icd.who.int/browse11 /l-m/en#/http://id.who.int/icd/entity/1448597234.

World of Warcraft. 2004. Irvine, CA: Blizzard Entertainment.

Xiuqin, Huang, Zhang Huimin, Li Mengchen, Wang Jinan, Zhang Ying, and Tao Ran. 2010. "Mental Health, Personality, and Parental Rearing Styles of Adolescents with Internet Addiction Disorder." *Cyberpsychology, Behavior, and Social Networking* 13 (4): 401–6.

Yee, Nick. 2006a. "The Demographics, Motivations, and Derived Experiences of Users of Massively Multi-User Online Graphical Environments." *Presence: Teleoperators and Virtual Environments* 15 (3): 309–29.

———. 2006b. "The Psychology of Massively Multi-User Online Role-Playing Games: Motivations, Emotional Investment, Relationships and Problematic Usage." In *Avatars at Work and Play*, edited by Ralph Schroeder and Ann-Sofie Axelsson, 187–207. Dordrecht, the Netherlands: Springer.

———. 2014. *The Proteus Paradox: How Online Games and Virtual Worlds Change Us and How They Don't*. New Haven, CT: Yale University Press.

Young, Kimberly S. 1998. "Internet Addiction: The Emergence of a New Clinical Disorder." *CyberPsychology & Behavior* 1 (3): 237–44.

Young, Kimberly S., and Robert C. Rogers. 1998. "The Relationship between Depression and Internet Addiction." *CyberPsychology & Behavior* 1 (1): 25–28.

INDEX

absorption, 25–26, 99, 112, 198–199.

addiction, 46, 72–74, 79, 188–191. *See also* problematic gaming.

alternative identity, 20, 37, 69–79; experimenting with, 130.

alternative reality, 152, 227n3.

American Psychiatric Association, 72–73. *See also* dissociative identity disorder. *See also* gaming disorder.

attention, 95, 134. *See also* dissociation.

avatar: as compensation for a disability or perceived deficiency, 74, 130; as ideal elf, 39–40, 147; in fiction, 1, 3, 15; history of, 4, 65–67; medium of escape, 186; sacred and secular, 2–3. *See also* self.

avatar therapeutics, xvi-xvii, 163, 187, 192–193, 202–203; through enhanced social standing, 125, 145–149.

Bhairuji, 51 *fig.*, 107–109. *See also* spiritual possession.

Bhat, 59–64; bard, 59; Bedami, 59, 60 *fig.*, 64–65, 81–84; conflicts with Ramu, 154–157; gender roles, 182; money narratives, 159–160; poems, 155; puppeteering, 120; use of performative language, 86–88.

bhav a gaya, 18, 50, 84. *See also* spiritual possession.

bhopas. *See* shaman. *See* spirit medium.

bhut. *See* malevolent spirit. *See* ghost illness.

Boddy, Janice, 142–144.

Candomblé, 30, 144–145.

Castronova, Edward: in relation to the magic circle, 20, 227n19; on immersion in video games, 26–27, 228n40, 230n87; on synthetic worlds, 68; on toxic immersion, 25, 228n30, 232n54.

casual gaming, 71, 75–77, 126–127, 147. *See also* gaming.

caste, 34, 59; changing professions of, 106; reversing the hierarchy of, 33, 197.

Chavanda Mata, 84–85. *See also* lineage goddess.

cognitive anthropology, 39–40.

cognitive dissonance, 35, 164, 188–192.

Counter-Strike Global Offensive, 78–79, 172–173; as a means of global connection, 168–169.

CS-GO. *See* Counter-Strike Global Offensive.

Csikszentmihalyi, Mihaly, 98–99. *See also* flow.

cultural consonance, 34–36, 148, 163–164, 180–181; by devaluing gaming, 190–191. *See also* Dressler, William.

cultural dissonance, 181, 185–186, 191–192, 196; alleviated through gaming, 186–187; alleviated through spiritual possession, 160–162, 185; caused by gaming, 188–189.

culture, 35–36, 39–45, 195; as manifested in a socially learned model, 34–35; norms, 31, 38.

Dalit, 59, 231n26.
D'Andrade, Roy, 153.
dashavatar, 4, 5–14 *illus.,* 47. *See also* Vishnu.
deprivation hypothesis, 57, 197. *See also* Lewis, I.M.
devi, 48 145; punishing, 54.
Dressler, William, 34–35, 67. *See also* cultural consonance
dissociation, 19, 37, 198–199; in gaming contexts, 99–101, 138–140, 187, 200; in spiritual contexts, 87, 109. *See also* attention. *See also* trance.
dissociative identity disorder, 27–28, 74, 195. *See also* American Psychiatric Association.
Dwyer, Graham, 57–58.

eating as metaphor, 85–86, 123, 155–156.
ecstasy, 19, 194–195.
Eliade, Mircea, 41.
escapism, 19–21, 73, 172–173.
ethnography, 41–42, 201–202; collaborative, 92–95; cultural-consensus analysis, 44; lone, 89; methods of, 165.
ethnomedicine, 16–17, 195.
eustress, 111–112; in gaming, 135, 150. *See also* positive stress. *See also* Selye, Hans. *See also* stress.

Festinger, Leon. *See* cognitive dissonance.
first person shooter, 78, 166 *fig.*
flow, 27, 98–99, 111–112. *See also* Csikszentmihalyi, Mihaly.
folklore institute, 118–119.
FPS. *See* first person shooter.

gaming: professional, 170–171; stigma against, 173. *See also* casual gaming. *See also* hardcore gaming.
gaming disorder, xiii–xiv, 46, 72; cultural context of, 187–188. *See also* American Psychiatric Association. *See also* problematic gaming. *See also* World Health Organization.
gaming zone, 78–79, 165, 166 *fig.;* alternative cultural norms, 171–172; as social gathering spaces, 167–168.

Geertz, Clifford, 39–40.
gender, 30, 130, 141–142, 179–184.
ghost illness, 23, 55–57.
Gibson, William, 1–2, 4.
Goodenough, Ward, 39–40, 42–43.
goddess. *See* devi.
guild, 70–71, 75, 147, 199–200; as collaborative, 129; hardcore, 150–151. *See also* Knights of Good.

hardcore gaming, 71, 75–78, 147; as problematic, 140; in Counter-Strike Global Offensive, 170; in World of Warcraft, 134–137. *See also* gaming.
healed healer, 19, 58, 109–110, 144–145, 178, 195.
health disparities, 32–33, 149. *See also* Marmot, Michael.
Higgins, Edward, 29. *See also* self-discrepancy theory.
Hinduism, 197; avatars in, 47–50; in hippie culture, 4.
Hinglish, 167, 169–170.

immersion, 68–70, 110, 198; and mental health, 73–75; toxic, 73–75, 149–150.
inclusivity: in the Knights of Good, 130–131; in Indian gamers, 168–169.
Islam, 102–105, 142–144.

jajmani, 119–121.

Kirmayer, Laurence, 25, 29, 152, 192.
Knights of Good, 75–77, 147–148; ethics of the, 126–131; minimize distress, 151. *See also* guild.
Krippner, Stanley, 25–26.
kuldevi. *See* lineage goddess.
Lévi-Strauss, Claude, 22.
Lewis, I.M., 30, 141–143. *See also* deprivation hypothesis.
lineage goddess, 53, 84; offerings to the, 81. *See also* Chavanda Mata.
Luhrmann, Tanya, 111.
Lynn, Chris, 26, 109.

magic circle, 20, 189.

magical flight, 21–22, 26, 178; similarities with gaming, 16, 21.

malevolent spirits, 53; as metaphor, 123; the casting out of, 104–106.

Marmot, Michael, 32–35, 146, 149. *See also* health disparities. *See also* status syndrome.

miraculous healing, 22, 85.

massively multiplayer online role-playing game, 3–4, 67–68, 90.

mental health. *See* stress. *See* well-being.

MMORPG. *See* massively multiplayer online role-playing game.

multiple personality disorder: *See* American Psychiatric Association. *See* dissociative identity disorder.

Obeyesekere, Gananath, 141–142, 186.

Ong, Aihwa, 142, 183–184.

pharaonic circumcision, 142–144.

plural subjectivity, 153.

positive stress, 98, 111. *See also* eustress.

problematic gaming, 139–140, 141 *fig.*, 149–150, 175–178, 200. *See also* gaming disorder. *See also* addiction.

psychological anthropology, 23–24, 42–43.

psychosocial well-being, 125–126, 153, 185.

raids, 75–76, 133–134; as collaborative problem solving, 129–130; as competitive, 131–132; promote dissociation, 152.

Rajasthan: Bhats in, 59, 61–63; gender norms, 30; spiritual possession in, 47–59.

raksas. *See* malevolent spirits.

sagasji baojis, 105–107. *See also* spiritual possession.

sakti, 49, 52–53, 87.

salary man, 119–120, 122–123; as security, 158–160.

second self, 68; as a bridge between worlds, 124–125; as ideal selves, 145, 149. *See also* avatar.

self: actual, 29, 31; ideal, 113, 149, 153; ought, 145, 148–149, 153. *See also* avatar.

Seligman, Rebecca. *See* Candomblé.

self-discrepancy theory, 29–32, 113, 145, 147–148, 153. *See also* Higgins, Edward.

Selye, Hans, 28, 39, 150, 229n49. *See also* eustress.

shaman, 21–22, 54,55, 178–179.

Shweder, Richard, 41.

spirit mediums, 56, 102–103; challenge gender norms, 141–145, 183–184; effectiveness depends on cultural context, 153, 179; in Brazil, 144–145; in South Asia, 141–142; in Southeast Asia, 142; in Sudan, 142–144.

spiritual possession, 17 *illus.*, 183; as a means of subversion, 141–144, 146, 180, 197; as protection, 103, 106, 160–161; Bedami's first, 81–84; in Catholicism, 179–180; in Hauka, 180; rationalizing contradictions of, 105; skepticism of, 85–86; Bhat utilization of, 156–157; to correct deviant behavior, 114–118. *See also* Bhairuji. *See also* bhav a gaya. *See also* sagasji baojis.

status syndrome, 146. *See also* Marmot, Michael.

stingy, 64–65, 115.

stress, 74; Bedami's, 123–124; in gaming, 134–137, 150–151. *See also* eustress.

subjective well-being, 100–101, 200.

tension, 106, 155–156.

therapeutic: avatars, 187; cultural context, 184, 200–201; gaming, 74, 96–97.

Tolkien, J.R.R., 68.

trance, 26, 28, 41, 102–103, 178, 197. *See also* dissociation.

tribals, 118–119; as an insult, 102.

Udaipur, 77, 197; Bhats in, 63–64; cultural views on gaming, 173–175; young adults in, 77, 172, 186.

untouchable, 59, 105.

Vishnu, 36–37, 47–49. *See also* dashavatar.

well-being: disruption of, 35; from online success, 138–139; through spiritual possession, 197–198.

Whitehall. *See* Marmot, Michael.

witchcraft, 54–55; stigma of, 102, 179–180. *See also* malevolent spirits.

World Health Organization, 72. *See also* gaming disorder.

World of Warcraft, 67–70; absorption in, 152; as a field site, 90–92.

Yee, Nick: on gaming motivations, 71–72, 232n43; on immersion in video games, 26–27, 39–40, 148, 228n40, 230n87, 236n31.